To Oakley & Joan
— with best wishes
for — Great Adventures!
and — Good Cooking!
Flying Tiger
Joe Rosbert

FLYING TIGER JOE'S
ADVENTURE STORY COOKBOOK

羅

斯

抜

Calligraphy by Ura Chen

ADVENTURE
STORY

COOKBOOK

by
C. JOSEPH ROSBERT

Published by Giant Poplar Press
452 Sylva Highway, Franklin, NC

Printed in the United States of America
by Copple House Books
Lakemont, Georgia 30552

DEDICATED
to my loving wife Lil
and
to our devoted son, Bob
and
to our daughter, Marie

TABLE OF CONTENTS

INTRODUCTION

The spirit of adventure is inherently inside each one of us. Sometimes it takes the occurence of unusual circumstances or the feeling of out-of-the-ordinary experiences to bring it out. That is what this book intends to do by roving the far reaches of the globe in search of adventure, whether it be in the cockpit of a fighter airplane over the skies of China, or simply in the confines of a kitchen at home.

To conceive of a cookbook, which is really a collection of culinary experiences, as an adventure story is beyond the usual connotation of the word. Adventure is defined as a remarkable and exciting experience. There is a risk involved. . . and imagination. . . and romance. This adventure story cookbook mixes the author's world-wide escapades with a concoction of all sorts of romantic and titillating dishes which can be duplicated right in your own kitchen.

As we travel the far-flung regions of the world, you will share the-*affaire d'amour* of each experience. This will inspire you not only to prepare interesting meals but also to feel the adventure of trying your own variations. That feel is what all good cooks and great chefs have. . . they do not measure in the usual cookbook style. Measurements are given to provide a base from which to start; but, as you acquire the spirit of adventure, feel will be your guide. At times, the risk will result in disaster. But, when you get it right, the satisfaction cannot be duplicated by following a routine measurement formula.

As the Spaniards say, *"Adelante! Y Buena Suerte!"*(Forward and Good Luck!)

ACKNOWLEDGEMENTS

Innumerable friends and associates have contributed to the completion of this book. Recipes are credited in each specific section. However, it is well to mention that Sue Hacker (formerly Buol) had a collection of many recipes from CAT personnel and friends of which she very kindly sent me a copy.

Some contributors; notably, Moon and Priscilla Chen and Charles Beauregard Davenport, sent many recipes and for that they deserve special thanks. Eddie Zee, Manager of the prestigious Grand Hotel in Taipei went even further. He mailed a uniquely bound red and gold book of recipes from the Chinese Cooking School operated in the Hotel during its early years, of which I was a student for three years. Milton Caniff, world-famous cartoonist, contributed a Steve Canyon sketch along with his unusual recipe.

William M. Leary, history professor at the University of Georgia and author of Perilous Missions (Civil Air Transport and CIA Covert Operations in Asia), University of Alabama Press, made a trip to our home in Franklin, North Carolina to read principal parts of the script. Many thanks for the suggestions and corrections.

This book would not have been possible at all without the support and help of family. First, thanks to Mom, Mae Saracino, who helped recollect the early days in Philadelphia. To our daughter-in-law, Effie, for her sketches. To our son, Bob, who realized that I was floundering with a little, old, broken-down typewriter and purchased a computer/word processor to write the manuscript. And to our daughter Marie for the final proofreading.

Finally, to my dear wife, Lil, who enjoyed with me the many years of adventure that went into the book; and, who suffered, during the writing, through the tantrums of what she called her "Hemming-Speare." Her sketches are noteworthy; but, most of all her long hours of editing resulted in a smoother and more accurate story than I could have ever hoped to do alone. Special Acknowledgement: It is impossible to express sufficiently my appreciation to Bob Andrade, instructor of the Palm Springs (California) High School VICA (Vocational Industrial Clubs of America) printing class, for typesetting the book. Many thanks to Bob and his students for this outstanding effort.

PART I: The Early Days

Chapter 1: Philadelphia and the Making of a Naval Aviator

Chapter 1

PHILADELPHIA AND THE MAKING

OF A NAVAL AVIATOR

How does one get from engineering school in Philadelphia to the cockpit of a fighter plane in the skies over China? First you have to devise a plan to attend college in the midst of the Great Depression with no ostensible funds. I made up my mind to put nose to the grindstone or, better still, in the school books and let fate take its course.

June, 1934: Assembly Hall, Roman Catholic High School, Philadelphia. We students were all seated on the stage facing relatives and friends in the audience. Their looks of admiration reflected our grand appearance in caps and gowns. The degree of excitement was measured by the fact that there was little comprehension of what was being said at the podium.

"For outstanding scholarship during his high school career," it was the voice of the Dean announcing, "The McMichan Scholarship goes to C.J. Rosbert."

It was hard to believe that I would be going to Michigan University! Through all the excitement it was a long time before I realized that the McMichan Scholarship was for four years at Villanova College just outside Philadelphia. That had the added advantage of being a "dayhop"; that is, a commuter, because there was no way that I could have paid to stay at a distant school. Lucky all around!

June, 1938: Another graduation. . . after four grueling years of chemical engineering studies. And, once again, a lucky event took place. A group of us students was gathered in the meeting hall to see, the announcement said, a movie shown by Naval Officers from the Philadelphia Navy Yard. They came in their impressive green aviators' uniforms and the movie they put on had the stirring, romantic title: "Pensacola, The Annapolis of The Air."

After seeing the student pilots flying those Navy planes, not to mention the beautiful beaches of the Gulf Coast and the palm trees waving in the breeze, I could hardly wait for the Officer to finish his talk before going up to volunteer for training to become a Naval Aviator!

During the ensuing weeks I was so excited I could hardly sleep. That almost turned into a disaster. During the intensive physical examination my blood pressure was high; too high, in fact, to be acceptable. The examining officer was understanding but he could not pass me. However, luck was with me, again.

13

"Go home and relax for a few days," he advised, "then come back the same time next week and we'll see."

As soon as I could get to a telephone I called Jerry Agnes who had been my buddy all through Villanova.

"Jerry, I've got a big problem," I explained. "Can you suggest something?"

"Sure," he said with his usual certainty, when he heard what had happened. "We'll call Pat."

I was hoping he would suggest that because his brother was a pharmacist! The upshot of all that was . . . Pat gave me some blood pressure medicine which calmed me down and I passed the physical with flying colors.

During the first thirty years or so of Naval Aviation, candidates for training came generally form officers who had passed through the Academy at Annapolis. About the midthirties a plan was devised in Washington to rain cadets who were college-educated. That made a large pool of candidates available for greatly expanding the air arm of the Navy.

Even though such a program was sorely needed, it went without saying that the hard core of regular Naval Officers did not like the idea. But Washington had its way. This did not eliminate the feeling that cadets were a lower breed than the regulars. And the friction popped up through the years even though thousands of Naval Aviators from the Cadet program made history during World War II, and other wars thereafter.

In 1939, by the time it was my turn, the Navy had become fairly accustomed to the fact that men educated in institutions other than the Academy could make good aviators. They made use of Naval Air Stations throughout the country as "elimination bases." And eliminate they did.

Just after being graduated in June, 1938, I pounded the streets of Philadelphia and surrounding areas. Can you imagine, knowing how engineers were recruited in later years, even before graduation, that a chemical engineer could find absolutely nothing in the way of employment. Luckily, through an uncle, El Brendel, who was starring as a Swedish comedian in Hollywood, I was placed as a very junior mechanical draftsman with a prominent Philadelphia architect (brother-in-law of Uncle El). It wasn't so lucky that I had to start at twenty-five dollars per month! That hardly paid for my lunch and carfare from South Philadelphia.

Several months later my salary was raised to the tremendous sum of thirty-five dollars per month. At the same time, a letter arrived from the Navy. I was so excited I could hardly get it open. It was notice to report to the Navy Yard in South Philly not but three miles from my home.

I had instant butterflies in my stomach. Imagine, the first milestone on the road to becoming a Naval Aviator! There was no secret enjoyment as I resigned my great position, my first big job.

Excitement filled the air as ten of us candidates gathered in the administrative office to sign up as Seamen Second Class. We made up the second class of that spring. One class had just completed its month and the successful ones would go to Pensacola. Our enthusiasm was dimmed somewhat when we heard that only two out of eleven had made it. But with the optimism of youth each one seemed to think that he would make it—I know I did.

In our new issue of khakis, with a cap like a Marine's with no insignia, we felt kind of cocky even though those were work clothes, the only kind we would wear during our training. A Seaman Second Class is low man on the totem pole, and an officer candidate, let alone potential Naval Aviator, is the lowest of the low. And we were pretty much treated that way: marching, learning Navy regulations and cleaning and scrubbing down the "Yellow Perils," the training planes we were so impatient to fly.

But once in a plane with an instructor the treatment was different; that is, different but by no means better. At times I thought that the vengeance of hell was falling on my head. At other times I felt like the dumbest creature on earth who would never get the hand of controlling that confounded flying machine. But the thrill of being at the controls overcame the brusqueness of that other man in the plane.

The month wore on.

"I don't, for the life of me," the instructor told me as we filled out the inspection sheet which was routine after each flight, "see how I can possibly pass you for solo with only one more hour of instruction. You haven't gotten the knack of control that is necessary."

With that he left me standing there.

"Dammit," I thought. "I know I can do it. I'll show him I can."

Needless to say, I worried the rest of the day and most of that night. The only small consolation was that all nine of the other students were in the same boat, no one seemed ready to solo.

The next day in the final hour of instruction I concentrated so hard on every maneuver that I almost busted a gut. When we landed and pulled up to the line there was a long silence.

"Against my better judgement," he smiled, "go ahead and take her up for one turn around the field, but land it on the ground, not thirty feet in the air."

I hardly heard the last part. And that "turn around the field" was over before I knew it. I must have made a smooth landing, on the ground not in the air, because everyone was cheering and waving as I pulled up to the line. My hand was shaking so much I could hardly complete the inspection sheet. I knew I was on the way to Pensacola. Only one other student, out of the class of ten, soloed to accompany me on my next adventure.

In the fall of 1939 Pensacola was a comparatively small town of about 50,000 people and the old San Carlos Hotel stood at the hub of the City, the intersection of Garden and Palafox Streets. When my companion, the only other survivor of our class, and I arrived on the train that was about all we saw as we passed in the bus on the way to the Naval Air Station. I did quickly note that the film we saw at Villanova did not lie, there were actually palm trees waving in the breeze! Maybe that was a good sign that the rest of the dream would come true.

The gate that we passed through at the Station was more like a guard house than the huge, impressive brick entrance that replaced it many years later. After about a mile the bus stopped at the Administration Building where we checked in and received, among other things, our bunk assignments. The large, red building that housed the cadets was a two-story brick structure with white colonial trimmings. My bunk and what was to be home for almost a year was in one of four wings on the ground floor of the building. There were dozens of other young fellows like myself from all over the country.

One of the first that I met was Tex Hill. He sure did measure up the name; a tall, sinewy, amiable type. He was in Class 121-C of the previous year and had only about a month to go to get his wings. Little did I realize then that we would meet again later in a far off land and become friends for life.

A class had started the month before, so I was in 129-C. It will be noted that there were a few numbers missing between the classes of Tex and me. Those were reserved for regular officers who had graduated from Annapolis. Besides having the designation 'O' after the class number, they were completely segregated from the cadets and we hardly ever encountered them during our sojourn at Pensacola.

The mess hall was located in a large area on the second floor. Taking a seat at one of the long tables, I noted that mess attendants were placing food on it family style. One quickly learned that, if a person wanted something, he said, 'Down potatoes,' for example. If anyone along the line ignored the request and kept on eating, the potatoes were more than likely just dropped on his plate. That served as a good sign to mind your manners and the other person's needs.

One dish that reminded me of home was, of all things, the fried oysters. They had a better taste than those up north; and, I found out later, had no preference for months but were in season all year-round.

That night, lying on my bunk, I felt a twinge of homesickness—it must have been the oysters. A long time went by before I fell asleep. It was a restive sleep with dreams of Philadelphia.

The City of Brotherly Love in the Twenties, staid as it appeared, would not be considered a place to spawn an adventurer. There were 'Blue Laws' which closed down everything on Sundays; people crossed the Delaware River to enjoy 'sin' on that sacred day of the week. Policemen walked the beat; they were part of the family scene. Few tall buildings and miles upon miles of row houses gave the town its nickname, 'The City of Homes.' But the seeds of adventure were there.

South Philadelphia, supposedly a collection of rough, tough neighborhoods, seemed to me a calm place to grow up in. There was no noticeable crime in the streets. In fact, many of those streets were wide with trees on each side and, here and there, one could relax in the pleasant green parks known as 'squares.' Picnics to the Zoo, Fairmount Park and Wissahickon in the summer were long-remembered. The airfield near Willow Grove Park held a certain mystery with those funny flying contraptions; the first autogiro experiments were performed there, and that led to my initial interest in aviation.

My first real contact with the outside world was Saint Monica's School, a 3-block walk from my home; nobody ever heard of a parent dropping a child off in a car! In fact, there were very few cars; deliveries of milk and bread were made by horse-drawn wagons. There were no school meals; everyone went home for hearty, nutritious lunch.

The nuns, known as 'Sisters,' were strict disciplinarians who did not spare the rod. Parents were called in to take part in the handling of any irregularities or to assist in ways to improve lagging grades.

And the hero of the decade lived right across 17th Street, between Ritner and Porter. Walking past the front window, we always tried to catch a glimpse of Tommy Loughran, the Light Heavyweight Champion of the World! That certainly was one of the seeds of adventure that entered my heart at that eaarly age.

What had all this to do with cooking and the makeup of a cookbook? There is no doubt that it created the atmosphere that nurtured the melting pot of immigrants from the Old World. Many of them, arriving in crowded New York, were advised to go on to Philadelphia where there was more of an opportunity to find a home and a job, or a business.

The Rosberts, up until the end of the 19th century, lived in the Alsace Lorraine area of France; sometimes, part of Germany. Grandfather Rosbert often ventured across the Saar River to Saarbrucken in Germany where he fell in love with and married Grandmother. The cuisines of both sides of the River came with them when they emigrated to America. A butcher's skill led to a business. And, possibly because they were also butchers, the Rosberts met the Hickens.

Grandmom Hicken came from the Irish side, her maiden name was Sullivan, from Delaware City, Delaware. There were trips on the ferry "Lord Baltimore" to the Port of Philadelphia. The tuxedo-clad waiters served European style meals on tables clad with white tablecloths and napkins. Mom told me that, as a little girl, she remembered those trips and the meals that were too large for any young one to handle. And she was taken, to and from the ship, by horse-drawn carriage.

A romance arose from the association of those two families, followed by the marriage of Mary and Camille. Yes, the French do saddle boys with such a name. It has always been kind of a secret, but they gave me the same name! When the realization hit, years later in high school, what that name could do to a man, I used my middle name "Joe" from then on.

The families and friends gathered together often. Everybody sang and many played musical instruments. We kids took turns pumping the player piano while the whole gang joined in harmonizing. Uncle Sam and Uncle Raymond were way before their time. They put on outlandish skits like an Abbott-Costello team while our sides ached with laughter. Especially hilarious was the act where Grandpop, arms held behind, was made to do all kinds of comic things through the maneuvering hands of Uncle Sam, with Uncle Raymond orchestrating the show.

The saying goes, "—a little rain must fall." Well, disaster struck when I was only four. The routine job on the railroad got too boring for Dad. Besides, vaudeville beckoned. He left home and went back to Keith's Circuit that he had experienced earlier in his life. His sister, Flo, was already performing with Uncle El, even though she was only in her teens; they were known as "Brendel and Bert." So, Dad was in his element with all the glitter and glamour, and was to remain in that profession almost the rest of his life.

In the meantime, Mom was desperate; with three children it was not easy, especially in those days. She soon married again. Needless to say, there was an air of confusion. I was only seven when Dad's sister prevailed upon Mom to take me to her home to convalesce from a childhood disease. But, it was not long before I realized that I would be there for a long time.

In the mid-twenties, Aunt Flo and Uncle El went to Hollywood to seek their fortune. It was amazing, especially during the Depression, that Uncle El became a star in a very short time. I was deeply impressed when, three years later, they appeared in front of our modest house with a brand new Stutz Bearcat; they had motored all the way across the United States!

For a 12-year old boy that was adventure in itself. I got to ride in that luxurious vehicle. But, the epitome of adventure—they took me to the Globe Theatre on Market Street to see their show. The ultimate in excitement was to go backstage to see them after their performance. With performers milling around, changing from their colorful costumes and removing stage makeup, the glittering atmosphere was overwhelming.

That was the beginning of a new life, another new adventure. There was a new kitchen attuned to the German and the French cuisines; Alsacian sausage, sauerkraut and pork, sauerbraten, German pot roast, chicken roasted or fricasseed, fried oysters, oyster stew, boiled Maryland crab by the dozens and all kinds of chowders. And, my first introduction to a gas stove with its own oven. It was my duty to keep it clean and scrub the kitchen floor in order to get a dime to go to the Saturday afternoon movie. What a treat that was!

Then, something astounding happened to lead us into the Thirties— . the Crash Came!

I did not know what that meant. There were conversations about the calamity but few people, if any, in our area owned shares in the Stock Market. Things seemed to go along as usual. However, that winter we did see men in the central area of the City selling apples, one by one, some peddling pencils and others roasting chestnuts. The latter were the lucky ones, they could warm themselves by the fire.

Thus ended one decade and another began. June of 1930 saw me on the graduation stage of Saint Monica's. Decked out in my first long pants, I really stood out; all the others were in short pants. Even then a tinge of adventure welled in me. I wondered what it meant, but the thought was interrupted by screams and yells. The graduation was over, as was a chapter in my life.

The oldest Catholic high school in the United States, Roman Catholic High School, three blocks north of City Hall, had impressive halls and corridors which seemed to cry out, "Study! Study!" I had plenty to sink my teeth into, concentrating on mathematics, physics and chemistry. That must have led to my beginnings in cooking; the mixing, heating and concocting.

In order to save the fifteen-cent round trip trolley fare, a gang of us would walk three and half miles each way. I always remembered dodging the pigeons going through City Hall. "Good luck" came an occasional direct hit by one of them.

Before setting out on those daily journeys, it was necessary to be properly fortified. There was always cereal; but not the dry variety. I had learn to cook oatmeal—without lumps! Then, a quick run around the corner where the storekeeper sliced enough sweet ham or Switzer cheese (the one with the holes) to make three sandwiches; the cost, five cents! That took care of lunch, there was no food service at school.

Watching Aunt Lena cook, I stored in my mind the preparation of many goodies. German Pot Roast was one of my favorites with its wonderful aroma laced with garlic and onions. Of course, like any other kid, it took quite a while to acquire a taste for those "smelly" vegetables. On the other hand, I liked liver right from the beginning, dipped in flour to give it a crisp, brown crust when fried; never overdone, always a little pink inside. And fried oyster sandwiches—they were heaven.

Many food items were purchased from hawkers in the alley that ran between the two rows of houses. The crab man would toss a couple of dozen fierce-looking crustaceans into a large tub which was quickly closed with a lid to prevent any escape. When they calmed down and a large pot of water was rapidly boiling on the fire, the lid was carefully lifted and those delectable creatures met a scalding doom which turned them flaming red within a few seconds. Then, a pleasant afternoon would be spent cracking and eating to our hearts' content. Many years later, the Chinese taught me the best sauce to accompany crab (see Page 227).

There was even a vender who carried a large grinder on his back along with a bag of horseradish roots which he ground to order for each customer. Boy! One smell of that would clear your brain for a week. An Italian-looking man with an accent hawked oranges, hollering what I thought was, "Orange-a, sweet-a down Jersy." It was a long time before I figured out that it translated to, "...sweet and juicy."

All stores, in those days, were specialty places of business. Oh, there were A & P's but they were grocery stores of The Great Atlantic and Pacific Tea Company, just a little larger than the others. The day of the supermarket was many years in the future.

There was a particular fragrance to each grocery store; the specific aroma depended upon the ethnic group. Especially etched in my memory was the little Italian store with its cheeses and salamis of all sizes and shapes hanging from the ceiling. Upon the order of a customer, a loaf of crusty bread was cut in half lengthwise and filled with tasty slices of whatever the heart desired. That was the inception of the Philadelphia

Hoagie.

Off Broad Street was the beginning of Passyunk Avenue. Walking along the first block or two, one observed two store fronts, one on each side. Displayed in the windows was a strange looking round, flat piece of dough with tomato sauce and a gooky-looking white substance with flecks of some kind of herb. It took a few years to become adventuresome enough to experience the joys of genuine Philadelphia Pizza and even venture into the taste of the explosive crushed red pepper.

My appetite for all kinds of food was matched by a thirst for knowledge. There was little outside counsel available; so, on my own, I chose difficult subjects: Physics, Chemistry and Mathematics which in turn led me to aviation. It became a passion manifested in the building of all sorts of model airplanes, and reading every book on the subject I could get my hands on.

One summer, after I had turned sixteen, the spirit of adventure sprouted. A schoolmate and I were struck by wanderlust. Early one morning, having told Aunt Lena that I was going with my companion to visit a relative's farm in Jersey, we set out hitchhiking southward. Our combined traveling fund consisted of less than two dollars in small change! Eventually, that ran out somewhere in Virginia. With our fortune depleted, we were forced to beg food and lodging at a local jail.

Through a series of hitches on various and sundry vehicles, we finally arrived in Philly one morning at three o'clock atop a truckload of melons; a few of which helped quell the pangs of hunger. That little trip made me appreciate the good cuisine at home and kindled the fire in my heart for travel and adventure. In the years to come I was to be the recipient of more than any one man's share of those diversions.

A loud fire bell rang in my ear rudely arousing me from the Philadelphia dream. That ill-mannered bell was the harsh method of waking up cadets to begin each day's routine. Sleepily, everyone made his way to the "Head" for the usual morning chores; shower, shave, —and other daily necessities. There was always a period of exercise on the veranda where some just wiggled their thumbs. Then off to the flight line to be berated over and over through the Gosport tube, that most excruciating and hardly understandable form of communication between the instructor's cockpit and that of the lowly cadet.

Things went well until advanced training in the Third Squadron where I received my first "Down." That meant that some nasty instructor, probably suffering from a hangover, did not appreciate my hour's performance. An extra period of instruction was permeated with epithets and the constant pronouncements that there was no way that I would ever become a Naval Aviator.

Luck was with me on the check ride because I did everything right to the consternation of the check pilot who had read all the negative reports about my performance up until then. He even smiled after the ride—and gave me an "Up."

I sailed through Patrol Plane instruction and, finally, the instrument flying phase. My PBY instructor always held my admiration because he had an antique Packard touring car that was polished and pampered to the degree that it always looked like a jewel.

"Do you have a need for a car?" He asked me one day when we had returned from a flight.

"I sure do. In fact, since completing Squadron Three, I have been thinking of buying one." I almost thought he was referring to the Packard.

"A month ago, I had a fancy to own a new Ford convertible. Now, I know it was a mistake; I love the old Packard. You can have the Ford just for the payments, no down payment!"

When I saw that red demon, I could not believe the deal he was offering me; no cash and a price of only eight hundred dollars.

"Let's go sign the papers." I wanted to get the contract formalized before he changed his mind.

A red Ford convertible was not only good transportation but it served me well in the pursuit of happiness with the ladies. I knew I had been missing something when I wound up dating two beauties at the same time; well, not exactly at the same time.

In April of 1940, Admiral A.C. Read, the Naval Aviator who made the first successful flight across the Atlantic in an NC-4, pinned on my own Naval Aviator's Wings. I was so elated that I did not remember packing and getting on my way to the West Coast for my first assignment in the Fleet at Sandpoint Naval Air Station on Lake Washington just outside Seattle.

Less than one year later, I was a Patrol Plane Commander in a newly-formed squadron based in San Diego, my first choice for duty before leaving Pensacola.

RECIPES

Philadelphia is famous for many things: Independence Hall, the Liberty Bell, Benjamin Franklin, among others. In the realm of culinary fancies are included: Philadelphia Pepper Pot, Scrapple, the Hoagie, Steak and Onion Sandwiches, and the myriad ethnic foods, expecially Italian. The development of the Pizza reached its pinnacle in South Philadelphia. Many of those and other recipes of the time are included now. Let's begin with the Hoagie.

THE HOAGIE

There are numerous stories about when and how the Hoagie was invented. The basic idea of a crusty loaf of bread, split in half lengthwise and stuffed with all kinds of goodies, originated in the Mediterranean countries of principally Italy, France and Spain. Little bars, grocery stores, produce markets, even the bakeries, made and sold them along with their other wares. In the early Thirties, I remember well the little Italian grocery store on Porter Street, one block off Broad Street, where Jerry Agnes and I gathered along with other cronies. Upon entering, one was greeted by aromas found in no other store in the area. And the salamis and cheeses hanging from the ceiling were a sight to behold. One of the Brancato brothers would take a loaf of Italian bread, the kind with the crispy crust; and, with one sweep of a sharp knife, cut it lengthwise, almost to the opposite side. Then at the slicer, operated by hand, he would cut the salamis and cheeses placing them in the loaf. If someone had a bottle of beer or some Italian wine (called "Dago Red") ,the repast was fit for a king. Later, bars and little restaurants began adding slices of tomato, onion and lettuce with some Italian dressing to "juice it up."

It has been said that Emil's, a little restaurant on the corner of Broad and Moore Streets, was the home of the original Hoagie because the name, presumably, was invented there about the mid-thirties.

So, there is no recipe for the Hoagie except: Use a crisp, crusty loaf of bread, Italian salami and cheese, fresh slices of tomato and onion, some lettuce and sprinkle it with Italian dressing (not the creamy kind) made with olive oil. In Tiger Joe's Restaurant (see PART VI), we also made several variations: Meatballs with Spaghetti Sauce, Tiger Joe's Homemade Italian Sausage and Peppers; and, of course, Steak and Onions.

STEAK AND ONION SANDWICH

This sandwich was made famous by Pasquale "Pat" Olivieri who, during the Depression, set up a little stand on a concrete triangle in the middle of Passayunk Avenue which ran diagonally in a northeast direction from south Broad Street to near the east end of Market Street. That stand is still there today, although it is closed in, not only to protect clients from the elements of the weather, but also to reduce vandalism. In recent years, Pat's Steak Sandwich Stand has been recognized as one of five Philadelphia landmarks which include Grace Kelly's Germantown home!

The steak, cut in thin strips, and the sliced onions were cooked in a little oil on a large grill for all standing customers to see. The tantalizing smell was enough for any hungry client to increase his order while waiting. A little salt and pepper and, with a sweep, the large, crisp roll was filled with the delightful mixture. When you make this sandwich at home, put the onions on the grill, or in the pan, first so that they will be brown and tender at the time that the steak is done. The latter should not be overcooked, it is tossed with the onions at the last moment.

PHILADELPHIA SCRAPPLE

This concoction was developed in the Amish country around the Lancaster area and was brought to the Philadelphia market, along with some other strange products like souse and head cheese. Scrapple was made from the pig's head thus completing the philosophy that everything from the pig was usable from the tail to the head. It was boiled with onions, salt and pepper until the meat could easily be taken from the bone. But you can use any cut of pork, and pork necks would be one of the most economical. Reserve the stock and pick all of the meat off the bones.

For each two pounds of pork bones, use 4 cups of stock. Bring to a boil and stir in one cup of cornmeal. Add the meat, chopped, 1 tbsp sage, 1 tsp white pepper, 1 tsp black pepper, ¼ tsp nutmeg and simmer over low heat for 10 minutes, stirring to prevent burning. Pour in bread pans which have been lined with wax paper. Chill. Slice and fry. I find that it browns more quickly and holds together better if it is coated with flour. Catsup goes well with Scrapple.

For quick Scrapple, use a one-pound package of pork sausage, broken up and browned with chopped onions. Use any stock; pork, chicken or beef and proceed as with the recipe above. Instead of cornmeal, try it with grits. It will be coarser but will have the same taste. Southerners usually do not eat scrapple because they think it is only for Yankees. If you tell them it is made from grits, they will probably love it! After all, they eat liver mush.

PHILADELPHIA PEPPER POT

This hearty soup is supposed to be flavor-hot but the seasoning can be adjusted to suit different tastes. It was devised to make use of tripe which is part of the stomach of the cow, preferably of the age that produces veal. Along with the tripe, buy a pound or two of veal breast and a quarter pound of salt pork. Bacon can be used if you like a smoky taste.

Dice the salt pork and saute it until browned. Drain and use the fat to saute:

1/2 cup each chopped celery and onion
1 or 2 green peppers, chopped

Cut the tripe into 1/2"squares; place in a large soup pot with the veal breast and water to cover. Add 1 bay leaf, 1 diced carrot and 1 chopped onion. After 1 hour, add the salt pork pieces and the onion-celery-pepper mixture. Season with salt to taste, 1 tbsp. thyme, 1 tsp. marjoram and 1 tbsp. black pepper. Simmer until the tripe is tender. At that point, you may choose to remove the breast and take off the meat. Add two or three potatoes, peeled and diced; and, when they are just tender, add the veal meat. Check for seasoning. If you desire a little thicker consistency, add flour or cornstarch mixed with water, stirring at the same time. Serve with homemade bread, preferably whole wheat or rye.

GRANDMOM'S SALMON CAKES

1 large can (15½ oz) salmon
1 each, chopped fine, green pepper, onion and celery stalk
20 saltines
1 egg, lightly beaten
3 tbsp chopped parsley
1 tsp black pepper
Bread crumbs for coating

Put salmon, with the juice, in a mixing bowl and break it up. Saute green pepper, onion and celery in 2 tbsp oil; cool. Roll the saltines to crumbs. Mix all the ingredients, except the bread crumbs, with the salmon in a bowl . Chill in the refrigerator. Form into 10 cakes and roll in bread crumbs. Fry in sufficient oil to come up to about half way on the cakes. Turn when brown and fry the other side. Drain on paper towels and serve. Pass the catsup and the tartar sauce.

GRANDMOM'S MARINATED CARROTS

1 lb cooked sliced carrots
½ onion, sliced and separated into rings
½ can tomato soup
¼ cup each vegetable oil, sugar and vinegar
½ green pepper, cut into strips
2 tbsp Worcestershire sauce
Salt and pepper to taste
Mix all ingredients thoroughly and refrigerate. Serve cold.

GRANDMOM'S BEEF AND BEER OVER NOODLES

4 lbs beef, cut into thin strips
⅓ cup flour
2 large onions, thinly sliced
2 green and/or red peppers, cut into strips
12 mushrooms, sliced
2 cups beer
1 ½ tbsp catsup
1 tbsp prepared mustard
Salt and pepper the meat and sprinkle it with the flour. Brown the meat in half oil and half butter. Stir in the beer, mustard and catsup. Simmer for an hour, or more, until the meat is tender. In the last half hour, add the onions, mushrooms and pepper strips. If needed, add more beer. Serve over hot egg noodles; with cold beer, what else!

SUNNILAND SUCCOTASH

This is an interesting variation of the usual lima bean and corn succotash found on family tables around the Thanksgiving and Christmas holidays. The recipe was given to my mother, Mae Saracino (nee Hicken), by the owner of a tourist spot in the Pocono Mountains called Sunniland.

Crush a large clove of garlic with the flat of a knife. Brown it lightly in about 1 ounce of olive oil. Remove the garlic and reserve it. Dice: 1 zucchini, 2 or 3 yellow summer squash, 2 pale yellow "Cuban" peppers, 1 bunch scallions with the tops, 1 large red pepper (or canned pimentos). Drain one can kidney beans. Saute peppers a few minutes; then, add the onions, squash, browned garlic and beans. Add the kernels from 3 or 4 uncooked ears of corn. Stir in 2 tsp black pepper. Cover and simmer for about 15 minutes until the vegetables are just barely tender. Top with two fresh tomatoes, chopped. Cover and cook another two minutes.

CRAB CAKES

In the Philadelphia area, there were as many recipes for Crab as there were cooks; each one had his own "secret." There are two basic ways of doing Crab Cakes or Deviled Crab. The recipes can be used for casseroles where additions can be made to your heart's content. Some cooks use various kinds of creamed soups, inside and on top; such as, mushroom, shrimp, etc.

RECIPE I

This is my favorite which uses a thick Bechamel Sauce as a base. For one pound of crab meat, melt four tbsp (half stick) butter and add 5 tbsp flour. After the mixture bubbles for a minute or two, add one cup milk and whisk quickly to make a smooth sauce; it should be very thick. Add salt, to taste, ½ tsp white pepper, dash of ground nutmeg, one tbsp each chopped parsley and green onion and a dash of hot sauce. Not everyone likes thyme but I add one tbsp. Fold in the crab meat; be sure it is picked over to remove pieces of shell. Refrigerate several hours or overnight. Form into eight cakes, roll in bread crumbs and fry in at least one inch of hot oil; turn to brown on the other side.

The recipe can be used for croquettes, formed in finger shape and rolled in bread crumbs; should be fried in deep fat, only until nicely browned. If, when you test the frying of one, the mixture is too soft and it leaks out; roll each one in beaten egg and another coating of bread crumbs. Another precaution; it is best to refrigerate the croquettes for at least an hour before deep frying.

Try using the recipe with chopped clams ("Deviled Clams"), chopped oysters or fish, or a combination.

RECIPE II: GRANDMOM'S CRAB CAKES

The base for this recipe is; eggs, bread and mayonnaise.
1 lb crab meat, remove any pieces of shell
1½ tsp baking powder
1 tbsp chopped parsley
1 tsp crab seasoning or white pepper and thyme

1 egg, beaten
1½ slices bread, crumbled and moistened with 1 tbsp milk
Dash of hot sauce
Mix well and add:
2 tbsp mayonnaise
1 tsp prepared mustard
½ tsp Worcestershire sauce
Form into 8 round cakes; do not flatten. Roll in bread crumbs and fry in about one inch of hot oil. Turn to brown on the other side.

NOTE: Chopped green and red pepper can be added to either of these recipes. If you like onion, it should be sauteed until soft before adding.

AUNT LENA'S GERMAN POT ROAST

The cheapest cuts of beef are best for this recipe; such as Chuck Roast, about four pounds will do for five or six persons. The same procedure can be used for Pork or Lamb. Use a heavy pot and brown the meat on all sides in about 2 tbsp oil. For the best taste, this should take at least 15 to 20 minutes.

Add one large onion, sliced, and brown lightly. Add salt and pepper, about one tsp each, 1 tbsp vinegar, 2 bay leaves, 1 tbsp Worcestershire sauce and about one half inch of liquid; half water and half brandy. Bring to a boil on high heat and then turn to the lowest heat. Simmer, covered, until the meat is tender (can take up to three hours depending on the cut and kind of meat; remember that pork or lamb will take less time). Garlic is essential for the taste of this dish. Add one or more chopped cloves (I use 4 or 5) during the simmering. Add quartered potatoes and carrots.

When the vegetables are tender, remove them and the meat to a warm platter. Stir in 1 tbsp cornstarch mixed with water until the desired thickness is obtained. A couple of tbsp sherry will do wonders to the taste. Serve with buttered green peas or other green vegetable. Hot, crusty bread is a must for that delicious gravy.

GRANDMOM'S CREAMY RICE PUDDING

¾ cup uncooked rice
3 cups boiling water
3 tbsp butter
3 cups milk, scalded
3 eggs, beaten

1 cup sugar
1 tsp vanilla
¼ tsp salt
½ cup raisins
nutmeg, cinnamon

Add rice, salt and butter to boiling water. Cover, simmer 15 minutes. Add milk and raisins, simmer 15 minutes longer. Thoroughly blend together eggs, sugar and vanilla.

Add small amount of hot rice to egg mixture and blend. Add to hot cooked rice and cook 5 minutes, stirring constantly to avoid burning. Serve hot or cold sprinkled with nutmeg and cinnamon. During the Great Depression, this was a very popular dessert; cheap and easy to make.

GRANDMOM'S APPLE CAKE

Pare and thinly slice 2 or 3 apples; sprinkle with 1 tbsp each of sugar, sherry, cinnamon and lemon juice. Let stand for one hour. Preheat the oven to 350 degrees. Butter a large tube pan. Mix at medium speed for ten minutes, the following:

1 cup oil
2 cups sugar
4 eggs
juice of one orange
2 tsp vanilla
3 tsp baking powder
3 cups flour

For an Italian flavor, add one tsp anise seed and 1 tsp grated orange rind. Pour one half batter in pan. Spread a layer of one half the apples, then the remainder of the batter and top with the other half of the apples. Bake one hour or more, insuring that it is dry to a toothpick test; otherwise, it might drop.

NOTE: All "Grandmom's" recipes in this section are from my mother, Mae Saracino (nee Hicken).

PART II: Flying Tigers of the AVG — American Volunteer Group

Chapter 2
RECRUITMENT

"Hey, Joe! Wake up!" Away in the distance, a voice aroused me from a deep sleep. Raising on one elbow, eye cocked, I noted the time.

"JJ, it's 3 o'clock in the middle of the night! What the hell are you doing waking me up at this hour? Besides you're drunk."

JJ was Ensign Lyons, my roommate in the Bachelor Officers Quarters on the Naval Air Station at North Island, San Diego.

Out of his drunken stupor came the words, haltingly, "There was shum guy in Rosie's Bar shaying he was recruiting pilots to go to China."

"Go to bed." I replied, angrily. "You're not only drunk; you're crazy!" Rolling over, I closed my eyes, oblivious of the further muttering of my floundering friend.

At that time there was no way a pilot could get out of the Navy short of doing something to get kicked out in disgrace. The Naval Aviators' program required three years of service in the Fleet after graduation from flight school. But, in recent months, an order from Washington had precluded indefinitely separations from the Service due to the war situation in Europe.

JJ nudged me again and I managed to hear, "No! Strue; . . . I think. Anyway; . . . he said he'll be on the Station t'morrow to splain."

With that he fell on his bed and almost immediately was asleep.

Finishing a routine patrol up the coast of California, I felt bored and depressed piloting the slow, cumbersome PBY back to North Island. It was June of 1941, only a few months before Pearl Harbor. For sometime I had been thinking that, with a good part of the world at war, there must be something I could be doing that was more important than trucking Navy patrol planes up and down the Pacific Coast. In Europe, France was a goner and England had been thrown off the Continent and was fighting for her life in Africa. It seemed that we were doing nothing but talking and what little fighting went on was among ourselves.

There was one interesting development. The Air Stations at San Diego, Alameda and Seattle had been alerted to patrol the entire Pacific Coast up to 400 miles at sea; . . . for Japanese ships! The newspaper headlines read: "Japanese Assets in US Frozen." At last we seemed to be getting a little smart.

One morning we had taken off at 4 AM. Hour upon hour we flew, straining our eyes for any speck on that great expanse of water. After fourteen hours, nothing had been sighted except a few of our own Navy patrol ships off the Golden Gate. So, with a feeling of dejection, we sat down on San Francisco Bay to spend the night at Alameda Naval Air Station.

33

The next day we flew north as far as Oregon then turned south and paralleled the coast, four hundred miles at sea.

"Looks like something there off to the right," my co-pilot shouted above the drone of the engines. Dropping down towards the small speck on the water, it turned out to be a Dutch liner headed west.

About midday, in line with San Francisco, another dot arose on the horizon.

"Let's have a look at that one," I yelled, pushing the nose down heading for the object.

"Hey, it's a Jap!" I hollered, excitedly. "Look at the rising sun and the name. . . it's the. . . Tatuta Maru!"

The ship was sitting still in the water and on its deck stood a fat, arrogant-looking Jap captain with his hands clasped behind his back. I could almost make out a sneer on his face and imagined him hissing through his teeth. Momentarily, that provoked an itchy feeling to use our machine guns to rake the deck from stem to stern; but, all we could do was report the name and position. Upon landing at North Island, it was discovered that we were the only ones to sight a hostile ship.

JJ appeared on the sea ramp as I emerged from the plane.

"That guy I told you about is a retired Commander and he's about to start a meeting in the ready room."

"Well, what are we waiting for, let's see what he's got to say," I shouted, already on the run.

The room was filled with familiar faces. The gray-haired gentleman spoke.

"I am Commander Irvine and I have an interesting offer to tell you about."

He proceeded to explain the proposition. An American Volunteer Group was being organized, complete with pilots, ground crew and P-40 Tomahawk fighter planes. That sent a thrill up and down my spine. I had always wanted to be a fighter pilot but had been stuck in a patrol bomber squadron for the last year and a half.

"You will be paid from six hundred to seven hundred and fifty dollars for wingmen, flight leaders and squadron commanders."

That was more than double our pay!

"And, although you will probably never see one, you will be paid five hundred dollars for every Jap plane shot down."

"Wow!" I thought. "This is right up my alley."

George Paxton's hand went up. "How are we going to get out of the Navy, under present circumstances?"

"That will be taken care of in due time," replied Irvine. "First, your application to Central Aircraft Manufacturing Company must be approved.

Take no further steps until that is formalized."

"Only then," he went on, "should your resignation from the Navy be submitted. We will handle any difficulties that may arise."

After a few more questions the meeting was over. A lot of buzzing was going on as I went up to the desk and signed an application. Immediately, ice water was thrown on my hot desire.

"You can send in your application," stated Irvine, "but we want only fighter pilots at this time. This is the First AVG; there will be another Group consisting of bomber pilots."

Dejected as I was, there was still hope. Tom Cole took me aside.

"There's a Chief Petty Office recruiting right now in Alameda; he's sympathetic to patrol plane pilots. Give him a call; you can't lose anything."

On my next run to Alameda, the Chief was there.

"If you're really that interested," he said after listening to my impassioned plea, "there's an Army type, Capt. Claiborne, who will be at March Field next week to formalize the contracts of several Army pilots. I'll do my best to get your application approved and have the word passed on to him."

As he jotted down the name, he added in departing, "Good luck. . . hope you make it."

The sun had set by the time I put the plane down at North Island; it was a couple of days after my little talk in Alameda. I was deep in thought mulling the whole thing over in my mind as I walked over to Operations to make my report.

JJ stopped me as I came off the field. "Here's a letter for you, Joe. I picked it up with my mail; it's from CAMCO."

CAMCO! I was almost afraid to open it. When I did, I gave a whoop that was heard all over the landing area.

Ensign Camille Joseph Rosbert
VP-44, Naval Air Station
San Diego, California

Dear Mr. Rosbert:

This is to inform you that your application for service in China has been accepted.
You will report to Captain Harry C. Claiborne at March Field, California, as soon as possible, to sign your contract. He will give you any further information necessary.

The Group is leaving San Francisco on or about September 1, and you will be required to report to the Bellevue Hotel in that City on August 28.

Yours truly,

Rutledge Irvine
Commander, US Navy (Ret)

All depression left me as I headed for my Commanding Officer's Office. I would have to resign my commission and that was not going to be easy.

As we were at peace with Japan, our Government could not countenance the recruiting of aviators for the Chinese Air Force. So, with approval of the plan by the Secretary of the Navy Knox and President Roosevelt, several retired Navy and Army Officers had been given "unofficial" permission to visit the various military air bases around the country to recruit the required contingent.

Naturally, Commanding Officers who had spent a great deal of time and effort to train personnel, were not very happy to see any of them go. In fact, several COs had refused to accept resignations, obliging the recruiters to refer to Washington. That always resulted in a cable to the obstreperous commander: "Resignations for this purpose must be accepted. Act accordingly."

My Commanding Officer had taken a special interest in me. Through his efforts, I made Patrol Plane Commander in less than a year after being commissioned, almost unheard of in those days. I expected him to object to my resignation, but he surprised me.

"OK, Rosbert," he merely said, "if that's what you want to do, go ahead, you have my blessing."

The wistful look in his eyes gave the impression that he, himself, would have done the same thing if he had been just a few years younger.

In the meantime, I drove like mad to make the appointment with Captain Claiborne at March Field, not far from Riverside. I heaved a sigh of relief as soon as both signatures were on the formal document. He reiterated what Commander Irvine had stated during the recruitment session back at North Island that the time spent in the AVG would count on our military records. That was later confirmed by others in the Group including its Commander, General Chennault, himself.

Years later, the military reneged on that pledge using the excuse that it was not in writing. The General spent years fighting an uphill battle, taking it all the way to Congress . . . to no avail. Obviously, the military was jealous of a small group of civilians who became world-famous heroes.

The San Francisco due date was not far off. There still remained the process of getting out of the Navy. The red tape and the paperwork were worse than getting in. Then, the final signature was affixed in the Naval District Headquarters in downtown San Diego and I was out . . . a civilian. Look out San Francisco!

As the plane took off from Lindbergh Field and flew out over San Diego Bay, I had a feeling of melancholy. The Navy had been a milestone, the first real big adventure of my life. Those thoughts soon gave way to my new connection with the AVG. It certainly was a mysterious business and none of the recruiting personnel had been willing to disclose many of the details. Our contracts stated that we were to perform any aviation job that the Company saw fit. There was no mention in the contract of the five hundred dollar bonus for each Jap plane shot down and nothing about our military service and record. Those items were part of an oral agreement. The Chinese Government came through on the bonus item; but the US Government failed us on the other commitment.

The business about our principal job being the patrol and protection of the Burma Road seemed like a cover-up for the fact that we were going to help China fight Japan. For my part, I was only too anxious to get into that kind of a scrimmage; all the better if it were with the Japs. China had been taking one hell of a beating from those devils and certainly deserved all the help she could get.

My thoughts were interrupted by the landing announcement. The familiar skyline of San Francisco came into view and, in a few minutes, the plane was on the ground.

The airport limousine whisked me into town to the Bellevue Hotel, our headquarters for the next few days. The desk clerk informed me that I had a room with Tom Cole, a Navy pilot and the friend from North Island who had steered me to the right person to get me into the AVG. I headed upstairs hoping to find Tom to see if he had learned anything further about our new job.

Tom was not there, but his trail was. Chairs, tables, beds and dresser were strewn with his clothes; and open suitcases lay all over the floor. I had to shove some of his stuff aside to make room for my two bags.

After a refreshing shower, I was just preparing to go downstairs for dinner, when Tom burst into the room. He was quite excited about the whole business but did not know anymore about the setup than I did.

"There will be a meeting tomorrow," he informed me. "A Mr. Spurgeon, the CAMCO rep here in Frisco, is gonna give us the poop."

Down below, we stopped in the bar for a drink. It was not long before we had collected more of the old gang from the Navy. Besides Tom and myself, "Catfish" Raines, Hank Gilbert, Ed Conant and Leo Houle made up the party.

It was a happy go lucky crowd that sat down to dinner that night, all of us determined to cut a wide swath in the last part of the United States that we would be seeing for a long time. Little did we know then that the "long time" would be forever for a few.

Tom pretty well settled the dinner menu for us. "The Company's paying the bill, boys, we might as well eat all the steaks we can. We probably won't be getting any where we're going."

We all laughed and everybody ordered Filet Mignons and huge salads. Tom's appetite for steaks seemed insatiable. During the days that followed he even ordered them for breakfast, confident that CAMCO was footing the bill.

The next morning, at the meeting with Spurgeon, I met the rest of the fellows, thirty-five in all. Some of the faces were familiar, the nine Navy pilots; Tom Cole, George Paxton, "Catfish" Raines, Hank Gilbert, Carl Brown, Ed Conant, Leo Houle, Morris Bohman and Dick White. The rest of the group were ground personnel, mostly from the Army.

Spurgeon, after a few introductory remarks, went on. "You will be sailing on the Klip Fontein, one of the newest ships in the Dutch merchant fleet. However, the boat has been delayed in loading its cargo and you will not be sailing for another three days or so."

That pleased most of the gang. But, a few, who had just said "Goodbye" to their families, were sad not to spend that few extra days together in Frisco.

Spurgeon was very vague about the purpose of our Group or what our work was to be, specifically. And when I went to the local office of the State Department to get my passport, I came away more mystified than ever. From the conversation, I guessed that we all were being steered to someone who had been thoroughly briefed.

"What occupation shall I put down?" asked the official, looking up from the passport he was preparing for me.

"Occupation?" I was confused. "Why, I'm an aviator, of course."

"That won't do. Let's see. . . will 'Builder' be all right?"

"Builder?" I queried, "I'm not going to be involved in any construction work."

"That doesn't matter," he replied. "No one is supposed to know who you are or what you are."

"Well, I suppose 'Builder' is as good as anything." By that time I was really puzzled, but the man could not, or would not, provide any further enlightenment.

The passport was for travel in the Far East only. Visas for Hong Kong and other places had already been arranged. I read every word in the little green book, trying to figure out the strange languages, including a large Chinese chop that was very mysterious to me. The names were fascinating; Batavia, Java, Burma, Rangoon, Singapore; thrilling places that, up to then, had been only half-remembered geography lessons. It seemed unreal to be headed into such an inscrutable region for the purpose of flying a plane in a genuine war.

Returning to the hotel that afternoon, Tom was waiting for me in the lobby.

"I just heard that guns are worth two or three hundred dollars in China." He was always a wealth of information. "Let's go buy a few!" Tom always thought in quantity.

There was no shortage of guns in the shops and we were surprised to find out how easy they were to purchase. I settled for a thirty-eight revolver and a neat little automatic. Tom, of course, would not settle for anything less than four different weapons. Walking down Market Street, we sure did look like an arsenal with guns sticking out of our pockets and under our arms; boxes of ammunition in our hands.

Besides arms and ammunition, we bought wildly everything we could think of that we might not be able to get in China. By that evening, our hotel room looked like a junk store.

"If everyone buys as much as we did," I mentioned to Tom, "the ship will probably sink."

"Don't worry," he assured me. "Besides, you'll thank me when you see how much this 'junk' is worth over there."

Spurgeon had informed me that there would be another meeting the day before sailing. However, days passed before we found out what was happening; a German raider had been reported in the Pacific causing the captain of our ship to change his departure date so that it would remain secret until the last minute.

In the meantime, we made the most of San Francisco. The St. Francis and the Fairmount Hotels were on our itinerary; and, of course, the fabulous Top O' The Mark overlooking the City with its expansive array of lights twinkling as far as the eye could see. There was Fishermen's Wharf, and all the foreign-looking places; everything seemed to take on a new interest as our departure time drew near. I felt a little uneasy at the thought . . . perhaps a little frightened.

On one of our last nights, Tom, George, Ed and I made the grand tour of Chinatown. The little shops fascinated us with their exotic sights, sounds and scents. A pleasant aroma indicated we were in front of a Chinese restaurant.

"Let's try some Chinese food." When it came to food, Tom was always ready to suggest eating.

"No time like the present," I replied, getting the urge to try something different.

As we entered, the fragrance of incense and the oriental atmosphere were intriguing. Once seated and served with steaming plates of food and bowls of rice, Tom dug in whole-heartedly. We followed his example, though a bit cautiously.

"Say, this is great!" I exclaimed.

The others assented but Tom was so busy shovelling it in that all he could do was grunt. I stopped a passing waiter to ask about the food in China because one of the dishes that had been suggested was Chow Mein.

"Allee same, China. Allee same, good food." He replied, grinning broadly. I later learned the reason for the grin; what a liar he was. What we were eating was tasty but it was not typical Chinese food as we were to experience.

Turning back to the table, I started to kid Tom. "Maybe you won't miss your steaks so much after all. . . " But he had disappeared.

"Now, where do you suppose he's gone?" I asked the others.

"You never can figure out Tom," George commented, "but maybe he just went to the Head."

A floor show started and we watched the Chinese dancers and singers. There were acrobats and a magician. It was half over when we spotted Tom, pushing his chunky body through the crowd at the bar, a big smile on his face and two big brown books under his arm.

"Whatcha got there?" George asked Tom as he sat down.

"We're going to learn Chinese. *Hao boo hao?*"

"What the hell are you mumbling about now?"

"Oh, that's Chinese," Tom replied, smugly. "You fellows are just ignorant!"

It turned out that Tom took up Chinese with a vengeance. . . for about a week. When we had the real opportunity to study with an Englishman aboard ship, his enthusiasm evaporated.

Although I had arrived in San Francisco on August 28th, it was not until the second of September that Spurgeon called a final meeting.

"Your sailing time has been set for ten tomorrow morning," he instructed. "Luggage is to be ready in the lobby at 7 AM."

Then he sprang his first surprise. "Now, about finances; each of you will receive an advance of one hundred dollars for expenses. The company has allowed five dollars a day, besides paying your hotel room; anything over that is to be paid by yourselves. I have here the food bills for the last few days; I've deducted the applicable amount from the hundred dollar advance."

I looked at Tom. Consternation showed all over his face. It looked like he was choking on all those steaks he had eaten as he went up to collect what little was left of his hundred dollars.

Then, came the other surprise.

"Someone has to be responsible for this group to see that you are delivered intact to your destination, Rangoon, Burma," Spurgeon announced. "The company has selected as your leader, Mr. Rosbert."

Looking around to see who the leader was, it finally dawned on me that I was the one! That really threw me for a moment. After all, both Paxton and Cole were senior to me in age and service. But, it was apparent that the company had made the decision before our arrival in San Francisco. I felt proud about the selection; but, at the same time, I could not say that the responsibility was welcomed.

"You'll find most of your questions answered here." He went on to explain as he passed out mimeographed sheets. "For anything else, you can refer to Mr. Rosbert."

"Refer to me," I thought, "what do I know?"

Spurgeon did give me a list of the group with something of their records and the jobs they were designated for in China. Five hundred dollars in cash was to cover inoculations by the ship's doctor, and other incidental expenses. That seemed hardly enough to get us beyond Honolulu.

The group consisted of ten pilots, listed as Wingmen at $600 per month, and twenty-five ground men, clerks, armorers, mechanics, radio men and mess supervisors, with salaries ranging from $150 to $300 per month.

Chapter 3

SAN FRANCISCO TO RANGOON

Before sailing, Spurgeon had introduced me to the jovial Purser, Mr. Vanderburg, with his white, short-cropped hair and military bearing, even though a little on the round side. Together we had all gone up to the private cabin and office of Captain Post, a very large man in white uniform. His serious posture was even more exaggerated by a thick Dutch accent. It was made clear that I was in charge of the group and any difficulties were to be conveyed to me for proper action, even including dismissal and the return home of the culprit. The Captain now felt assured and relieved because we almost had had our first casualty: at departure time, Murphy, one of the men, was still not on board. Just as the signal was being sounded to raise the gangplank, he appeared at its foot. Needless to say, Spurgeon had told him in no uncertain terms, that one more incident like that and he would be on his way home.

As the shoreline began to disappear, I went below to seek the Chief Steward and find out about taking care of my group for meals. Mr. Hassel was very friendly and proudly said that he would be glad to show me his dining room. He led the way up a few steps into a spacious chamber with two long tables and many other smaller ones which seated four. One of the large ones was the Captain's Table; so, I chose the other for the ground men and three of the smaller tables for the pilots. I remarked at the beautiful furnishings and he told me that the ship was only two years old and the newest in the Dutch merchant fleet. Little did we know then that, within a couple of years, that beautiful ship would be at the bottom of the sea at the hands of a German raider.

Down in my stateroom, Tom and George were already there. I chose a single bunk under the porthole while they had double bunks on the opposite wall. There were two washbowls and two closets which filled up rapidly as we unpacked. Hurriedly I showered and shaved in order to be first in the dining room to show the others to their places.

The diners presented an interesting picture as they began entering. In addition to a few Europeans, there were many from India, China and the Middle East, some in strange flowing robes usually seen only in the movies. I got my first picture of a native of India; a small, dark-skinned woman wore that form of dress called a *"sari"*, which consisted of a long rectangular piece of material wrapped around the body in such a manner as to preclude the need for buttons or pins.

We were amazed at the menu, especially Tom who was devouring all of it with his bulging eyes. There were: soups, salads, entrees, side dishes of vegetables, desserts and coffee with cheeses. The meals were served by Javanese native boys from the Island of Madera off the coast of Java.

43

Although shoeless (made for a quiet dining room!), they were impressive in their white uniforms decorated with red and gold, topped off with a turban. They spoke only Malay, a strange language peculiar to the Malay Peninsula and some of the surrounding region; so, we ordered by the numbers. An assistant steward was always hovering nearby to assist and explain any idiosyncracies of the menu.

The five-day run to Honolulu was like a dream; we were living in the lap of luxury. There was a swimming pool and a bar well-stocked with all kinds of goodies, including ice-cold Heineken beer. But there were other, more lofty things like a discussion group covering worldwide subjects. And we were fortunate to have on board Colonel Field of His Majesty's British Intelligence Service. He told me that he had spent fifteen years in and around Peking. He knew Chinese well and offered to teach me, and any others in the group, the language. As we talked, I saw a tall, thin middle aged man with many more experiences than he would care to discuss. We agreed on one lesson in the morning and one in the afternoon. We appreciated this much more later on when it helped further our communications and relations with the Chinese people with whom we came in contact.

Early morning of the sixth day saw us passing by Diamond Head. A PBY patrol plane, just before, had waved its wings in recognition and flown off on the early mission of the morning. Passing Waikiki Beach with the Royal Hawaiian and the Moana Hotels standing out, the ship was met by the pilot boat which led us through the narrow waterway to the Harbor. The thing that stood out above the numerous docks was a building with a tall tower, right on the waterfront. As we drew closer, I made out the word "Aloha," the Hawaiian greeting known everywhere.

Three glorious days in Honolulu; that was living. There was the sophistication of the Royal Hawaiian and the informality of the open courtyard of the Moana, where we sipped tall drinks and listened to the Hawaiian guitar players under the famed Banyan Tree.

On the last night, after dinner and entertainment, Tom said, "How's about a run over to Trader Vic's?"

"Sounds good." Several of us chimed, in unison. I had been to the one in the San Fransisco area and wanted to see the original. The tropical atmosphere and the exotic drinks served in their unusual containers left us in a euphoric mood.

"Let's go to Mamie Stover's," Hank announced. He was the youngest pilot in the Group and always seemed ready for any adventurous undertaking.

Off we went in a taxi to the old white, wooden mansion of Mamie Stover, the most famous madam west of California. The patrons were standing in a long line patiently awaiting their turn to engage in *combat d'amour* with the purveyors of the services of the oldest profession in the world.

The night air had cooled our passions somewhat and Hank and I were having a second beer while waiting to see what progress the line would make, when out of the background somewhere, there was a loud scream.

"Fire! Fire!"

Pandemonium reigned. Figures suddenly appeared in the doorways of the upper level; some with bare buns in the air as they struggled to get their pants up. I saw some with no pants on at all, just running with them in their hands, as the line below dispersed and everyone ran out the front and back doors to save their *derrieres*.

Hank and I stood off on the side to see where the fire was coming from.

"I don't see any smoke or flames, do you?" I asked Hank.

"No," he answered in a matter-of-fact way, "Some SOB prankster must be playing a trick to spoil the fun."

The next morning we could hardly tell the others the story for laughing at that Mack Sennet movie scene.

It was September thirteenth. Early that morning, there was   word for me to see the Purser.

"We shall be sailing this afternoon." He announced as I entered his office. "Everyone is to be on board no later than three o'clock."

I was in the dining room before breakfast awaiting everyone's arrival. The announcement was made as given to me by the Purser. Then Tom Cole and I went into town to do some last minute shopping and send off some cards.

At two o'clock I started checking off the names of those on board. By three o'clock two were still missing. Who were they? Of course the troublemakers, Dutch and Ringey. At three forty-five, I really began to worry; the captain had set the sailing time for four o'clock sharp.

"There they are," shouted George, "there, at the entrance to the dock." They seemed to be having trouble with the guard.

I rushed down the gangplank to the gate where I found them drunkenly arguing with him over a number of bottles of liquor in their possession.

"They have *okoulehao*," he directed his words to me, "and the Captain will not permit it on board." (Okoulehao: strong, distilled firewater, similar to moonshine)

"OK, let's get rid of the stuff." I said to them, angrily. "Those are the Captain's orders."

"Then we won't go aboard," Dutch said, drunkenly, "until we drink every drop." Ringey was nodding his head down to his chest.

Just as they both proceeded to carry out their threat, a native standing by whisked away the passport and wallet that Ringey was holding in his hand. He sobered up momentarily and went tearing off through the crowd which had gathered. The thief became frightened, threw the stolen goods into the water and disappeared among the warehouses. Another native immediately dove into the water and, very fortunately, retrieved the passport. Seizing the opportunity, I herded the two bedraggled individuals up the gangplank just as it was about to be raised. The ship's shrill horn sounded and we pulled away from the dock leaving the bottles of *okoulehao* standing there glistening in the sun.

Taking the two culprits off to the side, I really gave them hell. . . and they went off sheepishly to their cabin. With a sigh of relief, I accompanied Hank up on deck to watch the shores of Hawaii disappear as we sailed into the setting sun. A little way out, we picked up the silhouettes of two warships on the horizon. As we prepared to go to dinner, we felt relieved because we thought our ship was going to be convoyed to Manila, the next stop.

The next morning, the ships were nowhere in sight. It must have been decided somewhere higher up that the convoy was not necessary. Months later we heard that subsequent ships carrying AVG personnel did have convoy warships along for protection.

Things were going along smoothly, even the sea was pacific. Hank and I were in the midst of a checker game when someone shouted that a ship had been sighted. Just then ours swerved sharply as it changed course. We all ran to the rail and saw a small speck on the horizon. We never did know whose it was for we soon pulled away from its sight and then resumed course.

A few nights later, I was out on deck, fascinated by the phosphorescence of the glassy water, especially near the side of the ship where there was so much foam. The night was very bright from the light of a big silver moon. My reminiscences were interrupted by a ship's officer.

"Two of your men are trying to climb up to the crow's nest." He was talking very quickly, at the same time rushing me off to where the Captain was observing the shenanigans.

"Doss boyse of yours," he sputtered, "are going to kill themselves. Do sumpding!"

When they heard me shouting at them, having already attained the crow's nest, they contentedly decided it was time to descend. It seemed that they would fall at every step.

"We were," began Dutch, lamely, " only trying to be lookouts for

Japanese ships."

He and Ringey were marched off by a member of the crew to their cabin where they were confined for the next two days except for meals.

I muttered to Hank as we strode away, "I'll have gray hair before this trip is over!"

Link, the Assistant Purser, gave me some confidential information that we would be starting passage through the San Bernardino Strait later that day. Doing a little research, I found out that the Strait was the main route through the middle of the Philippines, skirting the southern border of Luzon; Samar Island being at the east end and Mindoro at the west.

About midafternoon, as I was straining my eyes for a landfall, shadows began to appear on the water. Drawing closer, a large form arose sharply out of the sea. It was San Bernardino Rock, on top of which stood the largest lighthouse in the archipelago. We were at the entrance to a large waterway. On one side, I spotted a native village with many thatched-roofed huts standing tall on stilts. A couple of junks with large sails were close to the shore. They attempted to come out to greet us but we soon passed them by. Then the thick, green jungle came down sharply to the water's edge; the terrain was very mountainous.

After dinner, darkness started to overtake us. All we had to guide our ship were the many-colored navigation lights. So, off to bed to be up in time to see our entrance into Manila Bay.

September twenty-eighth: I awoke with a start; a bright ray of light was shining in my eyes through the porthole. Looking out; there, very close, was the lush, green shore; we were moving very slowly. Up on deck, I ran into Mr. Vandenburg who informed me that we were picking our way through the mine fields that protected the entrance to Manila Bay. Looking over the bow, I noted that we were being led by a small pilot boat. The ship passed very close to Bataan Peninsula just opposite Corregidor; and, not too long after, the Naval Air Station at Cavite.

At first, the Bay was so large, one could not see across it. A large ship came toward us; as it passed, everybody waved. It was the same "President" liner we had seen in Honolulu. After passing a few more ships, the skyline of Manila came into view. Someone at the rail pointed out a large building standing out on the shore, the Manila Hotel. We had reached our second stop.

The City of Manila, with a population of more than half a million people who all seemed to be on the streets at the same time, was teeming with life. Tom, George, and I decided to go to town together. On the dock we encountered a whole barrage of native taxi drivers soliciting our business. Choosing one with a meter so as not to be gypped, we were propelled through the lines of strange cars, carriages and carts at breakneck speed. Our driver had three horns of different sounds which he used continously, and the other vehicles answered as a matter of custom. When we instructed our man to slow down, he looked hurt as if his only aim was to please us. Apparently he had seen too many American movies.

Inching our way down the narrow streets of the business district, we miraculously arrived safely at the Bank of New York. We were amazed at the fare; forty centavos which, at half a cent each, came to twenty cents!

In answer to my most important question, a bank officer informed me that there was no money from CAMCO. That was discouraging news. It did not bother Tom; he wired home some of his excess poker winnings. Poor George, always the loser, had to request that funds be sent out.

There were so many things to do in Manila, we hardly knew where to start.

"Let's find a Chinese restaurant." Suggested Tom, always a chow hound.

"Sounds good," I replied. "We can check it against that San Francisco fare and see how it measures up."

After strolling about two blocks through the crowds, we arrived at the entrance to a hotel. The sign which signified "Restaurant" had several intriguing Chinese characters. The dining room was on the top floor. A drink at the bar only made us hungrier. In the dining area we ran into two Chinese men who had been on the ship with us. Their assurance about the quality of the food was more than welcome.

The meal was served by a Chinese waiter who could scarcely speak English. I think we ordered enough food for six people. But that did not bother Tom in the least.

"This is great!" He mumbled through stuffed mouth; one would think that he had not eaten for a week.

Afterward, we all agreed that Tom's comment was a fair evaluation of the meal. It certainly was different and many times better than the "Chow Mein" type we experienced in San Francisco.

At the Manila Hotel, I pleaded in a radiogram to CAMCO for funds to carry us on to our final destination. The next stop would be Batavia and my hopes were high for some financial help to be there upon arrival.

The next day, we hired a taxi to visit the Naval Air Station at Cavite. I had met Jim Hogan, a Naval Avaitor from Sandpoint near Seattle, at the Army Navy Club. We were again surprised that our Navy identification, which had not been picked up at the time of separation was good at the gate, just as it had been at Pearl Harbor back in Honolulu.

Nearly all of the buildings on the Station were of open, tropical style architecture. That, with the humid, hot weather, gave us the feeling that we were getting closer to the area of our future home. Quite a few friends turned up that we knew in Pensacola and in the Fleet. Most of them asked how they could join us. Unfortunately there was no way; the CAMCO recruiting people never got beyond the States. That was the last time that we would see many of them; because, in those slow PBY s, they were sitting ducks for the Japanese.

It was Pappy Hendricks who introduced us to another taste experience.

"How about some Russian food?" He asked after we had had a couple of drinks at the Station's Officers Club. "I know a good place in town."

"Suits me." Tom agreed, as he always did when it came to food.

The small restaurant, not far from the Manila Hotel, was very plain and had only ten or twelve tables. The menu, handed us by a tall girl with straight blond hair, was all Greek to me. We deferred to Pappy's better judgment and experience. First, there was a hearty, wonderful soup which he said was *"Borsch."* The main course was *"Beef Stroganoff'* which we all consumed too much of, besides the shots of cold Vodka that went with it. Little did I realize that those dishes would become as familiar to me as roast beef and potatoes.

There was a visit to the Jai Alai, the most modern and interesting building we had seen. Inside, an elevator took us to the nightclub and restaurant area. Alongside was a long, corridor-like room with glass that curved outward over an immense court below where the game was played. Waiters placed bets and collected winnings for the patrons so that they did not have to be deterred from their entertainment.

Believe it or not, there was an "after that". Pappy took us to have a look at the dancing girls at the Santa Ana, purported to be the largest dance hall in the world. It was situated in a hangar-like structure, and there must have been a thousand girls who were taxi dancers. It did not take much of that to exhaust us. Sleep took over even during the rough taxi ride back to the ship. I did not even remember removing clothes to get into my bunk.

Early the next morning, September thirtieth, things were a little hazy but I managed to get organized enough to take a taxi to the bank. There had been time for money to arrive; that is, if CAMCO responded to my plea. George accompanied me and was elated when the bank officer informed him that his requested money was there. I was not too happy for him; with his luck he would lose it in the next few poker games. I was even less pleased with the word that nothing had been received for me.

Back at the ship, Vandenburg advised me that everyone should be on board by noon of the next day for an afternoon departure. Up on deck, I spotted Hank all dressed up in a white sharkskin suit.

"Hey sport, Where'd you get that spiffy suit?" I inquired.

"Believe it or not," he responded, "I found a tailor who made it in twenty-four hours and it only cost twenty pesos."

"Why, thats only ten bucks!" I exclaimed.

With the name and the directions to get there, I rushed down to tell Tom and George. The suits would be just the thing for tropical wear. We sped into town and climbed some rickety old steps in the rear of the shop. The upper level looked like an old attic with bolts of cloth strewn all over the place. When we asked the little Chinese tailor if he could make three suits by eleven o'clock the next moring, he looked doubtful but said he would enlist the help of his three sons, provided we returned at nine o'clock that night for a fitting.

At the appointed time, we were there. Amazement showed on our faces. The skeletons of the suits had been completed. A few minor adjustments were made and the tailor said they would be ready the next morning. At eleven a.m. we were rushing up the stairs to the funny old shop. All skepticism melted away when we gazed at the freshly pressed suits all ready to be wrapped. Our pleased looks brought a broad smile to his face displaying two sparkling gold teeth in the center of a fine set of very white ones.

Carrying our new suits as if they were little treasures, we took our final look at the City and were back on board the ship by twelve o'clock.

It seemed as though everyone had worn himself out during the three-day stay in port; because, when I checked my list, they were all there, to my great relief. At one thirty, the ship's horn sounded and we felt the movement which gradually widened the space between us and the dock. As we went slowly through the opening in the breakwater, I felt that we had learned a little of the Orient during our stay in Manila, especially about the dexterity and speed of the tailors; at least, one of them!

Passing through the mine fields in the vicinity of Corregidor, the ship headed south. Knowing that we were going to cross the Equator in about three days, Hank and I decided to play a practical joke on the others, especially the ones who had caused so much trouble. We spread the word that, when we crossed the imaginary line, a "line boat" would pull alongside to pick up mail. That got everyone to writing letters like mad; the story was made more plausible by having the purser in on it. Whenever anyone asked about the "line boat" he would substantiate the story.

We sailed past the Island of Palawan and, after three days, picked up the coast of Borneo. It was becoming hot and many of the group carried their bedding out on the forward deck to get the cool breezes at night. But the frequent tropical showers discouraged that. They had their letters ready but no "line boat" appeared. I stalled them until eleven o'clock saying that we had not crossed the line yet. Finally they gave up and went to bed.

The next morning Hank and I asked them why they had not waited up, adding that the "line boat" did indeed come alongside later that night and picked up our letters. Besides being very skeptical and disappointed, I don't think they ever believed me after that!

Batavia, originally the native Jacatra, was founded in 1619 by the Dutch on the site of the first European factory on the Island of Java. Our ship arrived in the harbor on the morning of October the seventh. Passing the lighthouse at the entrance, a sign read: "Java Pacific Lines, Netherlands East Indies", the Far Eastern home of the shipping line.

Dutch port officials came aboard and began checking our passports. One of them handed me a radiogram.

"At last," I said to Hank. "This should be word about the money."

Everyone was standing around anxiously awaiting the good news.

"Send itinerary", I was reading aloud, angrily, "will have money waiting at next port. What a load of BS; they know I can't send any information about our schedule."

The look on the faces of the entire group indicated that they felt it was my fault that they had no money. Now some of them would have to stay on board because of the lack of funds. I was tempted, right there and then, to divide all the money I had so that they could at least see the town. On second thought, it would be wise to wait a day or so. Then they could splurge it all just before leaving and would not be bothering me further, knowing that there was no more in the kitty.

Link arranged taxis for those that had the wherewithal to visit the city which lay fifteen miles inland. All the cabs were open touring cars and the charge for the entire afternoon was seven guilders, four dollars. We drove along a paved road which paralleled a wide canal. Large sailboats were carrying supplies to and from town. That day, the ones going toward the city were sailing with the wind while the others had to use long poles to push their way in the opposite direction. More than one had lines to the shore and were being pulled by stout water buffalo.

Passing through a native section with animals and naked children running in all directions, we suddenly came into the principal part of the old town. The main street was split in two by a wide canal which had little bridges at the cross streets. Each intersection had its funny little Javanese traffic policeman with his odd helmet, tight trousers and the antics of a circus performer. Javanese were doing their laundry and some were swimming in the canal.

Within a few blocks, another canal crossed at right angles. Around the corner, our taxi stopped at a low rambling building with the sign: "Des Indes Hotel". Walking under the brightly colored awnings and onto a large veranda, we were looking into the bar and dining room.

Having refreshed ourselves with some cool Dutch beer, Tom, George and I set off for the telegraph office. Everybody stared at us as we walked down the street; some even laughed. I guessed that our new white sharkskin suits caught their eyes. They didn't see why we should be so dressed up during the day, especially with that hot sun beating down.

Without giving any information about the ship's itinerary, I pleaded, once again, with CAMCO to have money for us in Singapore. After all, I was not asking for charity; it was our pay we wanted.

That night was for "doing the town" which meant visiting the Black Cat Nightclub. At the bar drinks were served by a woman bartender. Link, who joined us later as prearranged, told us that that was common practice in the Dutch bars. It was not long before we saw the entrance door filled with the large figure of Captain Post in his imposing white uniform. He was closely followed by his entourage of ship's officers. He invited us to join the group and a very happy time was had by all, especially since he paid. The drinks were good and music by the orchestra was suprisingly up-to-date.

The next day, Link said, "You cannot leave Batavia without experiencing the 'Reis Taffel'; it's the most famous type of dinner served in the Indies."

I tried to get more information out of him about his recommendation but, all he would answer was, "You will see. Just bring along at least a dozen of your friends."

The evening saw us back at the Des Indes Hotel. Our private dining room was splendidly decorated with various tropical flowers. The overhead fans made it pleasantly cool. Having had our drinks placed in front of us, Link said that the dinner was about to begin.

There was a grand entrance; not of a few, but twenty-four Javanese waiters! All very neat in their white uniforms decorated in red and gold, each carried a different serving platter of food. There was everything imaginable, from various fowl, other meat and seafood dishes to all kinds of fruits and vegetables, cooked in Oriental style. We did not even know what some of the things were but we ate them anyway. It was a great experience and one of the highlights of the trip. No wonder the feast is called:"Reis Taffel," meaning "Rice Table," because it is not just a dinner, but an entire table full of delicacies.

The next day, there was a knock on my cabin door. Opening it, I found Dutch standing there.

"How about coming over to our room for a drink and see what we've got?" He invited jovially.

I could see that he had already had a few drinks and was feeling no pain. I was suspicious; however, to humor him, I went along.

As we entered the room, I found myself ducking a number of objects that were flitting through the air. When I was able to focus my eyes, I identified two monkeys and one parrot.

"What the hell is going on here?" I demanded. "Are you trying to convert this ship into another Ark?"

"No." Said Ringey, matter-of-factly. "We just thought we'd start a zoo. And this ain't all; we're gonna bring a water buffalo on board, and lots of other animals."

"Yeh." added Dutch. "A native's bringing it down to the dock, right now."

With that they rushed out of the room. As I hurried up on deck to watch the procedings, there came along the dock a native boy leading a gigantic water buffalo. Dutch and Ringey immediately tried to coax the hapless animal up the gangplank. In the meantime, police were approaching; Captain Post was gesticulating from above. There was a big creature with a straw hat on his head being pulled up the incline by Dutch and Ringey. The police had hold of its tail and were pulling the other way, assisted by a couple of burly stevedores. Midst the screaming and yelling, and a lot of laughing from the spectators, my two charges lost the tug of war.

"Never a dull moment!" pronounced Hank who was standing alongside me. I nodded weakly and strode away.

"What's next." I thought, anticipating the worst.

From Batavia, the ship took us east along the north coast of Java, about two hundred and fifty miles, to the port city of Samarang. A short overnight stay saw us, the next morning, on our way to Singapore, the Hub of the Far East. It was miraculous that, during three days sailing, nothing untoward happened. It seemed as though my charges were getting a little worn out.

Singapore, with a population of over a half a million people, was the principal city of Singapore Island only 27 by 14 miles in size. After being in ruins for centuries, it was refounded by Sir Thomas Raffles in 1819 and became part of the British colonial system, only twenty years before their occupation of Hong Kong.

I had known for sometime that this was to be the end of the line for us on the Klip Fontein. It was sailing on to Ceylon. Vandenburg kept asking me how the men were going to pay all the bills they had run up. My only answer was that we would have to pray that our payroll would be waiting for us. I could visualize all of us being hauled off to some dark prison and never being heard from again.

With the help of a pilot, the ship inched its way through the intricate minefields. It passed a narrow entrance, both sides of which were protected by very large guns with camouflage netting suspended over them. The harbor was crowded with hundreds of vessels of all varieties, but the Captian found his place and we were soon tied fast.

British Customs officials called me into the lounge first and asked if any of the group had firearms. When I told them that we all had them, they informed me that all the guns would be collected and held until we left the city. In one way, that was a big relief for me because I could visualize my troublemakers shooting up the town,

When I turned to go, a young fellow in a white suit greeted me with a good old American accent.

"Aren't you the leader of this group?" His smile was reassuring.

"Yes!" I answered quickly. "Do you have any message for me?"

"Better than that. I'm with the City Bank of New York and we have your payroll in town!"

"Wow!" I blurted. "You're the man I came half way around the world to see." Then I added to those of the group who were standing around anxiously, 'I'm going to town with this gentleman to get your money."

At the bank, I was really overjoyed to get my hands on the payroll, and never let the bag out of my tight grip on the taxi ride back to the ship. As I went up the gangplank, I raised the bag high in the air for all of the men hanging over the rail to see. They let out a rousing cheer so loud that all the people on the dock looked up to see what the big celebration was.

Link helped me with the details of making the payments from the Purser's Office so that all of the individual ship's bills were liquidated. I felt sorry for a few who had very little left. However, they had enjoyed every minute of the six weeks we had been cruising.

Like a safari, our line of taxis pulled up to the famous Raffles Hotel. A huge Sikh, in white uniform and an immense turban, opened the door of my taxi and led me to the reception desk where the manager welcomed me. He also told me that he had room for only sixteen of us but that there were accommodations for the rest in the Adelpi Hotel about a half mile away. I selected all the ones who were prone to trouble and sent them to the other hotel.

To register, I had to fill out two pages in a record book, giving the history of my life. The others had to do the same. Then, there was another form to be completed for the police. George and I took a room

RAFFLES CAFE &
COCKTAIL BAR

1941

When and What to Drink

With Soup	..	Pale Sherry or Dry Madeira.
,, Fish	..	Champagne or Dry White Wine.
,, Entrees	..	Claret.
,, Roast or Game		Burgundy.
,, Poultry	..	Champagne, Bordeaux, Chablis, Hock.
,, Sweets	..	Sauternes.
,, Cheese or Fruit		Port, Brown Sherry or Sweet Madeira.
,, Curry	..	Beer.
,, Coffee	..	Liqueurs.

together, not too far from the desk. The rooms, fortunately, were large and made cooler by large overhead fans. The thing that surprised us most was the open plumbing in the bathroom; the water actually ran in a gutter from the wash basin and the shower to the outside. And the overhanging water closet proved to be very temperamental, coughing and squirting in the strangest manner whenever the chain was pulled. To make the odd setup complete, all the lights were very dull, like those that Edison made when he first invented the incandescent bulb. For a luxury hotel (?), strange indeed!

Imagine having a job that, in addition to a world cruise, involved visits to all kinds of intriguing places, including a week in Oriental Singapore, all with pay! Of course, I had worries on my mind and chores to perform. I spent one afternoon at the police station having all of our passports checked. Another was exhausted in negotiating with a Dutch shipping company, recommended by Link, for passage to Rangoon. The only thing available was a freighter, the Tarakan, which would be in port in about four days and would just barely take our group. But, there was no money for the passage!

So, the next day, I was welcomed by the Chinese Consul with tea and a friendly smile; that was about all, because he said he could do nothing to help. The American Consul did offer something. He prepared a message to CAMCO to go through diplomatic channels to Rangoon.

The remainder of that day was spent shopping with Hank. There were hundreds of places run by Indians and Chinese. They had everything imaginable; ivory and wood carvings, intricate silver filigree, jewelry with rubies and sapphires, silks and open-work linens. And, they were all cheap; if you learned how to dicker, and we did, very fast. After a few purchases, there was a two-mile ride back to the hotel in a 2-place ricksha. The coolie, with his pointed straw hat, looked so small, we were sure that he would never make it with our weight. But, plodding along at a steady pace, he got us there in due time.

Meals at the hotel were included in the bill; so, we had most of them there, except when invited out. But, they tended to be the same typical British fare. So frequently, there was the desire to try something different, like Chinese or Malay. The latter, called Satay, was usually obtained at sidewalk stalls and consisted of meat or seafood on skewers, marinated in a curry, peanut, coconut sauce, broiled over a wood fire. They went down very easily with Australian beer, even though it was warm.

Nightlife was always intriguing. For the mild, the after-dinner show at the hotel was entertaining. There was even an American dancing couple included. For the more adventuresome, there were several large nightclubs. Three of them stood out like Christmas trees with their thousands of lights; New World, Old World and Happy World. Experiencing the joys of those places meant getting acquainted with the men of Australian military forces. They were a rough, tough, happy, friendly bunch. All of us agreed that, if we had to fight, it would be with them on our side.

After one long night out, there was a message in my box at the hotel. The American Consul asked me to see him first thing next morning.

"I have something for you." He greeted me at the door to his office. "CAMCO has arranged for the bank to provide you with five thousand dollars for the rest of your trip to Rangoon."

I did not mean to upset the entire office but a war cry burst out automatically.

"You'll have to excuse me." I apologized. "But that just about solves all of my problems."

But my troubles were not over. The tranquility of my, so far, peaceful sojourn in Singapore was interrupted by a note from the Manager of the Adelphi Hotel to see him immediately.

"You will have to remove your rogues from this hotel, at once." He demanded as soon as I entered his office.

"What seems to be the trouble?" I asked in a very innocent voice, knowing full well that anything could have happened. I braced myself for the worst.

He managed to relate what had happened, spluttering many times in the process.

Dutch and Ringey had acquired a supply of scotch and beer with their paychecks and had gathered a number of friends in their room. The noise increased in volume with every drink; so, the Manager sent them a note to quiet down. That was, of course, ignored. In fact, it made things worse. They took to target practice, using empty bottles as ammunition and the passing taxicabs as targets.

The Manager thought he had the solution when he called the Military Police. But, Dutch and his group were not to be discouraged that easily. They invited the two fellows in and proceeded to get them drunk!

At that point, what little sense of humor the Manager had.. .disappeared. He strode up to the room to throw them out personally. The drunks ignored his repeated knocks on the door; until, finally, he had to get a passkey to force his way in.

In his stiff British accent, he shouted. "I say, you ruffians must leave this hotel, at once."

That demand did not deter the revelers, in the least. They only roared with laughter. Elmer, one of the largest in the group, and bolder when intoxicated, shook his finger in the poor fellow's face.

"Listen, bud!" He hollered. "We aims to raise hell and don't want anyone like you disturbing us."

With that, he grabbed the Manager by the collar and the seat of his pants and sent him sprawling through the door; to the loud cheers of his partners in crime.

During the course of the story, the Manager's face became redder and redder. He was furious. I managed to calm him down a little by promising to have the culprits out the first thing in the morning.

I kept my word. Fortunately, our freighter was in port. I had met the Captain and he was a rough old salt. After seeing that all the bills at the Adelphi were paid, I took the men to the ship and left them in charge of the Captain. He assured me that they would remain aboard from then on. By the look of him and the crew, I knew that there would be no further trouble. In fact, in the light of day and sobered up, they were sheepish and subdued.

The Tarakan had no luxuries. There were a few small cabins; George and I had one of them. The men were in a large room crammed with bunks. The Captain did suspend a large canvas on deck so that everyone could lounge around in the most casual, comfortable dress available. They seemed happier and more relaxed in the informal atmosphere. Two long tables served for meals. There was nothing fancy, just hearty Dutch meat-and-potatoes fare. And there was plenty of Dutch beer.

On October nineteenth, as we steamed out of the harbor and headed up the west coast of Malaya, I was sure that everyone was reminiscing about our week's stay in Singapore, the City that tells many fabulous stories of romance and dangerous adventure. We had experienced only a part of it but that was sufficient to whet our appetites for the unknown that lay ahead. It is interesting to note here that hardly four months would pass before the Japanese capture of, what the British maintained was, "The Impenetrable Fortress."

There was a loading stop at Port Swettenham, long enough to visit the charming Malayan Capital of Kuala Lumpur. That and the tin mines and lush rubber plantations, which we enjoyed seeing along the way, would all be abandoned to the Japanese within three months!

After an overnight stop at the Island of Penang (later taken by the Japanese in December of that year!) the Captain detoured across the Malacca Straits to the port city of Belawan on the Island of Sumatra. Some of us took a taxi fifteen miles to the Capital City of Medan. After taking in the sights and some of the shops, we stopped at a sidewalk cafe and obtained some beer by pointing to a bottle on the table of another patron.

It was midday and everyone was hungry. The menu was in Dutch and nobody spoke English.

"This looks interesting." Tom said, pointing to an item. "Seems to be some kind of steak; that's for me."

"What the hell is this?" Tom demanded of the uncomprehending fellow.

We all burst out laughing. The hamburger was uncooked and, in the center, there was a raw egg staring up at him! Getting nowhere with the native, Tom strode off to the kitchen carrying the plate. As we looked over his shoulder, he took out a cigarette lighter and waved the flame under the dish. Tom was fuming because the cook was laughing so hard, tears were streaming down his face. But he finally got the idea and threw the meat into a frying pan, to Tom's great relief and satisfaction.

Then, we all indicated to the waiter that we would take the same item. That was one of many examples of our naivete. The dish, of course, was Steak Tartar.

Early morning, October twenty-ninth, our ship entered the mouth of the Rangoon River on the southern end of Burma. That area of the world was just experiencing the termination of the monsoon season, during which it rains two to three hundred inches in the space of five or six months. No wonder everything was so green and lush.

The tropical rain came down in sheets for quite a while that morning; then, it stopped abruptly. The sun broke through the clouds and, thirty miles up the River, its rays struck a large, golden structure whose tall spire seemed to pierce the clouded sky. It looked like an immense gem set in the terraced hills, surrounded for miles by masses of green, tropical foliage.

"What is that beautiful edifice shining there in the sun?" I asked the Captain, who was standing beside me at the rail.

"That," he replied, "is the famous Shwe Dagon Pagoda, the most impressive sight in all of Burma. It is three hundred and sixty-eight feet high and, sitting on top of that hill, it dominates the entire City of Rangoon.

"Throughout the years," he continued, warming up to the story, "the natives have given generously in the form of gold leaf; so that, now, it is completely covered from its broad, round base to the very tip of the spire, with gold! And, in that spire, near the top, is encased an untold fortune in diamonds, rubies and sapphires!"

That intriguing story added to the feeling of mystery as we sailed up the River through that new and strange country. There were huge expanses of terraced rice fields (they fed a large portion of India, in addition to Burma), dotted here and there with coconut trees, palm trees and immense stands of bamboo that reached more than a hundred feet in height. We were in the land of tigers, leopards and elephants, which are employed to gather the huge teak logs from the vast forests. Also, the most famous ruby mines are situated in the middle of the country and almost all of the jade carved in China was obtained there.

Rangoon, the largest port in Burma, and only harbor feeding the Burma Road, lifeline to China, was taxed to the breaking point. All of the docks, on both sides of the River, had vessels tied up flying the colors of every allied nation. And the River itself was almost completely full of ships, anchored end-to-end, with only a narrow channel on each side for traffic. Our Captain performed the miraculous by putting his ship in its berth without a scratch.

There was a long delay of over three hours while customs officials checked everything, after which we finally set our feet on solid ground. We had lived on shipboard for almost two months, traveling twelve thousand miles, halfway around the world. As I gathered my group on the dock and was beginning to wonder what I was going to do with it, a middle-aged man in a white suit approached.

"I'm Ed Pawley." He announced. "I'll take that 'flock of sheep' off your hands."

"You can have it, gladly." I replied, with a sigh of relief. "It's a wonder I don't have gray hair herding them half way around the globe."

Not far from the dock area, sat the Strand Hotel, a white wooden building of the type you might see in the Florida Keys or in many areas of the South. The rooms were large with high ceilings and everywhere there were large, overhead fans which kept a nice breeze going.

Pawley had arranged a late lunch of curried chicken and rice. It had potatoes and hard-boiled eggs besides many other condiments. The sauce had a good curry taste but it was hot and I drank a lot of water. That was regretted later.

Anticipating what the men in these groups could be like, Pawley had wisely arranged to send them north on the afternoon train rather than have them spend the night in the big City. There was another problem; hotel rooms were in big demand with all the Burma Road activity that had built up in the past year or so. George was elected to get the group the rest of the way to our Burmese base. I had to remain behind to formalize a report on our trip and the attendant finances.

"Good luck." I wished George, as Pawley and I saw them off at the railroad station. "Hope the train survives the trip."

He laughed loudly. "Don't worry about a thing. We'll make it alright."

He was right about the last part; but, he told me later that my two wards, Dutch and Ringey, did not wait long to get into trouble. Each of them had a large supply of beer as they boarded the train. They found that, not only were the compartments independent of each other, but there was no corridor connecting them. What was worse, the two of them had been placed in different parts of the train.

The more beer Dutch drank, the greater desire he had to join his drinking buddy. So, he opened the window of the speeding train, climbed out and made his way like a monkey to the top of the car. Somehow, he located Ringey's compartment and let himself over the side. His kicking on the window was answered with two or three pairs of hands helping him inside. They went on, happily drinking their beer, as the train made its way north through the jungle.

Back at the Hotel, I showered and flopped into bed exhausted. There were six beds in a large room. All of them were canopied with mosquito netting hanging from the ceiling. I had just gotten mine securely tucked in and was reminiscing over the most interesting and exciting trip that I had ever made in my life, when the curry met the ice water in my gut and began to do strange things. Sleep went out the window with the first trip to the can and that was followed by numerous other trips all night long. A lesson was well learned and I vowed then and there; no more water with meals, only something out of a sealed bottle, like beer or wine!

I was glad to see daylight. By morning, the attacks had subsided and I knew that a good, hearty breakfast would further settle things down. Also, I had paperwork to attend to.

Ed joined me and, as I had thought, the food did the trick. Of course, there was hot tea instead of ice water! I had my paperwork in order. Putting my things together, I prepared for the train trip north.

After lunch at the Hotel, I was joined by Charlie Mott who had come over in the second group. He was a Naval Aviator of the Class 104-C, about a year before me at Pensacola. (Later shot down by Jap ground fire while on a strafing mission; I did not see him again until many years later in Okinawa and Taipei).

"Joe, I'll see you off at the station." He told me. "I have a little thing I want to get to the head ordnance man of the Group."

Later, at the train, he handed me an odd metal contraption.

"This is part of a gunsight I've been working on." He confided. "Our planes arrived with nothing of this sort."

"I'll guard it with my life." I vowed, superfluously. For the first time, I realized that there might be some real fighting. I was more anxious than ever to see and to fly the P-40.

Shortly before departure, a British officer, with enough baggage to fill the compartment, joined me as a fellow passenger. He was not much of a conversationalist; but, as he was getting his things stowed away, he did mention that his destination was Lashio, the northernmost end of the rail line. From there the Burma Road was the sole link to Kunming and all of southwest China.

I heard the compartment door bang shut and the ancient train started slowly on its way out of the station. Charlie waved as I settled back in my seat with thoughts about what lay ahead. Soon we were out of the City, passing through rice-paddies with the ever-present water buffalo, some of which were even too unambitious to disturb the tall white birds perched on their backs.

The numerous round pagodas, of all sizes, abounded everywhere. It was little more than an hour when a very tall one came into view.

"That's the Shwe-maw-daw pagoda." The officer commented. "It's 324 feet high, only a little shorter than the Shwe Dagon in Rangoon.

We were pulling into Pegu, the center of the region, a city on the Sittang River that existed from the time of Christ. The tea and toast, ordered by my companion, was welcomed. He noticed me hurrying with it.

"You don't have to rush, old boy." He advised. "The same company handles services all along the line; they will pick up the utensils at a later station."

"Thanks very much." I said, thinking, "old boy; that's odd, I'm neither old nor a boy!"

As we traveled along, I noticed hills beginning to appear on the horizon on both sides. They seemed to increase in height as we moved along.

"They continue to rise all the way through Burma," I was getting a geography lesson from my British teacher, "until the mountains become part of the mighty Himalayas."

When the sun went down, night started to come on fast. There was a stop long enough to have dinner. Then the officer took out his bedroll. He attempted to dispel my fear of missing my station by assuring me that someone would surely be there to meet me. Before I could ask how they would know what compartment I was in, he fell fast asleep.

Coming into each station, I strained my eyes to read the name, but was unsuccessful in the blackout. After about six hours, the train slowed down for another station. I heard some loud voices. I pounded on the locked compartment door. The latch moved.

"Looking for us, Joe?" A voice asked through the opening door; the face peering in was that of Hank Gilbert, my traveling buddy on the Klip Fontein. That face was joined by those of Tom and George, and a few unfamiliar ones.

"How did you guys know which compartment I was in?" I asked, much relieved over their discovery.

"It wasn't easy." Replied Hank. "Your name tag was hanging on the door!"

Soon, a station wagon was loaded with my things and we were on the way through the darkened town of Toungoo. It was difficult to see anything, but the forms of low buildings on each side of the main street were distinguishable.

Out of the village, we were riding on a narrow dirt road through the rice paddies. After a bumpy eight-mile trip, the gate of a fenced area appeared in front of us. A fierce looking native guard challenged us with a fixed bayonet! When he recognized the vehicle and the American occupants, he waved us through.

"What the hell kind of a soldier was that?" I inquired. "He certainly doesn't look like a Burmese."

"That's what is known as a Gurkha." Answered Tom. "They come from a country called Nepal; that's where Mt. Everest is. They love to fight, especially with those fiercesome looking curved knives. They are allowed to volunteer in the Indian Army, which is probably the best military break India ever got. There are quite a few of them around here as guards; when they challenge you, you had better stop or they will surely blow your head off."

"Don't worry, I will!" I assured him.

A long, thatched-roof building appeared in the darkness. Hank said the lights went out at ten o'clock but he went up a few wooden steps and turned on a porch light. Inside, both sides of the building were lined with bunks, covered with hanging mosquito nets. As I found mine, a man came down the aisle between the rows of sleeping figures.

"I'm Sandy Sandell, your Squadron Commander." He announced, in a low voice, not to disturb the others. "Welcome to the First, the best Squadron in the Group."

As he strode off to his bunk, I could tell that he was very proud of his position. With the mosquito net tightly tucked in, I tossed and turned for hours, living over again the phenomenal trip of adventures and amusing incidents that I had recently experienced. At the same time, I dreamed of the future and what it held for me.

The next morning, I was awakened by the bright sun streaming through the barracks. All the other bunks were empty with their nets tied up for the day. A small native bearer was standing patiently nearby to make up my bed. As I prepared to shower and shave, I noted that there were no windows in the building, only openings with covers propped up to allow the breeze to go through. The bearer took my laundry that had accumulated and I went off to the smaller building in the rear where there were three open showers and a long table with enamel wash pans under a number of faucets. The facilities were primitive but adequate for their purposes.

I felt refreshed as I finished dressing. The native boy pointed the way to the mess hall. On the way were a number of other buildings, all like mine. Off to the west, I could hear the sound of airplane engines. That was music to my ears and I was getting more anxious than ever to fly again, especially a fighter plane!

Seated at one of two long tables, with a make shift bar at the end of the room, I was served a typical American breakfast by a barefoot native boy in a plain white uniform. A couple of other pilots, who had the day off, joined me. One of them called for a station wagon and, soon we were off to the airfield about two miles away.

As we neared the end of the airstrip, there they were; three, sleek, sharp-nosed P-40s! In spite of what the military had said about them, they looked beautiful to me, with their four guns sticking out of the wings and two out of the nose. I was more than ready to fly, especially to try those guns and the capability of the plane.

Farther on were two corrugated metal hangars with thatched roofs. Pilots and ground men were standing around but we did not stop there. My destination was headquarters which consisted of a low metal building. Inside, several clerks were typing away. When I identified myself as the leader of the last group to arrive, one of the clerks told me that the "Colonel" would probably want to see me.

A heavyset, gray-haired man approached.

"I'm Harvey Greenlaw." He introduced himself. "I'll look in on the 'Old Man' to see if he's ready to see you."

In a moment, he beckoned for me to go in.

In the far corner, at a desk, sat a dark-haired man, working on some papers. A well-tanned, rugged face looked up and smiled; I could see from his appearance why he was known as "Old Leatherneck". Greenlaw introduced him as "Colonel Chennault." He took off his reading glasses and asked me about the trip over. I related the essential parts, particulary the fact that, in spite of the scarcity of financial assistance and the delays in getting it, I had brought the group through to Toungoo without a casualty. He thanked me for that and, without specifically saying so, indicated that CAMCO was not always amenable to parting with the necessary funds to support the program.

Then he became really enthusiastic as he related his plans to get a bombing section, SAVG (Second American Volunteer Group), and another fighter group, TAVG (the Third), each similar to the FAVG (the First), which had already been formed with three fighter squadrons. I left with the strong impression that Chennault was a man of vision who had the forcefulness to carry out his plans. It turned out that cataclysmic events would change all that and we would be the only Group, known as the AVG.

Greenlaw showed me to the hangar where all three squadron members congregated. To my surprise, there were many of my old friends from the Navy; Ed Rector, Chuck Older and Noel Bacon from my class at Pensacola; Tex Hill, Bus Keeton, Dick Rossi; and, many others that I had not met during our military duty. Those who had come over in my group, like Catfish Raines, George Paxton, Tom Cole, Hank Gilbert, Carl Brown, were mixed in with the crowd. Imagine meeting like that at a far off airstrip in the middle of the Burmese jungle on the other side of the world.

Then, too, there were Army Air Corps pilots; but, everything was informal with no distinguishing uniforms or bars so it was impossible to differentiate. That seemed to suit everyone just fine. Most wore khaki shorts and bush jackets with high mosquito boots, topped off by a jaunty looking pith helmet. Many carried guns on their hips, thus completing the moving-picture-like scene.

Soon, I was engrossed in a P-40 Handbook with which I had to be familiar before taking my first flight. It looked a day's job to learn all of the intricacies of the aircraft. With manual in hand, several visits to the plane were made to be sure of every detail. Carl and Hank told me they were ready to take their first flight the next day; I knew I would not be far behind.

Out of the nine pilots of my group, Carl, along with Bohman, White and me, were in the First Squadron; Hank and Catfish in the Third and the remainder, in the Second. Hank told me of the heat later in the day, usually up to 110 degrees in the shade by noontime. The planes were much too hot to work on, so afternoons were free. Off to the messhall we went to see what that had to offer.

The tables had been rearranged so that each squadron had its own. Chennault and his staff had another. Then, there was a smaller one which seemed to be for overflow. However, during the meal, it was occupied by three women! Carl told me the dark-haired one was Mrs. Olga Greenlaw. She looked sexy which could mean trouble, or fun, or—both. The other two were "our" nurses; Red Foster and Jo Stewart. They gave us a feeling of home.

That afternoon, the head flight surgeon, Doc Gentry, lent us his car to go into town to do some shopping. That presented the opportunity to see the town that I had passed through in the dark the night before. The shops were jammed together on both sides of the main street. Most of the proprietors were Burmese or Chinese.

"There are four things we must buy." Hank advised. "Light Khaki clothes; that is, shorts and short-sleeved bush jacket, pith helmet, mosquito boots, and, last but not least, a bicycle."

The town was doing a tremendous business since the arrival of the Americans and they were stocked with everything imaginable. Shopkeepers stood outside their doors to entice every available customer. However, we stuck to the essential items we had come for. Soon, we had everything but the boots.

"That looks like the bootmaker's place." I headed through a door where I saw all kinds of leather goods. After serving us some tea, the Chinese shopkeeper took off my shoes, put each foot on a piece of paper and, with a pencil, drew an outline. I put my name on the sheets and he indicated that my boots would be ready the next day.

"Now that's what I call service—fit for a king!" I laughed with delight and Hank agreed with a nod.

A loud gong almost knocked me out of bed; I thought I was having a nightmare. A light at the end of the building shone on the figure of Sandell banging away at a large Chinese gong hanging between two ornate wooden supports. Looking at my watch, it was five-thirty, the middle of the night! Somebody announced: "Breakfast at six."

"Are you ready to fly?" Bob Little asked me at the mess hall.

"I'll never be readier." Was my quick answer.

"We don't like to waste time, you're scheduled this morning."

The meal took on little importance; my stomach was already occupied by proverbial butterflies.

At the field, when I asked the supply man about flight gear, he answered by placing on the counter a parachute and a pair of earphones. That was it.

Bob Little accompanied me to the plane which took on a much larger size as we approached it. As I adjusted the chute and checked things in the cockpit, he came up on the wing for a last minute word.

"Careful when you taxi." He cautioned. "And don't land the thing thirty feet in the air, bring it right down to the ground."

The admonition was not taken lightly. First of all, I had not flown in over three months. Second, the P-40 cockpit was almost on ground level compared to the much larger PBY.

The engine started with a roar and I felt as though the plane was going to takeoff right then and there before I was ready. The crewchief signaled me to proceed. The long, sharp nose blocked out vision straight ahead. It was necessary to snake along to avoid collision with the other aircraft.

Then I was at the end of the strip. Parked at an angle so as to have a clear view of the runway, I ran up and checked the engine. Everything was OK.

"Here we go." I said to myself, as I released the brakes and the plane lurched forward with a terrific burst of power, pushing me back against the seat.

"Tail up." I coached.

I was in the air before I knew it, and was reluctant to start a turn until the wheels were fully retracted. Attaining flying speed, the plane zoomed up at more than two thousand feet per minute. At twelve thousand feet, I leveled off and had the opportunity to get the feel of the aircraft.

A steep dive and the speed picked up almost at a frightening rate. I knew, then, that nothing could catch it in that attitude. Back on the stick until I felt gray, over the top, looking down at the green jungle below, into the dive again and leveling off to complete the loop. Same thing over again; but, this time, at the top, a roll over to complete the Immelmann maneuver—level flight in the opposite direction. A few rolls, then a spin and recovery. I was exhilarated beyond description.

"This is what I came for." I said aloud as the wheels came down and touched the runway with a soft squeak.

"How'd you like it?" Little hollered as the propeller stopped turning.

"Couldn't be better." I smiled; it was hard to hold back the excitement.

Then, for the rest of the morning, I relaxed and watched the other pilots practice landings and other maneuvers. Some of them did not like the way the plane handled. Pilot Bohman, one of my group, had already decided to return home; as did White and Ringey. Those that liked the plane, as I did, were happy with the setup and looked to the future.

Chapter 4

FLYING TIGERS IN COMBAT

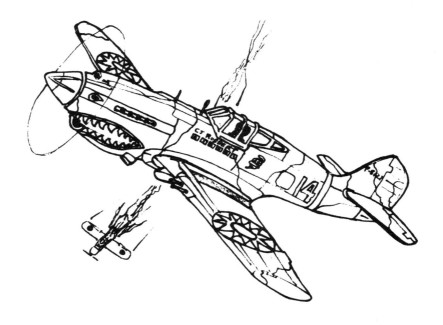

One Sunday, like the previous four or five, Dick Rossi, "Black Mac" McGarry and I found ourselves outside the church where Mass had just ended. The priests, who came from Europe, were always interesting to talk to. At least it was a diversion from our week-long activities at the base. It was December seventh (still Saturday, the sixth, in the States); a calm day.

On Monday at 5:30 AM, as was the custom, we were aroused from sleep by Sandy's rude gong. At the airfield, after breakfast, under an overcast sky, pilots lay around waiting for the flight schedule to go into effect.

There was a little Group paper which came out every Wednesday. So, we were all surprised to see the editor, himself, drive up and stuff a bunch of papers into the hands of one of the pilots, as he sped off towards headquarters.

When he yelled, "Holy hell! We're in a war!" Everyone mobbed him to get one of the freshly mimeographed sheets. There were only a few lines but the capital letters struck us like a blow.

"JAPS ATTACK PEARL HARBOR
OUR   RADIOMEN   ARE   IN   CONTACT   WITH
CORREGIDOR, HONOLULU AND OTHER PARTS OF THE
WORLD—WILL KEEP YOU POSTED."

I could see the excitement overcoming everybody. Some remarked that it was impossible that Pearl Harbor could be hit; it must have been Manila or some other place close to Japan.

Greenlaw appeared suddenly in his car.

"There's no mistake," he said, excitedly, "And Manila has been hit, also."

The Second Squadron was sent to the barracks to pick up their guns; we were next.

The alert shack became our daytime home; and, for those on emergency duty, nighttime, too. Meals were arranged at the airfield. We had cards and Acey Ducey; and Bob Little brought his record player for a little musical diversion.

That afternoon, the supply truck came by and issued all of us helmets and gas masks. The base had taken on a warlike look. It was Sunday, December the Seventh in the States!

The next day, if there was any doubt before, confirmed all that our communications personnel had told us; the United States declared war on Japan. Everybody was then convinced that he had made the correct decision in coming over with the AVG. I was especially sure, as were the other patrol plane pilots, anticipating that many of our fellow Naval Aviators would lose their lives in their slow, lumbering aircraft. Maybe some of them already had. We knew that Pearl Harbor had suffered many casualties and similar reports were coming in from Cavite in the Philippines.

Hank told me that he had thought, on more than one occasion, of returning to the States. Now, there was no turning back. There were others like him who, now, were fully committed.

The British prevailed upon Chennault, with the help of persuasion by Churchill, to send one of our squadrons to Rangoon. Their military forces in that area were in sad shape and, soon after, they turned out to be even worse than was thought. The Old Man decided that the protection of the harbor was important enough to accede to the request.

"We need two pilots to volunteer," Sandell was addressing our Squadron, "to accompany the Third to Rangoon."

"I'm in!" Hank was the first to agree to go.

My own decision was to stay and wait for orders to China, our original destination.

In the meantime, there was a flurry of activity, especially in completing the painting of sharks' mouths on the noses of the planes. Someone had seen a picture of RAF P-40s in North Africa with that design. It lent itself well to the long, sleek shape of our aircraft.

It was at that time that the individual squadron insignias evolved. Bill McGarry worked up a clever one for us. He sketched a figure of Eve chasing Adam inside a large apple entwined with a snake, designating the First Pursuit; The "Adam and Eve's." Members of the Third Squadron were painting the figure of a beautiful girl with wings and were calling themselves the "Hell's Angels." The second took the longest time but finally decided on the "Panda Bears."

The next morning, everyone was wishing the Third "Good Luck" on their venture in Rangoon. I singled out Hank to say "Good Bye." As the word was passed to man the planes, I walked with him to his plane.

"Everything will be OK," I assured him, shaking his hand and patting him on the back, "see you in China."

With a roar, the planes were taking off in pairs. Hank waved a last "Farewell" as he started down the runway.

The entire flight came over the field and pointed their sharks' mouths towards Rangoon. I wondered if we would ever see Hank again.

Ground personnel began packing equipment in trucks to be shipped up the Burma Road to Kunming. Everyone was becoming restless. There were long hours all day at the field and, at night too, when alert duty called. The night of the thirteenth, I got to bed late and fell into a deep sleep.

An eerie drone sounded way in the distance. My drowsy mind, soon, recognized the sound of a siren.

"Air Raid!" a voice screamed from somewhere in the barracks.

I began beating on the mosquito net in a frantic attempt to extricate myself. In a few seconds, although it seemed an eternity, I was free, fumbling madly to get my clothes on.

Someone turned on a light! It was doused immediately at the angry command of several voices.

A number of us were racing madly down the road with shirt tails flying. A car came by and we decked ourselves over the outside as it sped off madly to the field; it was all we could do to hang on.

Planes were taking off. The alert crew! We kept looking over our shoulders for enemy aircraft. I jumped into my plane and got the engine started, holding the brakes and waiting for radio instructions to take off.

It seemed like hours before "All Clear" was signaled. The sound of aircraft had been heard south of the field but nothing was sighted. For the first time, I was able to look at my watch; it was four o'clock!

At breakfast, much earlier than usual, we all laughed. In the dark, many had dived into mud holes for protection from the "attacking planes" and looked quite a mess as they came into the dining room.

"Hey, that's what we've got slit trenches for." Several of us chided as the "wounded ones" sheepishly went off to the washroom to clean up.

December tenth: Sandy passed on the word that the seventeenth was the date set for our departure for Kunming. The seasonal weather was improving in that area and the Japanese would be returning for another siege of bombing.

The next few days were spent packing. Everything would have to go by road. The P-40 had one small compartment which would take only the bare essentials. I dismanteled my bicycle, not knowing then that I would never see it again.

It became routine to live out of one suitcase. Everybody was keyed up for the appointed day. However, when the seventeenth came, Chennault announced that there would be a delay of one day because of bad weather. A CNAC (China National Aviation Corporation) DC-3 arrived to pick up the first group of ground personnel to take them to Kunming to meet our planes upon arrival. A second contingent was taken in the afternoon. We knew then that our departure was imminent, there was hardly anyone left to look after us.

On the eighteenth, as we awaited the final word to takeoff, a radio message from Kunming informed us that a formation of Jap planes was approaching the City! About thirty minutes later we received word to depart, just as the Japs were starting to bomb. We got forty-three planes of the First and Second Squadrons in the air, the most we would ever have flying again at the same time. What a pity we had not left the day before.

There were no maps! Each pilot had a small mimeographed sheet showing the route and the mileage. As we neared the area of Mandalay, a course change was made, heading us in the direction of our destination. The mountains looked even more rugged than the Rockies.

After covering over seven hundred miles, I began to worry about gas supply when the signal was given to go into single file. Almost immediately we followed the leader through a break in the clouds, coming out over a beautiful lake set like a jewel in the mountains. On the north shore was a flat area and adjacent to that, a large sprawling town. That was Kumming!

As we passed over the City on the approach to the airfield, I spotted a number of columns of smoke arising midst the buildings; the work of the Jap bombers.

The smiling face of my crew chief, Kenner, greeted me as I pulled up to the flight line. Opening the canopy, I got my first taste of the crisp, Kunming air. The sun was shining brightly but it was cold. We were at 6500 feet above sea level and winter had already begun.

My plane was almost immediately swarming with Chinese clad in quilted, indigo blue outfits. They were all smiling broadly enough to crack their faces. It was the first time they had ever seen such a large number of planes land at their airfield. When they measured the amount of gas remaining, it showed only five gallons, just enough to wet the bottom of the tank! Anyway, we had arrived in China, at last.

The three-mile drive to our quarters was rough and bumpy, and it was teeming with carts pulled by oxen or humans, and coolies carrying all kinds of vegetables and fruits, the largest I had ever seen. And the smell was outstanding. Col. Field, our Chinese teacher on the Klip Fontein, had told us it was the one thing about China that he remembered the most, even in his dreams! The ubiquitous, terraced fields were treated periodically with human excrement.

The station wagon passed the smiling guard at the gate to our new home. There were several buildings; some for the groundpersonnel, one for the mess hall, and those for the pilots. Out of the mob of houseboys, I found mine who showed me to my quarters. As we passed the length of a mud brick building, there was a door for each person. They were close together and, inside, sparse. The bed was little more than a cot. The cement floor was graced with a small grass rug. Over on one side, I spotted a low stand with an iron utensil in it. Since there was nothing else, I guessed that was the only source of heat.

There were noises in the next unit. By talking a little louder than usual through the thin partition, I could converse with my next door roommate, who happened to be Bill Bartling. I was just beginning to feel a chill when the houseboy brought in one of those metal containers with burning charcoal. The smell would take getting used to; and, at times, the brazier had to be left outside awhile to allow the carbon monoxide to burn off.

On the way to the mess hall, I passed several coolies carrying buckets of water on each end of a stick. They were headed in the direction of the washroom. Apparently, they were the supply line for the showers and other water necessities.

The talk around the tables centered on the bombing. A couple of the pilots had just returned from town and their story was grim. Usually, when the "Ching Pao" (air raid warning) was displayed, most of the population would leave the city for the protection of the open spaces. Since there had been no bombing for several months, most of the people had remained in town. About five hundred persons had been killed and many buildings destroyed. That hit home and made us realize why we were there. Without expressing it, everyone seemed to be thinking the same thought: "Bring on the Japs!"

It was very dark the next morning as our car approached the entrance to the airfield. A guard challenged us. Using the opportunity to use my Chinese, I shouted, "Mei kua jen" (American).

"Ding hao." He smiled and let the chain down for us to pass.

There were lights flashing on various parts of the field; the crew chiefs were warming up the engines. Turning on a light, Sandell announced that Chennault had decided on a dawn patrol to prevent any surprise attack by the Japs. He called off four names; I was one of them.

At the end of the takeoff area, when the crew chief shone a flashlight on the number, I found my plane. I almost broke my neck getting in, there was a little ice on the step. There was a cold blast of air on my face as the engine started off with a roar. The other three planes flashed their identification lights and we bounced down the runway together. As we reached our altitude, the first signs of dawn were showing in the East. For what seemed like hours, I strained my ears for some message from ground radio. There was nothing; we were called back to the field.

By late afternoon, we had given up on the Japs. Many speculated that maybe their spies had reported our arrival and would turn their efforts to other areas. That night, I got to bed early. I wanted the rest because I had a strong feeling that there would be action the next day. Was that wishful thinking?

The next morning, we went through the same procedure, except I did not have to fly the early patrol. I tried relaxing on one of the bunks in the alert shack but the noise of the games going on discouraged that. I was just getting interested in a game of Acey Ducey with John Dean when there was a screech of brakes outside and through the door burst Sandell.

"OK, men, this is it," he declared, a little breathless, "Jap planes have crossed the Indochina border and are headed this way. Stay in your planes and wait for the signal to take off."

There was a mad rush out the door and to the planes. Before I knew it, I was in my plane with the engine turning over, listening to the cracking sounds of ground radio. As I heard the broken voice say that the enemy aircraft were about a hundred miles away, an order was given for Jack Newkirk's Second Squadron to take off and intercept them.

"Dammit," I said aloud, angrily, "We should all go." Obviously, Chennault was worried about a second wave.

Again the voice in my ears, "Japs 75 miles out, no intercept yet."

Just as I was beginning to wonder if we were going to be bombed on the ground, I saw a red rocket go up. All fourteen planes of the First Squadron rushed down the field and into the air. With throttles bent forward, we headed through a break in the clouds. I was breathing heavily from trying to push the plane forward at a greater pace.

Just as we got above the clouds, I spotted a formation of planes silhouetted sharply against the bright, white background. I no sooner counted ten twin-engine bombers than Sandell was signaling for the strike. Unfortunately, my Flight Leader, Ed Leibolt, was ordered to ascend to a higher altitude and be on the lookout for Jap fighters.

Even though I was not in it, a big thrill went through me as I saw Sandell lead his flight into the enemy formation which was then headed the other way, towards home. With the first pass, one of the bombers began to smoke and trail the main formation. On the second run, it went down through the clouds and another burst into flames. The scene looked like a bunch of swarming bees. I wondered why our planes did not collide with each other, they looked so close.

Ed could not take it any longer. Knowing Sandell was preoccupied with the task at hand, he signaled that we were going into the fray. I tensed myself and followed him down, with my pucker string performing some strange gyrations. As the rear bomber loomed large in front of us, I pressed the gun button almost at the same time as Ed. Debris flew by as we dove down and away.

As we started in for a second run, I saw only six bombers. Ed was in the midst of the other planes and I could not make him out; so, I made the run alone. With a short burst, I knew the bomber had been hit, as I pulled away and down. Because the Japs, at that point had gotten right down on top of the cover, I went into the clouds on the dive. Emerging on the bottom side, I found myself over some very rugged mountains.

Not being able to recognize anything, I headed in a northwesterly direction. After crossing two ridges, I was just beginning to think about my next move, when another plane approached from the opposite direction. As he went by, I saw the shark's mouth. We joined up; it was Carl Brown, was I glad to see him. But, he threw up his hands indicating that he did not know where he was, either.

Heading east for the moment, we were joined by two more planes; one of them, Ed Leibolt. He signaled to follow him. With a sigh of relief, I saw ahead the second lake south of Kunming. Over the field, the order came for us to patrol until the others were refueled and rearmed. It seemed like hours that we were up there and my fuel gauge needle was approaching "Empty." I was about to leave the formation when we got the word to come in. We dove almost straight down and I landed with barely enough gas to taxi to the line!

I was immediately approached by a couple of anxious ground men who wanted to know how many I had shot down. I had to report that I could not claim any of them personally because the action went too fast and everyone got many shots at their targets.

I was rushed to the alert shack to make my combat report which was the procedure while everything was fresh in the mind. The other pilots were all busy with the same chore. Only four Jap planes had been seen to go down; but, later, Chinese Intelligence confirmed that only two of them had gotten back across the border. (NOTE: after the War, Chennault saw some Jap reports that stated that those two planes had crashed before making it to their base).

Joining my Flight Leader afterward, I asked, "Ed, did you know where you were when you picked us up out there over the mountains?"

"No!" Was his candid answer, "But it worked out alright, didn't it?"

We were all on Cloud Nine, especially when we heard that Ed Rector was OK. He had gotten low on gas and landed elsewhere. We all cheered at the good news. So, not one of us was harmed. There was not a mark on my plane: Number Thirteen; it was a great day!

But, the day was not over, yet. Sandell, unlike his usual seriousness, was exuberant. He shook the hands of the pilots and said that each one who had participated in the action would share credit for the four confirmed planes. That meant that I would have a fraction of a Jap plane in my record!

That afternoon, as we were all rehashing the experiences of the morning, Greenlaw came in the alert shack.

"Well, men," he announced, "you're heroes. The Chinese are coming out from the City to show you their appreciation for having turned back the Jap bombers from their homes, for the first time. Get straightened up a bit and look pretty."

Soon, we heard a band coming towards the field and a long procession appeared at the entrance. Led by the Mayor were hundreds of people, each one carrying something. He made a speech while we all stood in line listening. Although we could not understand, I could tell what he was saying by the thankful looks on the faces of those grateful people.

Little girls, with pretty faces crowned by neatly cut bangs, stepped up and placed long pieces of purple silk around our necks and bouquets of flowers in our hands. We were like a bunch of embarrased school boys. I could feel my face flush, along with the rest. What we had done seemed small to us; but, to them it meant a feeling of security in place of one of fear. The Chinese and American anthems were sung and gifts, which included native food, were distributed.

At dinner that evening, the Chinese boys treated us like royalty. Then, in town, our car was mobbed; everybody wanted to see the "Mei kuo jen." Looking back, as we started to walk down the main street, there was a large crowd following us. Everytime we went into a shop, there would be a dozen faces crowding the entrance just to get a glimpse of us. The news had spread like wild fire. It was not long before it was all over China.

When I arrived home that evening, I draped my purple piece of silk in the most conspicious spot in the room. I felt proud of it because of what is signified.

The next morning, there was a message of congratulations from the Generalissimo and Madame Chiang Kai-Shek, thanking us for all of China for the victory of the day before. They said that we were the liberators of the Chinese people from the plague of Japanese bombers. People were already calling us "Flying Tigers"; because the tiger was a symbol of the Chinese Government.

It is worth noting here that, for the entire remainder of the War, the Japanese never came back again to bomb Kunming.

There were a couple of days of quiet. On the afternoon of the twenty-third, Greenlaw brought us word that Ollie's (Arvid Olson) Third Squadron had run into a whole mess of Japs over Rangoon and shot down a half dozen of them. He added gravely that two pilots were missing. My heart jumped, I immediately thought of Hank.

That night I ran into Carl Brown.

"Did you hear the news?" He asked, gravely.

"It's Hank!" I exclaimed.

"You knew, then?"

"No, but I felt it."

"Neil Martin, also." Carl murmured, and, as he walked away, "Two down in the first engagement over Rangoon."

The sad news went to bed with me that night. I tossed and turned and did not sleep a wink.

Carl informed me later that Hank had told him confidentially, one night before he went to Rangoon, that he had gotten married two weeks before departure from the States. It sent a shiver up and down my spine.

Nothing was happening in our area; but, in Rangoon, the Third Squadron was in the thick of battle. During two days, Christmas Eve and the twenty-fifth, they shot down forty-four Japs. There were at least double that in probables. What a Christmas present!

But, there was a price. On the twenty-sixth, "Cokey" Hoffman was shot down. Now, both the youngest, Hank, and the oldest pilots had been lost. Cokey was the only enlisted pilot from the Navy in the Group. He was forty-five.

Early in January, Rossi and I went out to the field to talk to a couple of pilots from the Third Squadron who had just returned from the heavy fighting in Rangoon. We had dozens of questions about the action they had been in. We were most happy to hear that the P-40 was standing up far better than expected against odds as high as ten to one. However, we were very upset when they gave us the news that the Second Squadron had already been given orders to relieve the Third. That meant that we would have to wait another three or four weeks before we got our chance.

A week later, the sad news came in that Tom Cole had been shot down by ground fire while on a strafing mission. My old traveling buddy was gone; but, there was still some hope that somehow he would survive.

I was chafing at the bit to go to Rangoon. However, my luck would not allow it. All the pilots of the First could not go; so, one night, in the Squadron Leader's room, cards were drawn. I was one of the losers, but was told that in another couple of weeks, I could follow.

On February sixth, I had gone to the field before dawn for the usual alert duty. About eight o'clock, I received word to go back to the hostel, pack one bag and be ready to leave on a plane for Lashio by nine. Three other pilots and I almost broke our necks, packing and getting back to field. Jack Hennessey brought our Beechcraft around and we climbed aboard.

The red clay runway of Lashio airfield came into view and, after landing, we stepped out into the tropical sunshine. It was great to be warm again. We were just having a cold beer in the CNAC Hostel when Greenlaw entered with a very solemn face. Sandell had been killed while testing a P-40 that had been shot up by the Japanese. Bob Neale, Naval Aviator, would be our new Squadron Leader.

Late that night, we were put on the train to Rangoon. There was a stopover in Mandalay. We pulled into the station at Rangoon at ten o'clock one morning with the air raid sirens going. People were running in all directions. It was a madhouse. We managed to gather our baggage and push through the crowd in time to commandeer the last taxi. Natives piled all over the vehicle so that, soon, the driver could not see where he was going. We had to brandish our guns to get them off. The streets were being deserted quickly so it was not long before we were out in open country, on the way to Mingladon Aerodrome.

Dick Rossi met me to tell what a wonderful setup we had in two private homes of executives of the Burmah Oil Company. He and Mickelson were with Bill Tweedie, and Greg "Pappy" Boyington and I were in the home of Jimmy Adams. Both houses were very spacious and right next to each other. Servants would wake us with part of our breakfast (usually tea with a banana) in bed. And, greet us at night with cold drinks before dinner. This, in a war? Hard to believe!

It was the middle of February and most of the Malay Peninsula, including Singapore, had fallen to the Japanese who had pushed as far north as Moulmein, just one hundred miles across the Bay of Martaban from Rangoon. They had the British forces on the run. Because of those successes on the ground there were only occasional night bombing operations with the dock area and the airdrome as targets. We were close enough to the latter to hear the bombs exploding.

We could rest easily knowing that our planes were dispersed at two outlying airstrips; "Johnny Walker" and "Haig & Haig," we named them. The on-duty pilots would fly our aircraft there just before dark and drive back to their homes. Arising at four in the morning, the new crews would drive to the dispersal areas and bring the planes to Mingladon at dawn for the all-day alert.

On February twenty-fourth, five of our planes went to escort a flight of British Lancaster bombers on a mission to hit the Japanese ground forces just north of Moulmein. Except for the danger of being hit by anti-aircraft fire, the operation was fairly routine. So, we were surprised when one of our returning planes did a double victory roll over the field; that meant he had shot down two Japs. Soon the others came over also doing victory rolls. We had an excited discussion with the pilots. They were just heading back from the escort mission when they ran into a Japanese fighter patrol. Six enemy aircraft were shot down, for sure, with an equal number of probables. We were all keyed up with anticipation for further encounters with the Japs.

The following day, I was playing a game of Acey-Ducey with Dick Rossi. The other pilots were lounging on cots inside the alert shack or, outside, taking a sunbath in the hot tropical sun, in just their shorts. The afternoon quiet was pierced by the loud jangle of the telephone. We all turned to watch Bob Little's face as he picked up the receiver.

He said nothing to the other end but hollered, "Scramble!"

That was it; we all jammed the doorway like stampeding cattle. While I catapulted onto the wing of my plane, I saw, out of the corner of my eye, Boyington scrambling into his in just his khaki shorts. We tookoff in pairs in clouds of dust.

It seemed like hours to get to altitude, but was probably only about ten minutes. Bob Little waggled his wings and pointed south. I could tell from his devilish grin that we were in for something. Turning quickly, I saw two formations of twenty-seven bombers each headed for the airdrome.

I checked the gun switches "ON", then "OFF" and "ON" again just to be sure. I had a bomber picked out as my target and was getting my finger set on the gun button when we found ourselves in the midst of a group of fighters flying crazily in a bunch like bees. In a flash, one appeared in my sight, at close range; the two ugly red suns on the wings stood out. I managed one quick burst and almost immediately flew through the smoke and pieces that came from the plane. As I dove down and away, I saw him catch fire and spin earthward.

Pulling up to gain precious altitude, I looked around and all the planes seemed to have disappeared as if by magic. I took a heading towards Moulmein. Ahead and below, I spotted a foolhardy Nip pointed towards home. I closed on him with all guns blazing. Although white smoke appeared behind his engine, he made a sharp turn and went out of sight below me. Looking back, there were two of his mates trying to train their sights on me. I pushed the stick forward so hard I almost catapulted through the canopy. As I hurtled downward, I crouched down expecting at any moment the thud of bullets on the armor plate behind. Finally,

I looked back on both sides. Not only had I lost my pursuers, but there was nothing in sight.

With the all-clear message came the return of our flight, one by one. What a day! I had gotten my first Jap fighter and one probable. There was great excitement as we filled out our combat reports. Dick Rossi had gotten two planes. Our score; twenty-one confirmed and thirty probables. The Jap bombers had left a few craters on the field and killed one RAF man on the ground. But their losses must have convinced them that the AVG had, by no means, been destroyed as told by the Japanese propaganda machine.

That night, I could hardly get to sleep thinking of the luck of getting through that combat experience without a scratch. What might the morrow hold? Instead of sheep, I was counting planes going down in flames as sleep finally overcame me.

After picking up our planes at satellite field, Haig & Haig, we were back at Mingladon before the sun came up. Just as I was adjusting my Mae West in preparation for a strafing mission at Moulmein, the alarm sounded. Off again to hunt Japs! It seemed that they were making an attempt to surprise us.

But that was not to be. After searching the skies in vain, the order over the radio to proceed on the original mission. A seventh plane joined our flight; it was Dick Rossi.

Heading southeast over the Gulf of Martaban, we were soon approaching an airfield about twenty miles south of Moulmein. Since it was so early in the morning and our flight came in low, the Japs had not picked us up on their radio direction finders. It was a disappointment that there were only two planes on the airstrip. Each of us took shots at them as a few men on the ground scampered for cover.

We left the two planes in ruins as we quickly headed north. The east side of Moulmein was ridged with hills, so we made our initial approach over them directly out of the rising sun. As we came down from the ridge and neared the field, a wonderful sight met our eyes. The Japs had a little warning from the pass we had made over the auxiliary field. Some of them were just getting into their planes and others were already making their takeoff runs. It was a pitiful position for them to be in.

Going into single file, we dove on the "sonsabitches." I spotted a Jap at a thousand feet trying to gain altitude. Almost viciously I squeezed the button and with one spurt of all six guns, he rolled over and crashed into the hills next to the airport.

There were at least a dozen Japs that got into the air. That, with our seven planes milling around, made for a precarious situation, especially when all the big anticraft guns began to open up. The puffs of their exploding shells began to appear all around us. They did not seem to have any regard for the safety of their own planes.

When I started to gain altitude in preparation for another pass, I glanced at my fuel supply. Quickly calculating that there was just barely remaining sufficient gas to return to base, I advanced the throttle, at the same time pushing the nose over to pick up as much speed as possible. Down over the water, I streaked for home, rubbernecking for Jap planes the whole way.

Back on the ground, I discovered, from the accounts of the excited pilots, that we had shot down nine of the Jap planes. That, added to the destruction of the ones parked on the two airports, made for a very successful morning.

The lunch that was brought out to the field in a jeep was nothing to brag about. Since the City was becoming more abandoned every day, the mess supervisor had great trouble obtaining supplies for our daily necessities. We had no sooner finished eating the sparse meal than the alarm sounded again.

We managed to get twelve tired planes into the air. I wondered how long our equipment would hold out with no replacements or spare parts. The Japs really meant business; there were fifty-four fighters and fifty-four bombers! It looked as though this was their supreme effort to knock us out, and the airdrome, too.

In a moment, we were in the thick of battle. The first Jap I encountered went into a tight turn, but I had enough speed to pull up sufficiently to lead him for an instant. While I squeezed the gun button, he was blanked out of sight by the long nose of my plane. I pushed the plane over just in time to see him catch fire and head earthward.

Diving on through the fighters, their formation of bombers came into view. I picked the rear one on the right and made a diving quarter attack; but nothing happened, he stayed right in formation. I returned for two more passes. Smoke appeared from one of the engines but the plane just would not go down. Out of the corner of my eye, I spotted a number of Jap fighters approaching to protect the bombers. I immediately dove down and away.

As it always seemed to happen, when I returned to altitude, there was not a plane in sight. After heading east for a few minutes, I detected a speck on the horizon ahead. Closing in, it took the form of a Jap fighter. He was headed home without looking back. At about 250 yards, I squeezed the button and the barrage literally tore off part of his wing. He spun down crazily, crashing into the sea.

Taxiing up to the line after landing, my crew chief, Jake, approached the cockpit. I told him that I had shot down two for sure and two probables. A strange look came over his face.

"What's the matter with your tail?"

"I didn't know there was anything wrong with it." Was my comment. But, upon, glancing back, I saw that half of my rudder had been shot off. Those Nips had nearly found their mark! I had a weak feeling for a moment and probably even turned a little pale.

Jake pulled out some tape and began doing one of his miracle repair jobs as I joined the other pilots in the alert shack. That day we had confirmed twenty-three Japs with twice as many probables. The First Squadron had also made another record for two days continuous fighting; forty-four enemy planes with close to one hundred probables. And all that with only twelve available fighters!

That night I arrived at the almost deserted Adams' house with a dejected feeling that we were being abandoned in Rangoon. The Japs were only thirty miles away and nothing was in their way on the well-paved road leading into the City. I was awakened from a troubled sleep by a loud banging on the door.

"Get ready to leave," Jake advised, breathlessly. "The British have left the city without giving us any warning."

Among other things, they had taken the RDF radio equipment, the only means for detecting Jap planes as they approached our area.

"I'm taking you to the field, right now." Jake continued. "The planes will be ready to take off at dawn."

Speeding to the airdrome, we found the mechanics making last minute preparations, including the loading of trucks for the trip north. At first light we were off, as the trucks also started to pull out.

At Magwe Airport, I was met by some of the personnel of the Third Squadron who were back in Burma to relieve us for a much needed rest. On to Kunming via Loi Wing, we received word that all of our ground people had gotten out safely by road. Rangoon fell completely to the Japanese on March eighth.

One piece of disturbing news that I received was the recap of the action in Rangoon. The records that were given to Squadron Leader, Bob Neale, showed that I had only two confirmed Japs to my credit. I went over, in detail, all of the action as it had occurred. He confirmed my account with those of the other pilots who had been in the same engagements. After reviewing the situation with Chennault, it was agreed that I would be paid for downing four Japs. The supporting records never did arrive in Kumming; so, the official tally showed two planes instead of four. I had to content myself with the check for two thousand dollars which eventually arrived in my bank account in the States.

There was one other consolation; I was promoted to Flight Leader. The prestige was one thing; the raise, another.

On April fourteenth, I was chosen with five other pilots to make the long trip to Karachi, India to pick up six new P-40-Es, known as the Kittyhawk. An equal number had already arrived and they were formidable with their six fifty calibre guns free-firing from the wings.

While we were waiting for the CNAC airliner to come in, Clare Booth Luce came by. She was in China to get a story on the AVG for LIFE Magazine. It was the first time that we had heard the rumor that the famous career of the AVG was about to come to an end. She took pictures of the Group. It would be a long time before we saw them actually published in a big impressive layout in the Magazine.

The arrival at Dum Dum Airport that night was memorable. First, blackout restrictions were in effect, but all around for miles we could see lights flickering like millions of stars. Then, I never could figure out how the pilot found the field in the dark. Just before touching down, the bright lights of the airdrome went on briefly for touch-down.

Piling into a taxi, we were driven through the dark city of Calcutta to the Great Eastern hotel. The dining room was impressive with its English furnishings and large hanging crystal chandeliers. The waiter could not bring us enough chicken sandwiches; the remaining patrons just stared at the ravenous group of ruffians, gulping beer and scotch and sodas with each bite.

There was a small taste of the nightlife and the local beauties, and we all vowed to return. But, duty was calling and we were soon off to Karachi in a British flying boat.

Rushing out to Karachi Airport, we detected an attempt on the part of the Army to discourage us from getting off with the planes in a hurry. They told us that there were all kinds of things to be checked. However, we took the planes on a flight check to the beach area, tried out the guns and flew back over the field, buzzing the tent area in the process. An Army officer met us as we came off the line and told us, in no uncertain terms, that the General was mad as hell at such behavior. We smiled to ourselves.

That night we felt the ire of the General. We were given rope cots and a blanket to sleep on; no pillows. Early the next morning, we got off and, in formation, buzzed the General's tent area, blowing a number of them over in the process. We all laughed as we headed off in the direction of New Delhi.

From there, we flew over the Taj Mahal before heading for a last fling in Calcutta. It was then that we saw the news report of the Doolittle bombing raid over Tokyo.

Once the planes were checked, we headed over the breathtaking Himalaya Mountains. There was a stop in Loi Wing to drop off the extra gas tanks for some of our Group to use for long range missions into Burma and Thailand.

We learned of further details about the Doolittle operation. The crews had bailed out over China and every plane had been lost. Already, the men were turning up at various bases in southeastern China. Doolittle, himself, was in Chungking and a big party was being given for all the heroes who had assembled there.

One of the rumors of the time was that Chennault was being enticed into the Army with a commission as Brigadier General. He gathered us all together and explained the main problem. The Army would not supply us with spare parts and they had a plan to replace us with an Army Group. It did not make sense to us. The United States had pledged support to the Chinese Government and we were part of the Chinese Air Force. Besides, the AVG had invaluable experience and to replace it with a raw group seemed like nonsense to us.

In May, things deteriorated to the point where all of Burma was lost. For the first time all of our three squadrons were together. Bombing and strafing raids were made over the Salween River area. Those were dangerous and were done on a volunteer basis, ever since Jack Newkirk had been killed over Thailand. Tex Hill took over as leader of the Second Squadron. It was on one of those missions that my flying mate, Bob Little, was shot down near Pao Shan. One of our Navy Buddies, Ben Foshee, was killed on the ground at the same town. That added to the death of Frank Swartz as the result of a previous raid at Magwe.

During May, a few young Army Air Corps pilots arrived in Kunming. The U.S. military brass certainly did seem to be pushing the demise of our Group.

In June, with the cold, foggy season just about ended in the Chungking area; the Japs would be preparing for the summer bombing campaign. On the eighth, I was sent with the First Squadron to that City. Rossi and I had quarters together. Three days went by with nothing happening. Apparently, the Japanese spy network had reported our presence.

In the meantime, much was happening in Kweilin in southeast China. There was absolutely no air defense at that Airdrome except for a few antiaircraft guns. Every morning, the Japs had been sending over an observation plane, followed shortly by a formation of fighters and bombers. For them, it was more of a training program than anything else, as they encountered no opposition in their bombing forays.

On the afternoon of June eleventh, Chennault decided to put an end to their play. Eleven other pilots and myself were dispatched to that bombed city, arranging our arrival time just before darkness so that the Japanese would have the least possible oppurtunity to know we were there.

Arising two hours before dawn, we had our planes warmed up and everything in readiness. The Old Man had set up communications headquarters in a cave in a mountain just above the flight line near the end of the runway.

A short time before sunup, the Chinese Intelligence Officer answered the phone. Information had come from the warning net in the hills overlooking the airport at Canton, 250 miles away. Jap planes were taking off and heading in our direction. He placed little red pins on a large chart on the wall. As they were moved closer, Chennault gave the word to take off and engage the enemy aircraft, circling at twenty thousand feet until they were located.

It hardly seemed possible that, on such a calm sunny morning, we would soon be in mortal aerial combat. We were all straining our eyes for any telltale specks. In an instant, there they were off my right wing and a little below. Waggling my wings and, at the same time, firing a warning burst, our formation wheeled around and dove on the rear quarter of nine bombers. A short squirt of my guns and smoke appeared from one engine, but he did not go down.

Pulling up in preparation for another pass, I spotted three twin-engine planes scattered behind the other nine. Diving on the highest of the three; he, in turn, went into a dive. Then, to my amazement, he pulled up into a loop; but, at the top, rolled over and was headed in the opposite direction. Strange tactics for a bomber! Then, I recalled a recent intelligence report of a new Japanese twin-engine fighter — this was it.

Having sufficient speed, I was able to pull above and to the side of the plane and make another pass. Closing in, a quick burst of the six fifties tore off part of his wing and the Jap spun towards the sharp mountains below.

Directly in front of me, a bomber appeared, apparently unaware of my presence. My guns must have found a gas tank, because there was a gigantic explosion and the plane seemed to fall apart; pieces of it flying past my canopy.

Looking to the left, there was one of those twin-engine fighters chasing one of our P-40s. I turned to offer assistance, when the Jap made a head-on pass at me. He came so close, I had to depress my nose to avoid a collision. Again, he came around for the same kind of attack. In the meantime, the pilot I had come to assist had positioned himself on the tail of my attacker. Smoke and, then, flames appeared; another dead Jap.

Emerging from the cockpit, after arrival back at the airfield, I noticed something black right in the center of the fuselage at the base of the rudder. On closer inspection, I discovered that the spot was a large hole made by a twenty millimeter cannon. A few inches lower and the shell would have landed in my lap! A shiver went up and down my spine as I realized why the Jap had been so anxious to engage in head-on combat. When all of our pilots returned and reported , we had shot down nine Japs confirmed and five probables. That brought the First Squadron's total to 106, the Group's total rose to almost 300 with probables totaling over 500. I had 6.3 to my credit, although official record showed 4.3.

Incidently, the Japs never returned to Kweilin.

Towards the end of June, the Army sent representatives, in charge of a General Bissell, to our various bases to recruit the Group for the Air Corps. Instead of using Chennault for that delicate task, they attempted it themselves, with disastrous results. Only five of our experienced pilots signed up. Chennault had to send out a plea, asking us to stay on for another two weeks. During that time, two of our new pilots were lost.

Back at Kunming, before leaving China, the Generalissimo decorated us with the Fifth and Sixth Orders of the Flying Cloud Banner, the official decoration of China for war heroes.

Years later, during the CAT saga (Part IV: Civil Air Transport), General Chennault had the opportunity, during a visit to Japan, to look over Japanese military records about the AVG. They showed that; not three hundred planes, but nearly one thousand had been destroyed. That, with such a small group, which never had more than a couple dozen planes in the air at the same time! It was the inspiration for one of the Group to philosophize:

"There's nobody living today who knows how to do what we did."

That applied especially to the remarkable group of ground personnel who performed miraculous things under the worst of circumstances, even under fire, with a bare minimum of supplies. Enough cannot be said about their ingenuity and pride in what they were doing. They were the ones to keep the planes in the air so that we could make such an incomparable record.

雲南省政府歡讌

中國空軍美籍志願隊

民國三十一年四月二日

BANQUET

IN HONOUR OF

THE FIRST AMERICAN VOLUNTEER GROUP

of

THE CHINESE AIR FORCE

by

YUNNAN PROVINCIAL GOVERNMENT

THURSDAY THE SECOND APRIL 1942

MENU

Chicken soup with bamboo shoots

Green peas with ham

Spiced beef

Tiger palm mushroom with bean-sprouts

Chicken in Yunnan style

Eight precious pudding

Fruit

Tea

菜單

鷄　絲　竹　蒜　湯

火　腿　莞　荳

五　香　牛　肉

虎　掌　荳　芽

紙　包　　　鷄

八　寶　　　飯

鮮　　　　　菓

紅　　　　　茶

RECIPES

Kunming, in southwest China, is in the hearts of all Flying Tigers; it was our home and headquarters during the history of the AVG. A mysterious, walled city, it had high pagoda gates at the four cardinal points. Their huge, wooden doors which could be closed against invaders, opened onto the flat plain and beautiful Lake Tien Chih, 6,300 feet above sea level. The backdrop of surrounding mountains was spectacular. The city goes back almost four thousand years and I was sure that the huge cobblestones, about two by four feet, used for the narrow streets, had been there almost that long.

As the provincial capital of Yunnan, Kunming was known in ancient times as Yunnanfu, seat of the region. In addition to being the terminus of the Burma Road, it also was the main starting point for travelers and traders to Tibet. So, strange people were not unusual in the bustling streets, whose hundreds of shops catered to the thousands constantly milling about. It was all the more colorful with the ubiquitous red silk bunting and banners painted with decorative Chinese characters, usually in gold.

In China, food is probably more important to people in all walks of life than is Confucian philosophy. Restaurants abound and food stalls, preparing meals on the spot, are everywhere. Each region has its own specialties, in addition to the great gamut of Chinese cuisine which is found in even the smallest hamlets. Kunming was certainly no exception; the steamy vapors and tantalizing aromas were never to be forgotten memories of our sojourn there.

We found Yunnan ham an unusual treat processed in no other part of China. Since it was in such demand, the Yunnanese developed a canning process by which people in other parts of the country could enjoy that delicacy. Much of the uniqueness was attributed to the food grown in the area. Being at high altitude and, at the same time, in the latitude of the tropics, fruits and vegetables grew to an enormous size with unsurpassed quality and taste. That was reflected in the delicious pork produced there; hence the great ham. Yunnan Ham, in white sauce, with Chinese cabbage and bamboo shoots was a specialty of the Province.

Cheese was not made in China; that is, if by cheese is meant a product processed from fermented milk. However, the clever Yunnanese did develop a roquefort-like "cheese" from aged tofu, the great food made from soy beans.

Other things we learned by experience or by accident. Even years later, when we were again in Kunming under quite different circumstances, surprises were not uncommon.

My wife, Lil, was discussing dinner with our houseboy, Chin (pronounced "Gin"), whom we had brought with us from Shanghai.

"We have four—dinner tonight." She instructed. "You makee Chinese chow."

"Yes, missee."

"In Shanghai, we liked very much beef-green peppers." She continued. "You makee tonight."

"Missee mean led peppel." He objected.

"No, green pepper, like in Shanghai." She replied with finality.

As was his habit, Chin gave a conceding shrug of the shoulders, muttering, "Yes, missee," as he headed for the kitchen to prepare the meal.

The dinner had been resounding success through four courses: succulent shrimp sauteed in Chinese tomato sauce; steamed fresh fish from the Lake; Chinese vegetables, the likes of which can only be obtained in the Kunming area; and chicken with bamboo shoots and black mushrooms.

Then came the *piece de resistance*, a steaming platter of beef with green pepper. After placing it carefully on the table, Chin went to the door of the kitchen and stood there to watch the finish of another perfect dinner.

"To the new dish!" We all drank the warm Shiao Shing wine. Then all dove in with chopsticks and ate with relish. With relish? Hell, No! With Fire! There was a gasp from everyone.

One guest made a rush past Chin to the kitchen. Three of us grabbed for the wine; but that only made the fire worse since it was warm.

"Phew!" I choked. "Those damned peppers are hotter than any jalapeñas I've ever had in Mexico."

I looked at Lil. She was in discomfort but managed to blurt out. "But I told him green peppers."

"What is this?" I demanded of Chin."

"I tell missee 'led peppel,'" He said softly with that inscrutable smile of his. "Gleen peppel in Kunming velly hot, like file; led peppel velly sweet."

With that he left unceremoniously while we tried to recuperate. In a few minutes, Chin was back with a steaming platter.

"Led peppel." He pointed as he proudly set it on the table, removing the "gleen."

They were the sweetest red peppers we had ever eaten!

Now, let's continue with recipes from some Flying Tigers.

The adventure story of "Tex" Hill would take a book to cover. Born in the Kwangju area of Korea of Presbyterian missionary parents in the summer of 1915, he went early to San Antonio when the family was called there in 1921.

We first met at the end of the summer of 1939 in Pensacola where we bunked in the same wing of the Cadet living quarters. We were to develop a lasting friendship when we met two years later in the steamy little town of Toungoo, Burma. Adventurers seem to have a magnetic attraction for each other; evidenced by the fact that our paths have crossed many times in different parts of the world. Eventually we met beautiful Mazie, of Victoria, Texas whom Tex married when she was seventeen. They have parted with two of their favorite recipes which are now presented here.

"TEX" HILL'S *FRIJOLES*

Tex and Mazie say that this is known as: "Texas Caviar."
Assemble:
1 lb pinto beans
3 cloves garlic, minced
2 chicken cubes
2 Tbsp ground *Comino* (Cumin)
1 or 2 chopped Serrano peppers
Bacon rind, smoked ham hock or 3 Tbsp bacon grease
1 tsp salt, or to taste
Combine all ingredients in 4-quart pot with about 2½ quarts of water. Bring to a boil and simmer, covered, for about 4 hours.

Suggestion: The time can be cut to about half by, first, covering the beans with water; bring them to a boil, let them rest, covered, for one hour; then proceed with the above instructions.

"TEX" HILL'S ORIENTAL BARBECUED PORK RIBS

Assemble:
½ cup soy sauce
2 green onions, chopped
3 tbsp honey
2 cloves garlic, minced
1/2 tsp each powdered ginger and pepper
1 tbsp sesame seeds
3 racks pork ribs
Combine all ingredients, except the ribs, in a bowl and mix

thoroughly. Place the ribs in a pan (not aluminum). Pour sauce over them and marinate for 2 hours, turning frequently. Place ribs on a barbecue grill, not directly over the coals. Close lid and cook at low heat for 1½ to 2 hours until done. Pass the cold beer and lots of napkins!

Ed Rector, football player, aviator, *bon vivant* and ladies' man, is also quite a cook in his own right. Down through the years, from the time we first met as classmates at Pensacola, we have always been the best of friends. An ace in the Flying Tigers, he went on to a brilliant career in the Air Force in China and India. In Taipei, he was head of the Air Force Advisory Group. His last several years have been a joy in a large, beautiful house overlooking the Potomac River and all of Washington, DC. Lil and I have enjoyed Ed's unequaled hospitality on many a delightful occasion; and we have reciprocated in like manner. Most fitting is the Spanish saying, "Mi casa es tuya," My house is your house. And our visits always bring out the best in culin.ary achievement.

Ed's favorite creation is Beef Wellington which consists of a whole tenderloin of beef, roasted in the oven only until it is still rare. Since the tenderloin is tapered in shape, it should be tied up with string with the thin end folded over to make the entire piece have the same thickness. After it has cooled, spread with your favorite liver pate and roll in mushrooms which have been finely chopped and sauteed in butter. Encase this in an unsweetened pastry dough, brush with beaten egg and bake in a 350 degree oven until it turns a golden brown, about thirty minutes. Let it rest at least 20 minutes; then carve with a very sharp knife, or an electric one. The slices should each be thick enough to make one serving. Pass your favorite sauce; I like Bearnaise for this one. Ed's final word: "When I go to that kitchen in the sky I want my last meal to be Beef Wellington!"

Going from the sublime to the simple, Ed contributes the following:

ED RECTOR'S EASY (BUT DELICIOUS) FETTUCINE

8 oz sour cream
1 stick butter (Ed says, "No oleo.")
1/2 pint heavy cream
Mix together while heating but do not boil. At the same time, boil 8 oz egg noodles; drain when they reach the doneness you like. Add the cream mixture and toss with 1/2 cup grated parmesan cheese and 1/4 cup chopped chives. Salt and pepper at the table, to each one's liking.

Chuck Older was another classmate at Pensacola but he was a member of an elite group. Every class of Cadets had a few who had chosen to be in the Marine Corps. Of the sixty-six Naval Aviators in the Flying Tigers, about a half a dozen were Marines. A while after the disbandment of the AVG, Chuck returned to fight in China as a squadron commander and, together with his record in the Tigers, had credit for 18½ Japanese planes.

But Chuck was destined for still greater things. He became a Judge in Los Angeles and had the distinction of trying the Manson case. His lovely wife, Catie, contributed the following recipe:

CATIE'S *BOMBE MAISON*

1 quart Pistachio ice cream, slightly softened
1 oz unsweetened chocolate
7 oz semi-sweet chocolate
4 tbsp very strong coffee
6 tbsp dark rum
2 cups heavy cream
½ cup sugar

Chill a 2-quart bombe mold (Catie uses a spring form pan) and line it with the ice cream, firmly pressing against the sides; it should be about 1 to 1½" thick. Place in the freezer while preparing the filling. Melt both chocolates with the coffee over very low heat. Cool, then beat in the rum. Partially whip the cream; add sugar and continue beating until stiff. Fold in the chocolate mixture and blend gently but thoroughly. Remove bombe from the freezer and fill with chocolate mixture. Return to the freezer until the chocolate is frozen. To serve, unmold and cut into slices. Catie decorates the bombe with chocolate leaves or slivered almonds on top and adds: "I use mocha ice cream for a variation."

Robert (Bob) M. Smith was a radio station master for the Flying Tigers at BO-2 (station designation) in Cheng-Yi, China. At one point he had an opportunity to make the trip up the Burma Road. His diary is the basis of the book he wrote: WITH CHENNAULT IN CHINA: A FLYING TIGER DIARY, published by TAB BOOKS, Inc. It has over one hundred very interesting pictures of the AVG from that time. The recipe for chicken legs that is presented here was created by a famous Shanghai chef who escaped from the Japanese to Kunming in 1943. Bob says that he was first served the dish in an out-of-bounds restaurant operated by that chef. It was said that Madame and Generalissimo Chiang Kai-Shek always tried to visit the place when they were in Kunming because of the fame of the chef.

BOB SMITH'S CHICKEN LEGS WITH PINEAPPLE

Assemble:
12 chicken legs
1 can pineapple chunks, unsweetened
Flour, cornstarch and vegetable oil
Prepare marinade:
⅔ cup of pineapple juice from the can
½ cup soy sauce
1 tsp fresh grated ginger
3 tbsp sugar
Dash of pepper

Pour marinade into a 9 by 12 baking dish about 2" high. Put legs in and marinate for about 8 hours or overnight, turning occasionally. Remove legs and save marinade. Dip them in the flour and brown in the oil over high heat. Place legs in baking pan. In a pan, add 1 tbsp cornstarch to the marinade; bring to a boil to thicken. Put pineapple chunks over the chicken. Spoon sauce overall. Bake in a 350 degree oven until done, about one hour. Bob says that he serves the dish with brown rice cooked in chicken broth.

Robert "Moose" Moss, from the Army Air Corps, was in the Second Squadron of the AVG. Then we were friends in China National Aviation Corporation, flying over the "Hump" from India to China. Over the years, since that time, we have had occasion to visit "Moss Farms" in Doerun, south Georgia, not too many miles from the Florida border. I believe he is the only Flying Tiger who has a scientific pig-raising operation where the pigs live in the lap of luxury. Even though denied their usual wallowing around in the mud, they always looked happier, healthier and bigger than any pigs we had ever seen anywhere. Of course, he and his pretty wife, Janie, have, in addition to the pigs, many crops; peanuts, cotton, soy beans, etc., besides a few prize Charolais bulls. He has all the latest machinery and oversees the maintenance himself. If that were not enough to keep him busy; Moose, who is a great diving coach, develops youngsters, through his teaching program, into champion divers. Janie says that she sent the following pound cake recipe because, "I've never found one that could beat it."

POUND CAKE JANIE MOSS

1 lb butter or margarine
3 ½ cups sifted plain flour

8 tbsp (½ cup) coffee cream
2 ⅔ cup sugar
8 medium size eggs
1 tsp vanilla

Separate eggs. Whip the whites, adding 6 tbsp of the sugar; place in the refrigerator. Cream the butter, adding the remainder of the sugar gradually, beating until light. Add egg yolks, two at a time, beating after each addition. Add flour and cream alternately (about 10 minutes at low speed until very light). Add vanilla; then the egg whites, mixing only until well incorporated. Pour into a lightly greased tube pan and bake at 325 degrees, 50 or 60 minutes.

Carl Brown was from Class 135-C in Pensacola who joined me on the Klip Fontein in San Francisco to make the long trip to Rangoon. Later, we were in Squadron One together. After the AVG, Carl married Anne and together they scrimped and saved so that Carl could complete medical school and internship to become a doctor. As if that were not enough, they went through another siege and Carl completed law school to become a rare breed, a lawyer-medical doctor; or, was it a medical doctor-lawyer?! Anne says that Carl likes gumbo and submits the following recipe.

ANNE'S SEAFOOD GUMBO

Assemble:
2 tbsp each flour and oil
1 or 2 chopped onions
3 or 4 celery stalks, chopped
1 green pepper, chopped
1 can tomatoes
½ tsp liquid hot pepper sauce
2 pkg frozen okra
1 bay leaf
salt, pepper to taste
½ tsp thyme
lots of fresh or frozen shrimp or crab

The Roux:
Brown the flour in the oil, very carefully, on low heat to prevent burning; it takes a while. Add onions, celery and green pepper; saute until soft but not brown.

Add the tomatoes and about 2 quarts boiling water. Stir thoroughly while adding the hot pepper sauce and the other seasonings. Bring to a boil and simmer on low heat for ½ hour, stirring occasionally. Add the okra, cover and simmer for 1½ to 2 hours. Add the seafood before serving; cook only until the shrimp turns opaque.

Anne says, "The Southerners (Mobile area) cook the seafood longer, also they save it and have it the next day and it seems to get better and better with re-heating."

If you like oysters, do not hesitate to use them.

Serve over hot rice. *"A votre sante"*"with a glass of chilled white wine!

Ken Jernstedt is another of the Marine Aviators, from the Pensacola Class 131-C, who was with us in the Flying Tigers. Later on he was a member of the legislature of the State of Oregon, for a number of years. He complains of being twenty pounds overweight; and I can understand the reason after looking over the recipe he sent us. Here it is.

SENATOR J'S CHOCOLATE SPECIAL

LAYER I
1½ cups flour
1½ stick margarine, softened
1½ cups nuts
Mix and bake at 325 degrees for 25 minutes, then cool.

LAYER II
8 oz pkg cream cheese, softened
1 cup powdered sugar
1 cup cool whip
Mix cheese and sugar, then blend in cool whip. Spread on top of Layer I.

LAYER III
1 large pkg Instant chocolate pudding
1 large pkg Instant vanilla pudding
4½ cup milk
Blend and spread on top of Layer II. Top with cool whip and sprinkle with grated chocolate. Chill overnight. Diet strenuously before eating this in order to get a head start. Then, depending on the amount consumed, again diet accordingly.

Jim Howard was about a year before me at Pensacola Class 109-C. In the Flying Tigers he had credit for six Japanese planes. After the AVG was disbanded, he returned to the States where he signed up with the Air Force. Transferred to the European theatre, he was a Major in the 356th Fighter Squadron of the 354th Fighter Group. One day, in one action against the Germans, he shot down six enemy planes! He was given the Congressional Medal of Honor and later retired as a Brigadier General.

Jim has very kindly given us three of his favorite recipes. One of them that he uses all the time is from George Mardikian's book on cooking at his famous restaurant, Omar Khayyam's in San Francisco. He was an Armenian immigrant who built himself that magnificent establishment. One of the specialties there was the spinach salad.

OMAR'S RAW SPINACH SALAD

Remove the stems from the spinach. Wash very well in cold water adding a tsp of baking soda to the water to facilitate the cleaning. Drain and cut in strips about an inch wide. Season with salad oil and lemon juice and chill. When ready to serve, add chopped hard-boiled eggs and garnish with tomatoes and cold, cooked asparagus. Serve with:

OMAR'S DRESSING
2 eggs
1 tbsp sugar
1 tsp each of Worcestershire sauce and salt
½ tsp each of dry mustard and paprika
½ cup catsup
1 pint salad oil
½ cup vinegar
2/3 cup warm water

Rub a mixing bowl with a clove of garlic and mix all of the above ingredients except oil, vinegar and water. Stir them into a smooth paste. Add oil slowly, alternating with the vinegar. Beat with an electric mixer into a thick dressing, adding the warm water slowly. Keep in the refrigerator. Use as needed, will serve for several salads.

Jim's Spanish Omelette is similar to the one we made in Tiger Joe's Restaurant in North Carolina.
4 eggs (this makes a large omelette), beaten
2 tomatoes, 1 small onion, 1 green pepper, chopped

Saute the vegetables in 1 tbsp butter until soft. In your favorite omelette pan cook the beaten eggs until slightly brown on the bottom and done to the desired consistency. On top pour the vegetables and fold over. For lunch, Jim recommends garlic bread and fruit cup.

QUICK MEXICAN CHILI CASSEROLE

1 lb ground beef
1/2 cup chopped onion
1 envelope (1 to 1 3/4 oz) chili seasoning mix
1 16-oz can tomatoes, chopped
1 15-oz can kidney beans, drained and rinsed
1 1/2 cups shredded cheddar cheese
Sliced black olives

Brown the beef with the onion in a large skillet; pour off the fat. Stir in chili mix, tomatoes, and kidney beans. Simmer 10 minutes, stirring occasionally. Pour into serving dish and top with the cheese and olives. Pass the hot sauce.

Ed Goyette was another Naval Aviator, Class 108-C, who was one of us in the Flying Tigers. He had the distinction of working in Headquarters to help Col. Chennault in preserving as many P-40s as possible. During each day of familiarization flights, he would position himself at the landing end of the Toungoo landing strip in central Burma and make like a carrier landing officer; main object, get the pilots who had been flying much larger planes to land on the ground instead of 30 feet in the air. I think that only one casualty occurred. While Ed was waving frantically at a pilot who did not have the landing gear down, he landed anyway. After the screeching of metal on macadam had stopped and the dust was settling, the pilot jumped out of the plane.

"Why the hell didn't you watch my signals and go around?" Ed demanded.

"With that damned klaxon going in my ears," he answered sheepishly, "how did you expect me to concentrate on any signals." (Klaxon: Loud horn to signal that landing gear is not down).

It's a long way from there to South Florida where Ed is now retired from his real estate business. From there he sent the next recipe. He had one other one but Lil makes the best gazpacho I have ever tasted; for that you will have to refer to Part V, Page 277.

CHICKEN BREAST IN SOUR CREAM GOYETTE

4 or 6 chicken breasts
1 can cream of mushroom or celery soup
½ cup sherry
1 small can mushrooms, or fresh
1 cup sour cream

1 3-3½ oz pkg chipped beef
Paprika
Sliced ham, Swiss cheese and bacon
Flatten chicken breasts and roll each one with a slice of the ham and
Swiss cheese. Wrap each roll with a half slice of bacon, cut lengthwise.
Cover the bottom of a baking dish with the chipped beef and place the
chicken breasts on top. Mix well the soup, wine and sour cream and pour
over the chicken, covering it. Dust with paprika and bake at 350 degrees
for one hour. Pass the chilled white wine and enjoy!

Dick Rossi, of the San Francisco Rossi's, was a Naval Aviator of Class
134-C. After getting his wings, he was assigned as an instructor at the
Pensacola Naval Air Station. Very few aviators ever relished that job;
so, he was one of the first to volunteer when the AVG recruiter came by
the Station. We have been buddies since the Flying Tiger days, the
"Hump" operation (we had an apartment together in Calcutta, along
with Doc Richards), the beginnings of CAT and the early development
period of Son Vida in Mallorca. He is retired from The Flying Tiger Line
and with his wife, Lydia, lives on their avocado ranch in Fallbrook south
of Los Angeles. Here are three of his favorite recipes.

MEXICAN CASSEROLE ROSSI

1 7-oz pkg tortilla chips
1 lb ground beef
2 tsp instant minced onions
1/2 tsp garlic salt
1 can ripe olives drained and sliced
1 16-oz can tomato sauce
½ pint sour cream
½ pint cottage cheese
1 4½-oz can diced green chiles
½ lb grated jack cheese
Saute meat slightly and drain off the fat. Stir in onions, garlic salt,
tomato sauce and olives. Mix together sour cream, cottage cheese and
chiles. Crush tortilla chips, reserving a few for garnish. In a casserole,
place half the chips, half of the meat mixture, half of the sour cream mixture, then half of the grated cheese. Repeat the layers. Bake at 350
degrees (uncovered) until bubbly, about 25 minutes. Garnish with the
reserved chips and a few whole ripe olives. Serves 5 or 6.

DICK'S ZUCCHINI

6 small zucchini, shredded and salted lightly
2 large cloves of garlic, minced
2 tbsp butter
Dash of red pepper
12 oz jack cheese, shredded
Paprika

Saute the zucchini with the garlic in butter until crisp-tender. Transfer to shallow casserole, sprinkle with red pepper and cheese. Place under the broiler until the cheese melts. Sprinkle with paprika. Serves six.

POTATO CASSEROLE A LA ROSSI

6 medium potatoes, cooked in jackets, peeled, chilled
and then grated coarsely
1 cup cheddar cheese, grated
1 can cream of chicken soup
12 oz sour cream
8 green onions, chopped
1 cube butter, melted
Crushed corn flakes for topping

Stir together the soup and the melted butter. Add grated cheese, sour cream and onions. Toss with the shredded potatoes. Cover with some melted butter and the corn flakes. Bake at 325 degrees for 40 to 45 minutes. Serves 10 to 12.

Jim Cross was a pilot in the Adam and Eve (First) Squadron of the AVG contributing to the Flying Tiger record against the Japanese. Later, he distinguished himself for many years as a Captain for Pan American Airways before retiring, in recent years, in Palm Desert, California. This is his favorite recipe for Indian Curry accompanied by Sweet and Sour Lentils.

MUGHLIA BIRYAN-LAMB CURRY

½ stick butter
3 medium onions, chopped
2 garlic clove, minced
1 carrot, chopped
1 celery stalk, chopped (optional, American celery is unknown India)
½ green pepper, chopped
2 tbsp minced parsley

Saute all of the above until the onion is golden. Stir in one tbsp curry powder and cook on low heat for 3 or 4 minutes, stirring to prevent burning the powder. Gradually stir in 1½ cups beef stock (chicken stock for chicken or shrimp).

Brown 1½ cubes lamb in small quantity of oil. Can use chicken pieces of cubed beef. Place the meat in the prepared curry sauce and marinate for several hours, or overnight.

If using beef, especially one of the cheaper cuts, simmer the browned cubes in the sauce on low heat until the meat is tender.

Add the following to the sauce:

½ cup chopped tomato
½ cup coconut milk
¼ cup lime juice
3 tbsp chopped chutney
2 ½ tbsp brown sugar
1 tbsp ground coriander
1 tbsp ground ginger
2 tbsp raisins
¼ tsp ground cloves
1 bay leaf
½ tsp cinnamon
½ tsp cumin
dash of nutmeg
1 tbsp chopped orange peel
Salt and freshly ground pepper to taste.

Simmer the mixture on low heat until the meat is tender. About 15 minutes before the meat is done, add two chopped apples and ¼ cup plain yogurt.

For shrimp curry, shell 1 to 1½ lbs shrimp and cut half way through the back. After cooking all of the above ingredients in the sauce for 20 to 30 minutes, add the raw shrimp and cook only until just done; about 5 minutes.

Serve the curry on rice with lentils and condiments.

SWEET AND SOUR LENTILS

2 cups dried lentils
4 slices bacon
4 tbsp chopped onions
1 garlic clove, minced
2 tbsp wine vinegar
1 tbsp curry powder

2 tbsp sugar
¼ tsp nutmeg
1 tsp salt
Freshly ground black pepper

Simmer lentils in water until tender, about 30 minutes; add salt at the end. Drain lentils and keep hot; reserve broth. Saute bacon, remove and crumble. In the bacon fat, saute onion until golden; add the garlic at the end and the curry powder, cooking and stirring to avoid burning for about 4 or 5 minutes. Stir in one cup of reserved broth and cook until thick. Add the lentils and mix well; serve with crumbled bacon on top. The Indians eat lentils with chapatis, a round thin crisp bread made exactly like fried tortillas, using whole wheat flour instead of corn masa.

NOTE: The above two recipes as submitted by Jim Cross have thickening agents; flour in the meat curry, and cornstarch in the lentils. However, cooking the curry as instructed above, the sauce should thicken sufficiently. Also, note that the Americans and the British like the flavor of bacon in this type of dish but the Indians never use pork!

Condiments for Indian Curry can consist of any number of things served in individual dishes to be put on top of the curry as desired. Here are a few:

Chopped bananas, with lemon juice
Chopped apples, with lemon juice
Chopped onions, with lemon juice
Sliced onions fried very brown and crisp
Raisins, sauteed
Coconuts, toasted brown
Chopped hard-boiled eggs
Chopped tomato, green pepper and cucumber
Roasted peanuts, chopped
Chutney

NOTE: If curry hotter than the recipe is desired; add more curry powder in the cooking, or serve crushed red pepper or cayenne as a condiment.

Naval Aviator, Bob Neale, became my Squadron Leader early in the combat activities of the Flying Tigers when "Sandy" Sandell was killed testing a plane in Rangoon. He was a tall, very thin, wiry and nervous type guy who was bound to be a success leading the Adam and Eve First Squadron, evidenced by his becoming an ace several times over. He now lives with his wife, Fran, on Camono Island in Puget Sound, Washington. She says, "The recipe doesn't have a name." It is similar to quiche but differs in that it is made in a baking pan lined with bread rather than pastry.

NO-NAME SPINACH BAKE

Line a greased 14 x 9 x 2 pan with slices of buttered bakery bread (not the supermarket kind). Thaw a package of chopped spinach and squeeze it dry. Beat 3 large eggs in a large bowl; add:
The spinach
1 can cream of mushroom soup, undiluted
2 chopped onions
4 slices bacon, fried and crumbled
1 4-oz can mushroom pieces, browned in butter
½ cup milk
1 cup grated Swiss cheese
NOTE: For extra flavor, I like to add a couple of dashes of ground nutmeg.

Spread the mixture over the bread slices in the baking pan. Bake at 350 degrees for 35 to 45 minutes. When done, it should be puffy and a knife comes out clean when testing. A glass of chilled Chablis goes well with this dish.

PART III: CNAC — China National Aviation Corporation to FTL — Flying Tiger Line

Chapter 5

FLYING TIGERS GO TO CNAC

On July nineteenth, while waiting in Kunming for a CNAC plane to take us to India, Dick Rossi had some interesting information.

"There's a Panam Vice-President waiting in Dinjan to interview pilots to fly supplies over 'The Hump' from India to China."

"That's a smack in the face for the Air Corps." I noted. "You know the military powers that be may have precluded us from flying home since they control all air travel to the States."

The only other alternative was to wait for a boat from India and that meant facing German raiders in the Atlantic.

Bill Bond offered us a very enticing deal with CNAC, a subsidiary of Panam. They had just signed a contract with the U.S. Government to support Chennault in China. It was almost impossible to find pilots in the States; hence his presence to talk to the AVG pilots as they departed China after the dismal failure of General Bissell and his Air Corps recruiters. They thought they had us by the short hairs when they issued orders that no AVG s were to obtain air passage to the States.

The upshot of all those underhanded tactics was that Panam reaped most of the benefit. Seventeen AVG pilots signed up with CNAC. In addition, they obtained the superb services of "Doc" Lewis J. Richards as Flight Surgeon. The program was very attractive; two weeks of flying from Dinjan in upper Assam to Kunming, then two weeks off in Calcutta. The pay was excellent, much more than we had earned as fighter pilots, and there was anticipation of a vacation in the States within a few months.

Doc Richards found a large flat in a nice residential section of Calcutta. Dick Rossi and I went in with him. Several servants completed the setup. It seemed as though instant luxury was created out of what had looked like a bad situation when we departed China only a few days before.

On a clear day the Himalaya Range between India and China is an awesome spectacle. Afer takeoff from Dinjan, one could look back to the northwest and see the majestic peaks of Everest and Kanchenjunga rising above all the rest to more than twenty-eight thousand feet. To the east, Assam Province, Tibet, northern Burma and southwest Yunnan came together to form the area that we called "The Hump." It consisted of mountain ranges from fourteen to eighteen thousand feet. Bad weather was the rule and the constant presence of those jagged peaks hidden in the clouds was a fiercesome worry.

There were other concerns to the pilots. Weather reports were available only for the two terminals, Dinjan and Kunming. Enroute,

109

there existed no navigational aids. There was only one consolation in flying the bad weather, the Japs could not find us.

The Company had kept its promise. Vacations in the States were coordinated with the pickup of new planes. My turn had come in November. After a visit with family and a terrific 1942 New Year's Eve in the Stork Club in New York with my good friends Jeanne and Bus Loane, I found myself in Miami preparing to take a new Douglas C-53 back to India.

Eric Shilling, ex-AVG, had already brought his plane down from West Palm Beach where CNAC had set up a maintenance group to check out the new planes and install long range gas tanks for the transatlantic crossing. He went with me to pick up mine. The new C-53 was a cargo version of the DC-3 but still had the passenger door; later C-47 s had a double cargo door.

In the meantime, Bus Loane arrived. He introduced us to a south Florida delicacy. We were invited to Joe's Stone Crab Restaurant where we devoured large quantities of the succulent claws. It was a memorable meal, not to be repeated until many years later when our family lived near Key West.

Another item of use in India and China was cola syrup. It was sold in wooden casks, so I purchased one for friends who could not obtain the product in the Calcutta and Kunming areas.

Arriving at Natal, Brazil, via Puerto Rico, Trinidad, Georgetown (Capital of British Guiana) and Belem (near the mouth of the Amazon River), we prepared for the most critical part of the trip. The extra gas tanks were filled for the first time. We must have had at least four thousand pounds above the maximum allowable load. Takeoff for the ten-hour trip was set for eleven o'clock at night in order to arrive at our destination in the early morning hours.

Our destination; Ascension Island in the middle of the South Atlantic. The Island, only a small dot in the Ocean, nine by six miles, fortunately had a powerful navigational radio transmitter. With our overload, taxiing was very difficult on almost half-flattened tires. And, we went straight out over the water never gaining more than eight hundred feet of altitude for the first half of the flight. However, the trusty radio beam brought us straight into the long runway shortly after sunrise.

That left the same kind of a long trip to Accra, Capital of the Gold Coast in Africa. Then, several hops across the "Dark Continent" to Aden on the Red Sea. The rest of the journey took us along the south coast of Arabia, over the Indian Ocean to Karachi; finally, across India to our final destination, Calcutta.

It was a relief to finish all the traveling for awhile and enjoy two weeks off in our comfortable flat. But, the beginning of April, 1943, it was off to Assam to get back to work.

Spring of the year, in the Dinjan area, saw the beginning of the monsoon season. It was great for the cultivation of tea, which the region is noted for; but was critical for flying. Heavy precipitation, coinciding with lingering low temperatures of the winter period at the higher altitudes, made for the worst of icing conditions.

Such a day it was that early morning when Ridge Hammill and I took off with a load of medical supplies for Kunming. Ridge, who was from the Germantown area of Philadelphia, had just signed on with CNAC after a long service ferrying planes in Africa. It was his initiation on the run.

During the previous three months, CNAC had decided to put parachutes on the flights for the crew. On the other hand, de-icing boots for the wings had been removed. They gave the reason that the rubber rotted in the tropical sun of India. But, I suspected the reason was to utilize the weight saved in additional cargo.

Hardly thirty minutes out, at sixteen thousand feet, we encountered snow and ice which started to accumulate on the wings. Hammill looked grim.

"If we can make it halfway," I tried to reassure him, "we will be able to go all the way."

But that was not to be. Very soon, the ice built up to five or six inches and we were beginning to lose altitude.

"We've got to turn back." I announced.

Because of a predicted strong crosswind tending to blow us north towards the higher Himalayas, our heading was corrected to compensate. We never knew that the wind was about twice that anticipated.

Once under sixteen thousand feet, I had that empty feeling that we were going to get below some of the peaks in the area. When the plane approached fourteen thousand, I felt the hair on the back of my neck bristle.

"If we can hold out only ten or fifteen minutes more," I said, hopefully, "we should be in the clear."

Ridge just looked somber.

Ice had formed on the inside of the windshield. Using our hands to melt it, we could see nothing but snow. Then, suddenly, there was a swirl in the clouds. And, directly ahead, a mountain.

"My God!" I cried. "There's a mountain!"

Pulling into a tight turn to the right, there was almost instantly a scraping sound under the fuselage. The nose tipped down and we crashed into the mountain of snow.

There was a complete silence, except for the falling snow outside midst a whining wind.

Chapter 6

BEYOND THE LAST HORIZON

Shaking my head to get rid of the numb feeling, I sensed a cold wind. "There must be a hole in the plane." The thought occurred.

Just as I was beginning to wonder where the crew was, I heard a voice scream.

"Let's get the hell out of here!"

Looking back over my right shoulder, there was Ridge's head looking through the back door. He thought the plane was going to catch fire.

"Better get inside," I hollered, "You'll freeze to death out there."

Fumbling with the seat belt, I attempted to get up. There was a sharp pain shooting from my right ankle through the entire leg. I knew I had to get through the plane to survey our situation. There was debris all over and stumbling over it aggravated the injured ankle.

After what seemed like hours, I made it to the rear and slumped breathlessly on the floor next to where Ridge was. He seemed dazed. There was a large, bloody gash on the side of his face, and I was afraid to look at it for fear that he would notice my concerned stare.

"Do I look OK?" He inquired numbly.

"Yes." I lied to reassure him. "But, how do you feel?"

"I don't know. Feels like my ankle is sprained."

Then I realized that my radio operator was not in sight.

"I'll go up front," Ridge sensed my concern, "and see what happened to Wong."

I watched him crawl and stumble over the cargo. Up in the passageway to the cockpit, he bent over. There was a long silence.

"He's dead." Ridge cried.

I could only murmur. "Poor Wong."

Ridge just sat there on the floor for a long time.

"When you feel up to it, better come back here. See if you can bring one of the parachutes."

The lack of oxygen at fourteen thousand feet made it extremely difficult to do anything. But, Ridge eventually made it to the rear, dragging a parachute. When we finally got it open, it was unbelievable how much silk there was. It filled a good portion of the back of the plane. At least, it would keep us warm.

"As soon as I get my second wind," Ridge blurted out, "I'll get another one."

The parachute operation and looking for things we might use, occupied most of the day. All during that time the snow fell and the wind howled outside.

113

As darkness fell, the wind picked up with a roar. The plane rocked on the side of the mountain. Large amounts of snow broke loose and the avalanches threatened to carry us away. Sleep was impossible. There were a few obscure moments when it seemed like we dozed.

Dawn eventually came. The scene outside was unbelievable. In the clear light of morning, there was snow everywhere, surrounded by three sharp mountain peaks. The two behind were joined by a saddle which we had clipped just enough to slow the plane down and drop us in the snow, abruptly.

"What luck!" I exclaimed. "Look at that peak ahead of us. If we hadn't been slowed by hitting that ridge behind us, we would've crashed straight into that mountain."

The third peak was not more than two hundred yards directly in front of us; a gigantic wall of ice and snow. We just sat there, looking silly, smiling at each other at our good fortune.

"Even on a clear day like this," Ridge commented, "no one could put a plane down in this spot and get out alive."

"Well, we're alive, but there's no way we can walk away in our condition. We'll have to wait at least a few days to see how our ankles do."

Wait, we did. What does one do at fourteen thousand feet in the snows of the Himalaya Mountains? There was a deck of cards and, fortunately, a bottle of the cola syrup that I had purchased in Miami. We played gin rummy and drank "Snow Cokes," made by mixing syrup with the virgin snow. And, we kept score: Ah, the optimism of youth.

After several more storm-filled nights with frightening shows of avalanches, dawn of the seventh day broke clear.

"This is it." I told Ridge. "Once we leave there's no turning back."

We had made a futile attempt on the fourth day; but, after half a day stumbling in the deep snow, we had struggled back to the protection of the plane.

Plywood strips helped support our ankles. We used parachute nylon to wrap them tightly. The parachute shrouds could come in handy, so we each carried a coil. The door from the plane served as a sled until we lost it over the side of a precipice after two hours. Then, we slid on our butts.

Shortly before arriving at the snow line, the canyon we were following, came to an abrupt end. There was a drop of over fifty feet. That's where the parachute shrouds did their duty. Tying them together and to a rock, we let ourselves over the side, dropping the last ten feet into the final stretch of snow.

Following the stream seemed best but it meant sloshing along in the cold water, soaking our feet and most of the lower parts of our bodies. There was still a lot of snow and very often snowball avalanches pounded us on our backs while we waited for them to subside.

Once away from the snow, there were only two worries. First, the Japanese had taken most of Burma and we had to hope that we were far enough north not to stumble onto any of their positions. Then, there was the ever-present danger of starving to death before encountering anyone.

Gourmet note: One day we found a dead bird. It appeared to have flown into the trunk of a tree, breaking its neck. I had the remnants of a tube of soup concentrate which had broken in the pocket of my shirt during the rough descent through the snow. Removing the feathers and rubbing the scrawny bird on the turned out pocket, we experienced our first gourmet Himalayan meal.

The lack of food caused a constant thirst. The sound of another stream ahead was the cause of anxious anticipation. It was the seventh day out of the plane. Coming over the opposite bank of a rivulet, there ahead was Ridge on his knees. As I approached, he said nothing but stared ahead.

"What is it?" I asked, apprehensively. Still no answer

Looking in the distance, I saw the reason. There was a long, thatched-roof bamboo hut on short stilts. And there was smoke rising from the roof! I fell alongside Ridge and neither of us said a word for several minutes.

Nearing the hut, it appeared locked up; there was nobody around. Locating a door at the far end, we forced our way in. After becoming accustomed to the semi-darkness, we could make out a long corridor on the right side with compartments on the left. But they were all empty, except for the last.

Huddled around a fire in the middle of the room were several children and two old women, all with straggly black hair and smoky, oriental complexions. The children, eyes flashing in fear, were jabbering at the old women whose eyes indicated they were blind. They certainly were explaining that we were creatures from another world.

When their fears subsided, they put an iron utensil on the fire. After a few minutes, the grains that they had added began to pop. So the first real food that we had had in two weeks was popcorn! Then they put crushed corn, with water, in the same pot and boiled up a kind of mush. Although coarser, it reminded me of good old Philadelphia cornmeal mush. We devoured it as if it were the best gourmet meal we had ever eaten in our lives.

Incidentally, those two "dishes" proved to be the extent of their cuisine. After four days of such a diet, we had our first bowel movement in almost three weeks. That started my belief in a high fiber diet.

On that fourth day, something else happened. We noticed that two of the children were gone. Even the next day, there was no sign of them. The morning after that, we were sitting on the step of the hut when, in the distance, coming up the trail, were the two kids. Following them were three men; but, men like we had never seen before. They looked like creatures out of the Stone Age; long black hair, G-string, abbreviated vest-like back cover with a pouch on one side and a long knife on the other.

They approached us suspiciously and motioned us into the hut. We all gathered in the next to the last compartment where we had been staying. After looking us over very carefully, they laughed at our boots. Cautiously one tried them on. Clopping around, he thought it hilarious. The other tried on my flight jacket. The zipper was a great mystery. He couldn't believe that up, it was closed and down, it was open.

During our brief stay at the hut, we had learned a few words of the language. The men got across to us that we would have to walk to the next hut, a day's travel away; an excruciating thought.

Early the following morning, we set out on our next hike, after having had the inevitable corn mush for breakfast. It was difficult to get used to our boots again and it was not long before our ankles were throbbing with pain. The men were very patient with us and held down the pace to what was a leisurely one for them.

The ups and downs of the rugged mountains was a terrible grind for us. By noontime, they signaled for a rest, indicating that we had covered about half of the journey. A couple more natives came out of the thick undergrowth to join us. They had some bananas which we all ate ravenously.

Shortly after that, we were passing through a large patch of poppies. One of the men showed us how they sliced the bulbs on the stems and extracted the sap which was absorbed on strips of heavy cloth carried on a string around their waists. They called it *"ganee,"* their word for opium!

"Do you think we'll ever get to where we're going?" I asked Ridge, late in the afternoon.

Instead of an answer I got a grunt, meaning, "I'll be dammed if I know."

About the time we were about to give up, an elderly man came down a hill to greet us. Pointing to himself, he indicated that his name was Dayno. He led the way over the next ridge and there, below, lay another bamboo hut just like the one we had left early that morning. It was the first one we had seen that entire day.

More natives appeared, surrounding us, to see who the strange characters were. The women stayed in the background and peered between the men. When we reached the steps of the hut, we crawled through the doorway and collapsed inside.

"That's the last time I'm going to walk." I gasped.

"You're so right." Ridge agreed, completely exhausted. "They're going to have to carry us out, before I walk again."

The only apparent difference inside the hut was the two fires; one in the half of the compartment nearer the door for the men, and the other for the women. The latter wore clothing that covered most of the body and, for decoration, silver coins around the neck. Within a short time they were passing around bowls of the inevitable corn mush.

"This should make you feel right at home." I said, smiling.

"It's not exactly homecooking," Ridge replied, wryly, "like in Philladelphia, but it'll do for now."

"I just remembered reading in the Calcutta newspaper about a tribe like this called the Mishmis. did you see that section on our map called the Mishmi Hills?

"If you're right," Ridge said, looking at the map we had brought along, "we're about fifty miles north of where we thought."

"That accounts for not seeing any Japs." I concluded. "We were sure lucky, at least, in that respect."

The Mishmi Hills were in the most mountainous area of northern Burma and northeast India, bordering on Tibet. The people were related to the Burmese and Tibetans. The women went out all day to work in the fields while the men sat around and talked. They were inveterate smokers using a Chinese-type water pipe. A main section of bamboo had a smaller tube inserted near the bottom. A piece of dried leaves was placed on top of the small section and lit with a hot coal from the fire. The smoke passed through water in the bottom of the main tube. The smoker handled the hot coals from the fire with his bare hand. Needless to say, they had very calloused fingers.

We were great curiosities. Visitors were constantly passing by to view the "strangers from outer space." Our boots and flight jackets with their mysterious zippers were of great interest, as was Ridge with his blond hair. One day, a visiting native tried on Ridge's jacket. Before we knew it he disappeared.

"Must have gone to show his friends." I remarked.

"I think he stole it." Ridge said accusingly.

Incidentally, from our hut, there was not another one in sight; and we never knew from how far visitors had come.

Not to offend our hosts, I accepted the water pipe and joined in with the other men, although I was not a smoker. One evening, we noticed Dayno going through quite a ritual. He sliced up banana leaves and browned them over the fire. Then he took one of the strips of cloth hanging form his waist and dipped it into hot water in a bamboo tube.

"*Ganee.*" He said as he dipped the leaves into the extract. Rolling them into a ball, he broke off a small piece and placed it on the end of the water pipe. A hot coal was held over it as he inhaled the smoke. Nothing spectacular happened but, later, we did notice that he went to sleep with a smile on his face.

"I wonder if that would work for us, Ridge?"

"It's worth a try."

We had developed a strange malady from sleeping on the ground and being constantly wet for so long. Our skin was very painful to touch and sleep was difficult, if not impossible. So, when Dayno offered the pipe, we tried it out of politeness. Besides, his machete-like knife always looked menacing. However, we never did notice any improvement in sleeping. That was our introduction to opium smoking.

Days became routine. We were almost part of the family. Actually, the Mishmis lived in septs, a group of families in one hut. There were no villages, but rather isolated structures like the one we were in.

One day, two strangers appeared and joined us around the fire. The older one, whose name was Ma Lon, had a woven rattan hat and a pouch from which he took some tea and a quantity of rice. The younger wore a neat, black turban and carried a gun that looked like an old blunderbuss of the type used by the Pilgrims. He was obviously a headman by the way everyone listened to his every word. They called him Ah Shaw.

After sampling the tea and the rice, I began adding a couple of new words to the back of my map. Ah Shaw was immediately interested. He made some frantic motions.

"What do you suppose he wants?" Ridge asked.

"Probably wants the map for a souvenir."

When I tore off a piece and handed it to him, he was not satisfied, but kept pointing to my pencil.

"Do you suppose he wants the autographs of two celebrities?" Ridge asked facetiously.

Taking the piece back, I wrote:

"To Ah Shaw and Ma Lon from two pilots crashed in the mountains."

He no sooner got the scrap in his hands than he was on his feet and, without further formality, was out the door. We watched as he disappeared, dashing down the trail like a graceful deer.

Three days later, Ah Shaw appeared in the doorway. He was grinning from ear to ear. Seating himself by the fire, he took four eggs out of his pack and gave them to us.

"Well," Ridge reacted, "looks like our autograph was worth four eggs. At that rate our whole map should be worth its weight in food!"

After a short while, Ah Shaw arose and went outside.

"Hope he's not leaving again, so soon." I remarked.

But, he hadn't left. He came back and handed me, sort of as an afterthought, an envelope.

"Ridge! Look!" I fairly screamed.

It was an official Indian telegraph envelope, sealed with red sealing wax.

With my heart pounding and my hands shaking, I ripped open the envelope.

TO PILOTS AWSHAW AND MALON
SENDING RATIONS WITH MESSAGE STOP DOCTOR
·ARRIVING TWO DAYS LATER WITH AID STOP
MAJOR PHEIFFER AND CAPT LAX

If we could have danced, we would have. As it was, we just sat there, our faces beaming. Ah Shaw's round face was one big grin; he was as happy as we were.

We plied him with questions, but we were so excited that we forgot our few words of Mishmi and it took us quite a while to find out that he had run all the way to a British scouting party four-days' march away, to deliver the note that we thought was wanted as a souvenir. He had traveled so fast that he made the eight-days' trip in less than four. The porter with the rations didn't arrive until late that afternoon.

NOTE: It was sometime later that we discovered that, due to the way the officer in charge of the scouting party had interpreted the note, it was thought that our names were Ahshaw and Malon. Inquiries to the Army and CNAC brought negative answers about such pilots being missing. This was further complicated by the fact that, when the inquiry was put to Washington, the names had gotten changed to O'Shaw and Malone! Consequently, there remained considerable mystery about our rescue until sometime later when communications were established.

That evening, after the rations arrived, there was a big celebration. We gave everyone cigarettes and matches. The latter went into a cache to be saved like treasures. The head of the house brought out a kind of a beer made from corn, called "bawsee." There was tea, and rice. The canned rations completed the gourmet feast. All the hardships of the last few weeks were dissipated in the joy of at last making contact with civilization. It was much later before we realized how hopeless our situation had really been. That night we slept better than anytime since the crash.

Two days later, on a nice sunny afternoon, Ridge and I, sitting outside, experienced a strange sight. Snaking its way along the mountain trail below was a safari of about thirty people. As it slowly drew closer, we could make out a British officer leading the single file. It seemed to take ages for them to negotiate the last approach to our hut.

"I'm Doctor Lax." Came the British accent, as he stretched out his hand in greeting.

He almost lost his British composure as we practically hugged him like a couple of bears. After we settled down in the hut, he went over us thoroughly.

"Your ankle," he directed his diagnosis to me, "is dislocated and broken in several places."

He indicated that I might be crippled; that was grave news, especially for a pilot. Ridge fared a little better in that his sprained ankle had healed fairly well.

"I hate to tell you this." The Doctor advised. "But, the only way to get out of here is to walk."

That was even more excruciating news. The scouting party had set up a camp about three-days' travel from where we were. The monsoon rains were to get worse so it was imperative to depart almost immediately; early the next morning.

During the festivities that went on that evening, Ridge and I joined Dayno and the others in "a pipe."

"How long have you been doing that?" Doctor Lax asked when he saw what was going on.

"Oh! About a week."

"You'd better stop." Was his only comment.

Our various experiences during and since the crash had accustomed us to miracles, but the Doctor added more to the story. He told us no white man had ever been that far up in those mountains and that it was quite by accident that a British scouting party came even as near as four-days' march.

"Our patrols," he went on, "only go through this area about once in three or four years. My appearance just happened to coincide with that of you chaps, quite by chance!"

The next morning at dawn, there was a great gathering in the clearing in front of the hut. Doctor Lax handed over to us more than three hundred silver rupees. This, in turn, we delivered to Naykur, the head of the sept. Jubilation shone on all their faces because that quantity of silver was a lifetime fortune for them.

It was time to leave "our hut" and the gentle people who had been so kind to us. We felt sad for we had acquired quite an affection for them. The pain was eased when Ah Shaw and Dayno decided to go along to see us through to the end.

In the first few hours, the narrow trail dropped about a thousand feet to the Gulum River. We picked our way through its gorge, detouring now and then to miss impassable areas.

After two full days of rough going, we were looking down at the juncture of the Gulum and Tullo Rivers. The latter was much wider and swifter moving. On the other side, we could see the small figures and the huts of the British camp. While an overnight camp was being set up, Ridge and I surveyed the mode of negotiating the river.

Across the torrent were strung several strands of wire between two wooden superstructures on each side.

"You think we're supposed to cross on that dinky thing?" Ridge asked, incredulously.

"It does look impossible."

Doctor Lax was listening. "Not impossible. I was a nonbeliever, a few days ago, but that's the way we came over to reach you.

The next morning, Ah Shaw showed the way by going first. Facing the sky in a loop of rattan that went over and around the cable, he started with his head pointed towards the other side. The early going was easy as the cable sloped down to the center. The rest of the uphill way, hand-over-hand, took a monumental effort. Soon, he was on the other side, waving to us as if to show us how easy it was!

For us, the rattan loop was brought back with a wire attached.

As I climbed in the loop to make my crossing the Doctor instructed, "Don't look down and you'll be across before you know it."

Hanging on for dear life, I zipped rapidly to the middle, then seemed to stop for the longest while. The natives on the other side had to take up the slack in the wire. In the meantime, I did look down   at the raging torrent.

"Brother! Get me out of here." I screamed.

But, of course, no one could hear anything above the roar of the river. It seemed like ages before the natives, huffing and puffing, pulled me up to the other wooden structure. They all smiled as they lifted me out of the loop. It was hours before the last man had crossed.

Major Pheiffer and his men gave us a rousing welcome. Although the quarters were the inevitable bamboo huts, it was like heaven to us because of the blankets, waterproof covers and, of course, the British food.

While we settled down for a much needed rest, the Mishmis and the porters of the British party began to clear a long strip on a flat area above the river. The Major had word that it might be possible to get a small plane in to take us out.

After the arduous trip, Ridge began to feel strange. He was nervous and irritable, at times downright mean. Doc Lax took a look at him.

"Seems to me you had too much of that pipe. A few days of rest and some good food and you'll be alright."

He turned out to be right. Ridge had withdrawal symptoms and within a short time, was OK again. It was strange, but I never did feel anything untoward.

The waiting made us anxious but there were diversions, mostly culinary. The scouting party consisted of three groups; the British with their European cuisine, the Moslems who did not eat pork and Hindus who ate neither pork nor beef. So, there were three separate kitchens! And, off on the side, our few Mishmi friends had their usual fare.

In the evening, after savoring a nice British meal, we would sneak off and visit the other messes. Although, most of the time, we had no knowledge of what we were eating, there were many interesting dishes spiced with curries and chutneys. And, they had the best chapattis which are like crisp tortillas but made of whole wheat. We even dropped in on the Mishmis to see if the corn mush was up to standard! When they found out, the officers never stopped wondering about our voracious appetites and cast iron stomachs. They could not fully realize what we had gone through during the previous many weeks.

The next day we were awakened with the news that the monsoon weather was breaking a little and a plane would be able to reach us.

"This is it." Ridge said over breakfast. "Finally, we're going to get out of this god-forsaken place."

"I wouldn't be too sure." I cautioned. "This gorge is very treacherous and he's going to need a clear break in the clouds to get in."

"Ah, he's sure to make it."

But, he didn't make it; we heard the engine noise and thought we saw him briefly through a small hole in the overcast. After a short time, the sound began to retreat and...then, disappear altogether.

"Maybe he'll come back later." Ridge murmured

"I doubt it." It was Major Pheiffer. "The forecast indicates a worsening of the situation. I'm sorry to say that we have to break camp and move out of here before the monsoon traps us for the entire season."

Ridge looked so hopeless, I really felt sorry for him.

As we prepared to get under way, Doc Lax told us that it was about a hundred-mile walk to the approaches to Sadiya, the last town of the upper Brahmaputra River. We cringed at that news; that meant at least ten to twelve days more, over rugged mountains. And, with the monsoon, it meant traveling through almost constant rain.

"The Mishmis offered to carry you over the rough spots." Doc Lax tried to offer some consolation .

"How in the world can those little fellows carry us?" I asked. "They're only five feet tall. Even though we've lost a lot of weight, we must still be one hundred thirty-five or forty pounds."

"You shall see." Was his only comment.

It was not long before we got our first demonstration. Everything was packed and the porters were moving along the trail with heavy loads on their backs. We had reached a particularly rough, rocky section. Two of the muscular mountain men took off their turbans. A knot was tied in the heavy black cloth, making a large loop. One of them put his around my waist and lowered it under my butt. Then with his back to me, he stooped down and placed the knot over his forehead. Standing up with a grunt, he had me off the ground, on his back; even though my feet were almost dragging the surface.

In a moment, he was off over the rough rocks, followed by his companion carrying Ridge. It was almost like a race to see who could cover the most ground in the shortest time. They had a big toe which was somewhat separated from the others and was used to grip rocks and other protrusions.

Grunting with each step, it was miraculous the way they covered that rough section, without once stumbling. They set us down once we reached easier going.

"That's the damndest ride I've ever had in my life." Ridge sat on the ground laughing.

"Doc Lax sure was right. I never would have believed it, if I hadn't experienced it."

If we had admiration for the Mishmis before, we now thought they were nothing short of miracle men.

All went well for the next few days, as we passed through some beautiful mountainous country with deep gorges and rushing rivers. Those were crossed on swaying bamboo bridges which I wouldn't dare tackle even under the best of circumstances. My ankle tired easily and I knew that I was giving it a bad beating.

The little, muscular Mishmis performed the impossible, carrying us piggyback over the roughest country I had ever seen in my life. They laughed as they took turns and never seemed to think it was a task; but, rather a contest. Soon we came to a very steep area along the river and had to go straight up to get around it.

"Boy," I confided in Ridge, "I hope they can do this without dropping us over the side of that gorge."

"Sure looks scary." Was Ridge's only comment.

One of the Mishmis took a bamboo tube down to the river's edge and brought it back with some water, while our two carriers were taking strips of cloth from around their waists. They let them soak in the liquid and, at the same time, prepared us in the slings. When we were properly positioned on their backs, they drank the "ganee" extract and, believe it or not zipped several hundred feet up the steep cliff and deposited us at the top as if it were nothing.

"Wow!" I exclaimed. "I don't believe we did that."

Ridge lay on the ground in hysterics, while the other Mishmis gathered around and laughed and cheered as though it were a picnic.

Suddenly, the monsoon broke with a vengeance. The heavens opened up and punished us with all-day rains. Doctor Lax calculated that, in one 24-hour period, it rained twenty-four inches!

The river and its streams became swollen and torrents of water rushed through the gorges with a fury that took everything with it. The natives went ahead of us to prepare crossings at the least dangerous spots. It was a race against time.

It was also a battle against the leeches. The more it rained, the more of them appeared. They hung from every branch and bush. At the end of each day's travel, we would strip everything off and tear off the leeches. Poor Doc Lax! He was of very fair skin and would pick up dozens. I was lucky in encountering only one or two each day. They left scars that I would have as evidence for the rest of my life.

On the eighth day of the monsoon, we finally escaped the river gorge and headed up the last of the mountains. On top of the ridge, we were greeted by an American Signal Unit that had been waiting for us for more than a week. They had prepared an American feast. There was, among other things, Southern Fried Chicken, American coffee and homemade apple pie! We ate so much, we were almost sick; but, the pleasant feeling as we lay in our bunks that night, was well worth it.

Early the next morning, a good omen...the monsoon eased up temporarily and, as we started down the other side of the mountain, there lay in front of us the valley of the Brahmaputra River winding its way down from the Himalaya Mountains in Tibet. Farther down the River, we could make out the area where Dinjan was located, the base where we had taken off forty-six days before. We were on the dividing line between the primitive world and civilization. We had walked 150 miles!

Along with the thrill of actually escaping from the arms of death, there had to be a sad note. We had to take leave of Ah Shaw and Dayno and the rest of our Mishmi friends. They had worked so hard and done their utmost to return us safely to our own people. They stood in the trail watching as we disappeared into the valley below.

The next morning, a truck took us to Sadya on the River, where a small plane took us to Dinjan. It was not long before a CNAC plane had us in Calcutta where Doc Richards told me that I would have to go to the

States to have my ankle overhauled.

There was one interesting aftermath. When a plane went down over the "Hump", it was given up for lost. Someone was appointed to distribute the crew's clothes and send their valuables home. When the impossible happened, and Ridge and I returned, there was a mad flurry to return our things. We got clothes back; but, the majority of them were the clothes of others because the originals could no longer be located. Many were much too loose, only a few were too tight.

Chapter 7

CNAC TO FTL

It's a long way from the Mishmi Hills to Seattle. A Doctor Anderson in The Swedish Hospital had been recommended as one of the few men who might rectify all the punishment that had been heaped upon my poor right ankle. He was the inventor of the original metal splints in the orthopedic treatment of broken bones, especially the joints.

A six-hour operation and thirty days in the hospital, saw the removal of the erector-set structure in and around the ankle. They used tools not unlike those employed by a carpenter. Three months later, in Dr. Anderson's office, I was forced to stretch the Achilles Tendon and almost passed out; but, from then on it was all downhill. He told me, only then, that he had been concerned that I would never walk normally. The operation involved taking the joint apart and scraping away all the callous which had formed inside.

One year later, in the Hollywood Hills, I was walking fairly normally and began the long road back to flying. In those days, even with all the experience I had had, it was necessary to start from scratch. I joined the Civil Air Patrol and studied all the written part of the regulations and, then, took flight lessons at Independence north of the Mojave Desert area. Finally, flight tests at Baker, California and I had a Commercial License and Instrument Rating.

But, there were no jobs. In the spring of 1945, Harvey Greenlaw, who was living in Beverly Hills with Harmon and Ising of movie cartoon fame, invited me out to his house to discuss a proposition.

"Joe," he explained, "Paramount Studios is planning to do a picture called 'Calcutta' about flying the 'Hump' and they need a technical advisor. It will be directed by John Farrow and star Alan Ladd and William Bendix. Would you be interested?"

"Would I? Of course, I'd take anything right now; and, it might lead to something else."

"Don't count on that; it's only for three or four months, then it ends."

Well, it did lead to something, but not what I thought.

The work was extremely interesting. Paramount acquired a surplus Douglas C-47 cut it in half lengthwise, and mounted it on large, hydraulic pistons to simulate the motion of flying. When it appeared that Alan Ladd was flying, I was working the controls on the side, out of camera range.

We went on location for a 24-hour stint at Saugus Airfield at the extreme end of the San Fernando Valley. I even got a chance to act in the picture, even if only for a brief moment, as a crew chief, directing the plane into the flight line.

But, as always happens, all things must come to an end. It was in May, of 1945, during the last few days of work, that a call came into the Studios for me.

"This is Bob Prescott, here in Washington." The familiar voice said.

Hardly giving me a chance to say "Hello," my Flying Tiger friend of the First Squadron went on.

"I have an option, with a few Californian businessmen, to purchase fourteen cargo planes. I need ten of the old guys to put up ten thousand dollars each to form a cargo airline. Can I count on you?"

"You sure can." I was way out on a limb, because I had less then four thousand dollars to my name.

"Good. I'm going ahead with the deal and I'll be back on the West Coast in a few days to formalize the whole thing."

When he hung up, I called "Catfish" Raines who had been one of my group on the Klip Fontein. Prescott had already informed me that he had committed himself. I explained my predicament.

"I can lend you some money so you can participate fully in the deal."

While thanking him, I thought, "It sure is nice to have a friend to come through like that in the time of need."

The next day we went to the Bank of America and signed an IOU and I was virtually an equal partner in what eventually became the Flying Tiger Line, the largest all-cargo airline in the world!

The meeting took place in the home of Allen Chase in Pasadena. Sam Mosher, the President of Signal Oil Company, did most of the talking.

"I understand," he began, "that you fellows have ninety thousand dollars—we will match that. Also, I recommend that Prescott be given his ten thousand shares in return for his efforts in obtaining the planes for this operation."

Everybody was agreeable to that and the Company was formed with one hundred and eighty thousand dollars, the bulk of which was used to purchase fourteen Budd "Conestoga" cargo planes. They were made of stainless steel and had been turned down by the Navy for what was purported to be "minor defects." Those defects turned out to be major; however, because the war was still going on, the planes were the only ones available and they enabled us to get started in the airline cargo business.

The next day, in a room in the Biltmore Hotel, in downtown Los Angeles, "Catfish" and I joined Prescott and the other Flying Tigers participating in the Company which, incidentally, was known, in the beginning, as the National Skyway Freight Corporation. "Duke" Hedman was our first Chief Pilot and I was appointed Superintendent of Flight Operations. In spite of those impressive positions, we would all work as pilots along with the others; including, "Link" Laughlin, Bill Bartling, "Cliff" Groh and "Catfish." Dick Rossi was one of the investors but was still flying in China.

Prescott, of course, was President, heading the operations at our first headquarters at Long Beach Airport. He used an old friend, "Tony" Miller, Packard salesman, as head of the Sales Department to drum up cargo. Our first loads were cut flowers, lettuce and strawberries from southern California to the Chicago and New York areas. Our planes were overloaded, to please clients, and the Budds gave us all kinds of difficulties; stainless steel fittings broke from metal fatigue and exhaust stacks fell off the engines, causing fires on more than one occasion.

With a load of furniture, out of Detroit, an engine caught fire and the pilot just barely got the plane back to the airport before it burned completely. On the first flight of our biggest contract to fly Newsweek Magazine to Los Angeles, the plane crashed, in a snowstorm, on top of a mesa out of Albuquerque, leaving "Doc" Lewis, Flight Engineer, as the only survivor.

Besides those catastrophes, many as a result of the purported "minor defects," the major airlines started a campaign to eliminate us from the business. One of the largest actually appointed a Vice-President, whose sole objective was to see that our existence was short-lived.

But, we survived. It seemed like the instincts which we had developed over the skies of China served us in the vicious war declared on us by the airline industry.

During that period, I had my own harrowing experience. It was New Year's Eve, 1945. I had delivered a load of California strawberries to New York and was in Washington, D.C. scouting the airport for passengers for the return trip. I managed to sell passage to seven sailors who were returning to duty after the holidays. I met Tom Haywood in the weather office. He had just completed his eastbound run and told me that the weather was bad over the Appalachians, snow and sleet, but the tops of the storm were at approximately ten thousand feet, about right for the Conestoga. So, we headed out for Memphis.

After two hours, we were flying "on top," having climbed above the snow and sleet. But, as we headed into the area of the mountains, the tops of the clouds began to rise and the plane was in, then out of, the ice which began, little by little, to deposit on the surfaces. Especially the antenna was affected and radio reception began to deteriorate. That was notably bad for bringing in the radio ranges, our mainstay for navigation and letting down through the poor weather. Then, we had a little bit of luck.

"I think we've got the Knoxville range." I hollered over to John Pinney, my co-pilot. "We'll make a try at a letdown."

The descent through the storm was rough and there was no sign of anything, except darkness. For some reason, I put on the landing lights. In a moment, there was a swirling of clouds.

"Jesus!" I hollered. The landing lights shone on nothing but a snow-covered mountain and bare trees. The hair bristled on the back of my neck as I abruptly pulled the plane up and advanced the throttles all the way forward. We were almost immediately back in the clouds and there was a long, tense silence before we could even breathe normally.

"Goddam, that was close." I looked over at Pinney and he was as white as a sheet. "We're heading back east to see if we can pick up an airport that might be in the clear."

But, no such luck. A couple of towns went by, evidenced by a few flickering lights below the overcast. However, no sign of an airport. Another worry...gas supply was getting low.

"The next sign of a town, I'm going to circle down and take a look." Pinney just nodded at my remark.

By the time the next telltale lights came into view, I had to make a big decision.

"Whatever we see," I announced, "We're going to have to find a place to land."

That turned out to be not as easy as it sounded. Below the clouds, we found ourselves in what appeared to be the bottom of a teacup. Everything was snow-covered and there were mountains all around. A few lights flickered here and there.

"I'm going to have a look over there at that spot." I shouted at Pinney. "Looks like a road. Look for obstructions."

Coming around, I prepared to land. The flight engineer had prepared the passengers for the jolt.

"Wait!" I heard my copilot scream as he pointed across my face to the left. "Over there looks like a better place."

"We're sure to run out of gas." I blurted out, but decided to take the chance.

As I wheeled around in a sharp turn to line up with the newly-chosen site , the engines sputtered.

"Out of gas on that side." I cried, as I reached the cross-feed and frantically switched to the last tank, whose needle gauge was already bouncing off zero.

Into a steep slip, we went; and, at the last moment, I straightened it out and pulled the nose up, as we touched surprisingly softly and went sliding over the snow.

With the landing gear up, the plane stopped rather quickly and everything became very quiet except for the snow falling on the fuselage outside. A flash went through my mind of a similar situation in a far off land in the Himalayas.

The tranquility was broken.

"Let me outta here!" A voice screamed and there was pounding on the side of the plane. Looking around, I saw that it was the flight engineer who had gone a little berserk as he saw the reflection of the landing lights on the snow and thought we had caught fire.

I got the door open and he immediately calmed down when he saw the way out. Stepping into the snow, I was making my way toward the edge of the lighted area around the plane.

"Here, you'll need this!" A voice came out of the dark circle. An arm appeared in the light and a bottle of whiskey was handed to me by a tuxedo-clad gentleman who had stepped forward from the crowd of formally dressed people.

"What is this?" Was all I could think to say.

"You're on the golf course of the Bluefield Country Club!"

After the cheering had subsided, we were led up a hill to the Club where we joined in the New Year's Eve festivities that had been abruptly interrupted by our dropping in.

For more than thirty years, the plane stayed on that golf course in West Virginia as a caddy house. The stainless steel structure remained a non-corrosive, shining monument to adventure, and golfers tipped their hats as they passed by playing their rounds each day.

When I finally got the CAA on the phone, they congratulated me for getting the plane down safely through the snow storm, and I felt pretty good. That is, until I reached Prescott in Long Beach.

"When is this going to stop?" He asked, in anguish.

"You ought to appreciate that we all got out of this alive and without a scratch." I answered angrily. Of course, he had his worries as President; my plane was the fourth one lost, thus far.

All of this culminated in two things; one, I stopped flying, temporarily, to devote full time to my operations job, and the Company made the decision to start purchasing surplus C-47 s which had become available with the ending of the War.

In the Fall of 1946, General Chennault paid us a visit at Mines Field (later Los Angeles International Airport) where we had set up new headquarters. The Old Man had just been awarded a franchise for an airline in China in return for his outstanding efforts on behalf of the Government before and during the War. Our discussions with him included the possibility of a joint venture between the two airlines. Catfish and I became especially interested and committed ourselves to joining the General's operation when it was ready.

The quirks of fate are strange. The combined operation could have been one of the greatest in the world. Prescott appointed his brother, an accountant with the Flying Tiger Line, to proceed to China and check over the financial aspects of the new airline. If everything appeared in order, the two companies were to join forces. Prescott advanced $20,000 for expenses which meant that we original stockholders already had a stake in the venture.

George Prescott's first layover was in Manila. That evening, he was sitting in the lobby of the Manila Hotel having a cool drink. A car screeched to a halt outside the entrance and from it two men emerged. Ascending the steps to the hallway, to the horror of the onlookers they sprayed machine gun fire into the area and fled as quickly as they had come.

George lay in a pool of blood on the floor where he had fallen from his chair. He had died instantly. The gangsters, in search of an enemy, had murdered an innocent bystander, by mistake.

Needless to say, that ended abruptly any interest that Bob Prescott had had in the new venture. However, Catfish and I were still interested. Bob was very upset with our decision, but there was no deterring us.

Another development occurred which convinced us that our move was the right one. F.T.L. had been awarded a much sought after contract with the Air Force to fly their Pacific runs. Prescott had employed a few "professionals" from T.W.A. to take over key positions in the airline. He took the stance that we were only pilots and he needed executives. But, he had been "only a pilot." And when you got right down to it, most of the executives in all the major airlines had been "only pilots" to start with. I was more than a little bitter over that attitude.

Catfish and I were on a plane to Honolulu just after Christmas, 1946. Dick Rossi was at the airport to meet us.

"When are we leaving for China?" I asked enthusiastically.

"Not so fast." He told us. "The planes won't be ready for at least four weeks, and probally not for six. So, relax and enjoy your stay. After all, we're on per diem and hotel expenses are paid."

That satisfied us and we proceeded to do just that, enjoy our stay in Honolulu. It's seldom in life that one has the opportunity to get a job where there's a six-weeks' vacation, with all expenses paid, especially in Hawaii!

With our headquarters in the old, charming, wooden Moana Hotel on the beach at Waikiki, we basked in the sun and enjoyed the beauties of

Hawaii. There was an occasional trip to Wheeler Field where seventeen C-46 s were being prepared for the long trip to Canton, China.

The Royal Hawaiian Hotel, next door, was bringing over Joe Reichman and his orchestra for the event. He was an old friend of mine from San Fernando Valley, who had permanent billing at the Biltmore Hotel in Los Angeles where a gang of us used to attend the dinner dances that were so popular there.

One evening, over a roast lamb dinner at Coconut Island, Allen Chase's executive hideaway in Kaneohe Bay, he mentioned that his sister would be visiting soon. Allen was Director on the FTL Board and a member of the Sam Mosher group.

"How about escorting Betty and go with Celie and me to the Grand Opening at the Royal?" He offered.

"Sounds great" I accepted, but with a reservation. "Isn't it formal?"

"Don't worry about that, I've got an extra outfit."

On the big evening, a boy brought the suit to the room; complete with shirt, tie, studs, everything. Everything—except I had no black shoes.

"Dammit!" I exclaimed to Catfish. "No black shoes and they are waiting in the lobby for me."

"So, what do you want me to do?" Giving the impresion that there was absolutely nothing he could do.

"I'll tell you what you can do." I had an idea.

Picking up the phone, I called Joe Reichman. Fortunately, he was still in his room getting ready for the big event.

"Joe, have you got an extra pair of black shoes?" I felt silly asking. "I'll explain later."

"Yes," he replied, laughing, "send someone over to pick them up."

The rest was almost like "Comedy Capers." Catfish rushed downstairs, smiling in quick recognition as he passed the Chase party.

He was back rather quickly.

"Where the hell's the shoes?" I demanded when I saw his empty hands.

"They wouldn't let me through the gate." He explained lamely.

"Joe," I said meekly over the phone, "could you, please, call the guard at the entrance and tell them to let Catfish in." I could hear him laughing as he agreed and hung up the phone.

"Get the shoes." I commanded, pushing him out the door.

As I paced up and down in my socks, biting my nails, the phone rang. It was Allen.

"What the hell's taking you so long." He demanded. "The gals are getting nervous."

He was not appeased; and, I was sure that he must have thought we were a bunch of nuts when Catfish went by for the fourth time; this time carrying...a pair of shoes!

The evening was a gala affair, with a sumptuous dinner, entertaining company and great music for dancing. All through the festivities, every time I danced by the bandstand, Joe Reichman at the piano, would lift his foot high in the air and laugh like a fool. And, Allen and the party went into hysterics when I finally had to explain what had happened.

RECIPES

Milton Caniff is a fellow member of the Flying Tigers Association. He is considered "one of us" especially because of his depiction of the many exploits of the Flying Tigers and the pilots of C.N.A.C. in his two famous comic strips: TERRY AND THE PIRATES and STEVE CANYON.

While Milton Caniff's favorite menu consists of such disparate gourmet foods as; Spanish Gazpacho, African Lobster Tails, Deep South Greens and Hong Kong Melon, his cartoon strip hero, Steve Canyon, lives a more precarious existence. After a parachute landing in dense jungle, Steve broils a boa constrictor filet. Caniff says it tastes like chicken! Here's how he did it.

CONSTRICTEUR ROTI A LA NECESSITE

NOTE: This is a last ditch survivor's attempt; only for adventurers in dire straits.

Catch one medium-size boa constrictor, any python will do.

Remove head and skin; cut into portions the size of a chicken breast. Broil over wood coals for about ten minutes until tender but juicy, basting with pure water, boiled or treated with halazone tablets.

Serve with fresh bamboo shoots, if available, or cooked leaves of the taro plant. The root of the taro plant is the "potato" of the tropics and may be served baked, boiled of roasted.

As a substitute for wine, serve water which still smells of chlorine 15 minutes after halazone tablets have been added.

Pray!

Charlie Uban was a C.N.A.C. pilot flying the Hump along with the rest of us. After the War, he moved with the Company to Shanghai. Ever since those days we have been very good friends, visiting each other as travel opportunities have presented themselves. He and his lovely wife, Emma Jo, settled in Waterloo, Iowa where Charlie served for awhile as State Congressman. They have sent the following recipe which, although not as "last-ditch-survivor's" as Milton Caniff's boa constrictor, is still rather unusual.

ROAST CAMEL

1 Camel leg or fillet steak

One day before grilling camel meat, marinate all day in a good teriyaki sauce, basting frequently. Use a grill with a lid. When the fire is ready, brown the meat well, basting to keep it moist. Close the lid and allow camel to roast; continue basting. Cook as long as beef roast; time depends upon size. When a long pronged fork is inserted in the center of the meat and comes out very hot to the back of the hand, the camel is done. The finished result is superb!

NOTE: The Ubans give a tip on recognizing camel meat, if you ever find it for sale: "When jabbing finger into the raw meat, it will not give, but remains firm."

ABOUT *SATAY*

Satay is a dish prepared throughout Malaysia and the Malay Peninsula. The meat or seafood is marinated in a sauce which has as its main elements; dark soy sauce, lemon or lime juice, garlic, ground coriander, black pepper and crushed red pepper or cayenne. Recipes have to be adjusted for piquancy to suit individual palates. For guests, employ a minimum of hot pepper in the marinade and the serving sauces; use a separate bowl of the hot stuff for the more adventuresome. Curry powder, ground peanuts (you can try other nuts, too) and ground ginger are varied in the sauces. Ground sesame seeds are often used in place of or with nuts. I like ground coconut in the sauce for shrimp or fish.

The meats are usually; beef, pork, lamb or chicken. You can try chicken livers. Shrimp and bite-size pieces of fish make succulent *Satay*. All these items are placed in the marinade in the raw state, then skewered on bamboo sticks and cooked over an open fire. The meat should be put on the sticks in such a way that the pieces are together and lie flat, rather than round or cubical; keep this in mind when doing the cutting. Instead of giving a large number of recipes with each kind of meat and seafood, here are two basic recipes; do not be reluctant to try variations in the sauces.

MEAT *SATAY*

Cut the meat into 1½ inch squares about ½ inch thick and put in marinade:

¼ cup dark soy sauce
3 tbsp lemon juice
1 tbsp sugar
2 cloves chopped garlic
2 tbsp ground coriander
Cayenne to your taste

1 tsp curry powder
½ tsp ground ginger (can use fresh, chopped)
ground black pepper

Reserve some of the sauce for serving. If two sauces are desired, make a variation by using ground sesame seeds in place of the peanuts. Weave the meat onto the skewers, sprinkle with oil and grill close to the fire. The meat should brown but not be dry and overcooked. Since the meat is not thick, it will take only a few minutes to cook. Pork will take a little longer; chicken takes the least time.

Serve hot with the sauces.

SEAFOOD *SATAY*

Use peeled raw shrimp or fish cut into 1½ inch squares about an inch thick.

Vary the marinating sauce by substituting; lime juice for lemon, ground sesame seeds with or in place of the peanuts and add about 2 tbsp ground coconut.

Remember, shrimp and fish cook very quickly over a hot fire. The secret is to cook only until they turn opaque, about two minutes on each side.

For *Satay*, have lots of cold beer or chilled wine to calm the fiery aftereffects.,

ABOUT CURRY

India and Burma make up the center for what I call "Curry Cuisine." That includes the Island of Sri Lanka, formerly Ceylon. Curry serves two purposes; the spices preserve food in an area where refrigeration has always been lacking, and the piquant characteristic causes perspiration which serves to cool in that tropical area.

The spices in curry powder and curry paste are indigenous to the region. They consist of many exotic plants, seeds and roots; some of which are described here.

Fenugreek was cultivated by the Greeks for cattle fodder, hence the name. It serves the same purpose today in India. The seeds are ground for one of the components of curry. The plant is related to ginger.

Turmeric, along with cardamon, is also in the ginger family. It produces the vivid orange yellow color of curry; and incidentally, is also used in the preparation of mustard.

The heat, or piquancy, in curry is produced by ground red peppers known as cayenne. Ground pepper corns complement this. By the way, truly black pepper comes from the outside hull of the corn and white pepper from the inside. A similar situation exists with the nut of the nutmeg tree; the lace-like outside is ground to give mace, and the inside nut produces nutmeg, also used in curry.

Other spices in curry are cinnamon and cloves. The difference between powder and paste is the latter contains almonds. Powders and pastes are ground daily and for that reason it is difficult to equal the authentic flavor and taste of curry outside the region. Use any good imported curry powder; the paste is very hard to find. If you want to approximate a paste, add almonds ground with a mortar and pestle, or in the blender.

There are as many, or more, recipes for curry as there are cooks; so, specific recipes will not be given here, only a few hints. For a detailed recipe see the contribution of Flying Tiger Jim Cross on page 102.

Almost every curry recipe begins with onions and garlic. The onions are chopped or sliced and sauteed in butter (Indians use "ghee" which is a little on the rancid side) or half butter and half oil. If you concern yourself with animal fat, eliminate the butter. The onions should just start to turn brown, some recipes say "golden." Add as many chopped garlic cloves as you like. Garlic may be anathema to romance; but, the saying goes that it is good for the heart!

With the pan on low or medium heat, add the curry powder, at least 2 or 3 tbsp, and cook for two or three minutes. It must be stirred constantly because it is very easy to burn. While stirring, add 1 or 2 cups of stock, beef or chicken. The resulting basic sauce will be slightly thickened and will become thicker as the cooking proceeds. For this reason, thickeners such as flour and cornstarch are seldom used in genuine curries. The curry powder itself will take away any watery consistency and that is all that is necessary. Remember, the curry will be served over rice and you do not want a "starchy" dish with rice. At the same time, I have encountered potatoes in a few Indian Curries.

The meat or fish to be used is then marinated in the basic sauce, for hours or overnight. Meat can be added as is or browned first; the taste is different either way, try each one. Shrimp or fish are added at the end of the complete cooking process, they take only a few minutes to cook.

The cooking then proceeds at a simmer, like making a stew which is basically what a curry is. Many things can be added at this point. Turmeric enhances the bright orange yellow color. Chopped orange peel adds fragrance. Coconut milk, or ground coconut gives a nice flavor especially to shrimp and fish. Try a can of peeled tomatoes squeezed into the pot, juice included. Something sweet is needed; sugar, chutney, chopped apple or a combination. Sometimes, chopped fresh mint is added as in the case of a lamb curry.

You can use any kind of meat for curry; but, keep in mind that Moslems do not eat pork and Hindus eat neither pork nor beef. So, if you have Indian friends, take care.

Serve curry over rice accompanied by many small dishes of condiments (see page104). Things like chopped fresh vegetables, fruits and nuts complement the dish and help dilute the fiery taste. Of course, you can regulate the degree of "fire" by the amount of curry powder used in the preparation. Just be sure that you do not reduce it too much because curry must be spicy.

Bob Conrath, very appropriately, belongs in the part about CNAC and the Flying Tiger Line because he was a pilot in both airlines. However, he took time out from Shanghai in the early part of 1947 to fly one of CAT's newly acquired C-46 s to the Far East. After spending many years with FTL, he retired with his wife Martha in Encino, California. She has contributed the following three recipes.   The first one is remembered from her mother's kitchen

CREAMED CHICKEN A LA MARTHA'S MOTHER

Boil one chicken with: bay leaf, one onion and one or two carrots, salt to taste, until the meat is not quite done. Cut into serving size and brown the pieces in butter with some chopped onion. Just before serving, pour cream on top and simmer for 5 to 10 minutes. Serve on boiled potatoes, rice or noodles. Sprinkle with dill or chopped parsley. Use the broth for making soup.

MARTHA'S POTATO KRUGEL

3 eggs, beaten
4 tbsp melted butter or other shortening
3 cups grated and drained potatoes (Red are best)
1/3 cup flour (Potato flour, if you have it)
1½ tsp salt, ½ tsp baking powder
3 tbsp grated onion, 1/8 tsp pepper

Beat eggs first and then stir in the other ingredients. Bake in 1½ quart casserole for one hour at 350 degrees. Serve hot. When cold, can be sliced and fried.

MARTHA'S GERMAN PANCAKE

½ cup sifted flour
1 tbsp sugar
1 cup milk
Dash of salt
4 eggs, well beaten

Mix as listed, folding in the eggs last. Fry in a large frying pan with butter, browning on both sides. Sprinkle with sugar and serve with jam or sauteed apples with brown sugar.

NOTE: We had such a pancake in a small place in the Olympic Village of Cortina d'Ampezzo in the Italian Alps. The Chef put the apples in the pancake mixture before frying. Yum! Yum!

Jerre Shrawder was one of the CNAC pilots who later joined CAT. He is now retired with his beautiful wife, Angela, in Hemet in Southern California. She has contributed two of her favorite recipes which she has assured, "are tried and true."

CALIFORNIA SALAD

1 pkg lime jello
1 cup boiling water
3 tbsp sugar
6 oz cream cheese
¼ cup mayonnaise
1 cup cream, whipped
1 No. 2 can crushed pineapple, drained
¼ cup pecans, chopped

Pour boiling water over lime jello; add sugar. Cream the cheese with mayonnaise. Pour jello over cheese mixture; blend in whipped cream. Add crushed pineapple and pecans. Pour into mold and refrigerate several hours or overnight. Serves eight.

CARROT CAKE

2 cups flour
2 cups sugar
2 tsp salt
1 tsp soda
4 eggs, beaten
1½ cups vegetable oil
3 cups grated carrots
1 tsp cinnamon

Mix ingredients well and bake in three round cake tins, greased and floured, at 350 degrees for 30 minutes. Cool and cover layers and sides of cake with frosting; 8 oz cream cheese, 1 stick butter, 1 box powdered sugar, 1 cup chopped walnuts and 2 tsp vanilla.

William C. McDonald, Jr. flew as part of Chennault's trio of precision fliers who performed all kinds of intricate aerobatics with their wings tied together, to demonstrate the versatility of fighter planes to the Signal Corps, forerunner of the Air Corps. Later, Mac joined CNAC in its early days. When we Flying Tigers signed up with the Airline in 1942, he taught us the intricacies of instrument flying pertaining to the "Hump" operation. For many years of his later life, he was retired in a beautiful house on a hill overlooking all of Birmingham, until his recent death. The following recipe from his wife, Peggy, is dedicated to Mac.

Neuro

Neuro is the Chinese word for beef. The story goes that this recipe is from Shantung Province which was taken to Japan by emigrants. There, it was prepared, with variations, and was called Sukyaki.

For six to ten people, prepare:

6 lbs lean beef, sliced thin
4 bunches green onions, cut in 1-inch pieces
1 large head   Chinese cabbage (Napa), cut up
Sauce
6 eggs beaten with 6 tsp soy sauce and 6 tsp Brandy

The guests sit around a hibachi and the host cooks the ingredients in oil, adding soy sauce and stock as he proceeds. Each guest has a bowl of rice and a bowl with a portion of the sauce. When the meat reaches the desired degree of doneness, the host serves the guests, using chopsticks. The sauce in the pan improves as the cooking progresses and is used on the rice.

NOTE: Various vegetables can be used and other meats; such as, chicken and pork can be included.

Roy Farrell was one of our more intrepid CNAC pilots who got the brilliant idea of buying a Douglas C-47 in the States. He loaded it with sundries and flew to Shanghai where he disposed of his various wares and used the proceeds and the plane to start Cathay Pacific Airways along with another CNAC pilot, Australian Sid DeKantzow. His success was made complete when the Airline was bought out by Hong Kong Airways. His wife, Margie, contributed the next two recipes.

BREASTS OF CHICKEN WITH SHERRY

8 chicken breasts
2 cans cream of chicken soup
2 cans sliced mushrooms
1 pint sour cream
½ cup sherry
1 tbsp Worcestershire sauce
¼ cup butter, melted
2 tsp salt
dash garlic powder

Place the chicken breasts in a lightly greased baking dish. Combine the remaining ingredients and pour over the chicken. Bake, covered, for 1 ½ hours at 350 degrees. Uncover and bake 30 minutes more.

NOTE: Chicken breasts cook very quickly; I like to reduce the total time to about one to 1 ¼ hours.

ITALIAN RICE

2½ cups rice, cooked
½ cup oil
½ cup instant minced onions
½ tsp granulated garlic
2 chicken cubes dissolved in 1 cup hot water
1 cup dry white wine
1 cup evaporated milk
¼ cup butter
½ tsp each basil, oregano and pepper
2 tsp salt
1 cup sliced almonds, toasted

In a large bowl, combine all the ingredients. Transfer to a lightly greased baking dish and bake at 350 degrees for one hour. Serves 10 to 12. Margie says, "Great for buffet suppers!"

Fletcher Hanks was a CNAC pilot who is now retired from a successful business that he later developed for the harvesting of clams in Chesapeake Bay. By his latest report, he and his wife, Jane, are heavily into exercise and healthful life-style. He is rated Number One by the Oxford (Maryland) Triathlon Association in the Marathon for his age group, 65 to 69. Jane was Emma Jane Foster, one of our nurses in the AVG. We all lovingly call her "Red." She has a neat, quick recipe for wild duck

Skin two wild ducks; Fletcher says picking is very boring. Place in a browning bag, sprinkle with rosemary and roast in the microwave oven on high for 13 minutes. Rare and good!

Muskrat is another favorite. Remove the fat from the meat. Cut in pieces if large, and in half if small. Dip in flour seasond with salt, pepper and garlic powder. Brown the pieces quickly at high heat. Roast, covered, in a 350 degree oven for about an hour. The meat should fall off the bones.

Photographs

146

1924

148

150

152

153

維斯柏先生紀念

155

165

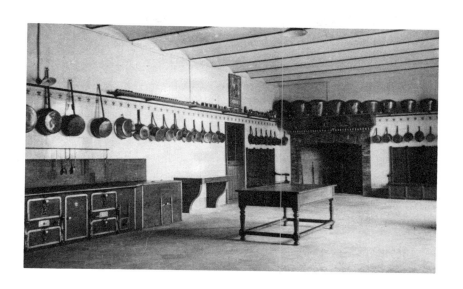

172

PART IV: CAT, Civil Air Transport

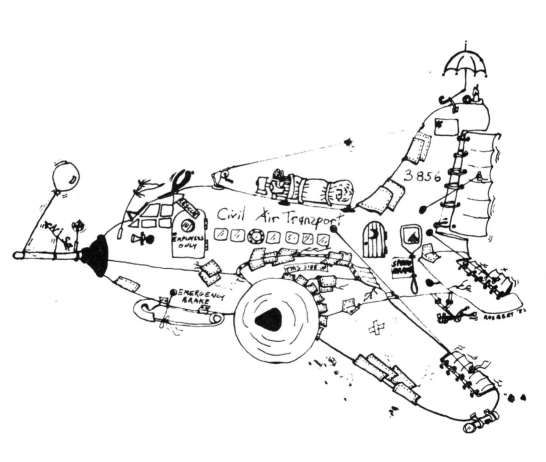

Chapter 8

OFF TO CHINA — AND ROMANCE

In October of 1946, CAT was born as CNRRA Air Transport. CNRRA was the Chinese counterpart of UNRRA, the United Nations relief organization. There were already two Chinese airlines, CNAC (Chinese National Aviation Corporation) and CATC (Central Air Transport Corporation). The CNRRA connection was somewhat of a political ploy to get around anticipated objections by CNAC, principally Panam; and by Moon Chin, the founder of CATC. Both organizations had powerful friends in the Chinese Government and it was no small miracle that Chennault managed the franchise for CAT. Also, it was inevitable that the pressure against him would continue for some time. Only a fluke of history later eliminated that pressure. It was ironic that the Communists, whom Chennault considered mortal enemies, would turn out to be the ones to erase the pressure from CNAC and CATC; thus, unwittingly, doing the Old Man a very large favor.

No attempt will be made to do a history of CAT in this book. That history has been covered in many places and probably the best and most comprehensive coverage is in the book by my friend   Bill Leary, PERILOUS MISSIONS.

When I arrived in Shanghai, early in 1947, I went to see the General in the head office of CAT, located on the Bund, overlooking the Whangpoo River. He introduced me to his partner, Whitey Willauer. For several years, he was to be Chennault's right hand man, until he went to serve as Ambassador to Honduras.

Dick Rossi, "Catfish" Raines, Bob Conrath, Felix Smith and I had departed Honolulu with the first three of fifteen Curtiss C-46s (two of the original seventeen had been cannibalized for spare parts). We made the long journey to Shanghai via Johnston Island, Wake Island, Guam, Manila and Canton. Dick invited Catfish and me to stay in his beautiful flat in the French Concession until we could get situated. Among other things, it had heat which most places in Shanghai did not have because the Japanese had robbed the radiators to send to Japan to make ammunition.

We found out how inconvenient that could be when the Company found temporary accommodations for us in the York Hotel, across the street from the Italian Club. There was some heat, but on a reduced scale because of the plundering by the Japanese. We accepted the discomfort until one day Catfish and I went to visit Roger Shreffler. He had been a communications expert with the AVG and had come over to China again to join us in the CAT operation

"This is really warm." Catfish remarked when we entered the room.

"And no wonder!" I exclaimed, seeing Roge and his roommate in their undershorts and, on each side of them, a fan blowing on the only two radiators in the room.

"You can see what the wonders of technology can do." Roge laughed.

Of course, the fans were taking the maximum heat from the two radiators, leaving very little for the other rooms.

"Well, I'll be damned!" Was all I could add.

In spite of some inconveniences, Shanghai was full of wonders. It was divided into sections. There was, of course, the old Chinese section, Nan Tao, with its Oriental architecture and mysterious buildings on narrow alleys. But, the major part of the City was divided into sections; such as, the French Concession, and the International Settlement, which included British and Americans. Each had its own administration and police force. So, a different flavor was to be had just traveling from one section to the other. And, that was usually done by pedicab, a kind of ricksha for two, mechanized by a three-wheel bicycle and propelled by a muscular coolie, complete with Chinese bamboo hat.

"Meet Mark Kaufman." Dick Rossi introduced me to the famous LIFE photographer. He had invited us to the Foreign Correspondents' Club on the top of the Broadway Mansions, the tallest building in Shanghai. The City was stretched out in front of us and, directly below, was Soochow Creek teeming with all kinds of sampans. And there on the left was the Bund and hundreds of vessels in the Whangpoo River, some moving in and out, others tied up at the edge.

Mark showed us his apartment, one floor below. The correspondents had the two top stories of the building and all the other twelve floors were occupied by the American military.

"You fellows sure have it soft." I commented about the neat arrangement they had. "You should have a look at the York Hotel; this is a palace in comparison."

Dinner in the dining room was a distinct change from the fare we had been experiencing at the hotel. There was an Oriental atmosphere with the rattan furniture and straw decorations. The meal was served faultlessly by Chinese waiters who moved about so quietly they were hardly noticed. There was a wonderful yellow fish, done Chinese style, and juicy Tournedos with grilled mushrooms. We had both white and red wines. I was feeling in high spirits by the time the evening was over.

"Let's get together for a night on the town." Mark extended the invitation to me because Dick was going on a trip.

"Sure thing!" I was delighted. "What have you got in mind?"

"I'll arrange a couple of dates. We'll have a few drinks and dinner. Afterward, we'll go dancing."

"Sounds great. Give me a call and let me know the details."

June 18, 1947 was a most memorable date. Something happened that, although it could not change that which had already transpired in my life, would decide the course of it for the rest of my days.

Mark and I were sitting in the bar of the Cathay Mansions sipping Gimlets. Our conversation was interesting enough that we did not notice the two attractive young ladies that had come in the entrance almost behind us. They were just turning around to leave when Mark glanced in that direction.

"That's them!" He exclaimed, getting off the bar stool and heading towards the door.

He returned in a moment holding the two ladies by the arm.

"This is Lisa." He said, introducing the dark-haired one.

I was not looking at her but at the tall, statuesque blond. Her greenish yellow eyes held my gaze as I heard Mark's voice.

"This is Lydia."

The name hardly seemed important as I took her arm and seated her beside me. I don't know if it's called electricity or magnetism, or what; but, there was some kind of a tingling sensation going on inside me that was never to leave.

There was dinner but I never remembered what we had. However, I did learn a lot about Lydia.

"You can call me Lil." She said with that infectious laugh of hers; and I thought it was especially appropriate since she was from Shanghai, although born in Harbin, Manchuria, of White Russian parents. Her father had been the dentist in the Chinese military compound there.

"Shanghai Lil! That's what I'm going to call you."

When the evening finished after several hours of dancing (Yes, Lil was a great dancer) I knew that something had happened to me that I had never experienced before. Was it Love? That remained to be seen.

My agreement with the Old Man was to fly that first year with CAT because he had already employed sufficient administrative people. Although flying in China could be very interesting, it now took on all the characteristics of a chore. Each time, leaving Shanghai, it seemed to me that I would be gone for weeks rather than the few days it actually took.

I even did some very silly things, like the time I took Lil in the plane with me to Tsingtao and stayed in the "Castle", the pilots' house there. She went with me on a couple of flights to Weihsien and I taught her a few things about flying.

There was always that yen to get back to Shanghai and, of course, to

Lil. The culmination of all the flying and almost my future with CAT occurred when I wanted to get back to Shanghai from Tsingtao for a special date with Lil (they all seemed to be special). The weather was marginal. The Director of Operations, Chuck Hunter, ordered me to cancel the flight.

After checking with CNAC and NWA, both of whom had landed planes at Lunghwa, Shanghai's main airport, I decided to exercise pilot's discretion and make a try at it. I ignored Hunter's orders to return to Tsingtao after I had taken off.

Luck was with me. I broke out at Lunghwa at five hundred feet and was able to steer a course to Hungjao where CAT had its base of operations. Although in and out of the low hanging clouds, I broke through over the airstrip and came around for a perfect landing.

"You think you're pretty smart, don't you?" Hunter was red-faced in his rage. "You haven't heard the last of this."

I hardly heard what he said as I took off in a jeep to keep my date with Lil.

The upshot of the affair was that I was called into the General's office. I was sure I was going to be fired.

"That was quite a decision you had to make exercising pilot's discretion." He started with that twinkle in his eyes. "I pay my pilots to do a job."

I was about to make some stupid comment when he went on.

"I've been thinking for some time about our conversation in LA about you doing an executive job. I think the time has come. What would you think about taking over the job as Director of Operations?"

In accepting, I could just barely hold back all my emotions; and, I could hardly wait to tell Lil.

There came a period of trial and error. Some pilots do not care at all for a desk job. Others think they do and then find out that it is not for them. There is a third type that knows that he wants the executive activity and thrives on it. After a try or two, I finally found one of the latter for my Chief Pilot. He was Bob Rousselot.

Bob was born in Noel, Missouri, and later moved to Joplin and went through pre-med schooling. He became a Naval Aviator at Corpus Christi. He chose the Marine Corps because it was "a tougher Service." Among other experiences, he ran into "Pappy" Boyington in the Pacific and saw evidence of what we had noted in the AVG; he (Boyington) always wanted to wrestle, expecially when he got inebriated. Bob said that he saw him trying to wrestle a General Moore, after a drinking bout.

After the war, Bob volunteered for extra duty in Peking in order to save money for Medical School. After a few months he heard that

General Chennault was going to form a freight airline. He arranged a flight to Shanghai.

"Yes, Lieutenant, we're interested in pilots but never had much luck with Marines." Chennault said with a stern face.

When he saw Bob's face fall, he continued. "Had a guy named Boyington who ruined two or three of our P-40s in the AVG."

Bob was getting more discouraged by the minute, but his eyes lit up when the General laughed and said, "You go ahead and complete your application, you don't look like any Boyington to me."

That was the beginning of a business association, and a long friendship that continued for many years.

At dinner, one night, Lil reported on her visit to Doc Richards who had his CNAC office in Shanghai since the end of the war.

"I went to see Doc about the worms." Everybody seemed to be getting worms those days.

"Well, what did he say?" I asked, matter-of-factly.

"He said. 'You don't have worms, you have just one worm." She became more grave. "I'm pregnant!"

My stomach did a flip-flop and then fell; I felt numb.

"What are we going to do?" I had confided in her shortly after our first meeting that I was married.

"I could have an abortion." Lil offered the solution in her usual, realistic Russian manner.

"No, at least, not yet." I said hopefully. "Maybe something will happen."

"But what?" She asked, knowing there was little chance of anything that could solve our entangled situation. Needless to say, there were many sleepless nights after that.

"I can't believe this!" I exclaimed, sometime later, as I tore open an envelope with a letter from a lawyer in Las Vegas.

"What is it?" Lil was as puzzled as I was.

"Well, I'll be dammed." Was all I could say for quite a few moments. "He says that my wife is getting a divorce; do you know what that means?"

There were tears in our eyes and all we could do was hold each other in our arms for the longest time. The baby had been saved!

The marriage was a simple ceremony which took place in the living room of our dear friend, Mary Strauss. Lil's mother was there and Bob Rousselot was the best man. The minister's name was Mortenson, the same one who had married the General and Anna Chennault.

"General," I said over the phone, "Lil and I just got married."

"The hell you did." Was all he could say for a moment; then, "Anna and I will be right over."

They came along with Louise and Whitey Willauer and several close friends. Lil's and my fate had been sealed that day, November 13, 1948, but we always remember June 18th of the previous year as the most important in our lives, the day we fell in love.

If our lives were to become harried, it began that night. Guests started to depart to beat the ten o'clock curfew. When most of them were gone we had a last glass of champagne with Mary and Bob. That turned out to be a mistake. As we took them to the door, it was apparent that the barriers had already been put in place. Lil's Maid-of-Honor and my Best Man had to spend the night with the newlyweds!

We had a call the next morning. Two other friends were caught in the curfew and spent the night in jail! Those were the days.

"The communists are coming!"

We heard that everywhere.

CAT set up an evacuation operation in Mukden, Manchuria; we got thousands of refugees out before the communists came. But, the sad facts of life were in evidence; Peiping fell and, soon, the communists were down to the Yangtze River.

Shanghai was still a gay city. The Columbia Country Club, fun center for the Americans, was in full swing. The British and French Clubs went on as if nothing were happening. The only noticeable change at the Foreign Correspondents Club was the presence of those who had held posts in northern areas. Most notable of those was Spencer Moosa of the Associated Press; we were to be the best of friends for many years on Taiwan. There was also Joe Fromm of the US News and World Reports (He is, at this writing, Assistant Editor for that Magazine), among many others, all concentrated in the center of world news for that moment.

Oh yes, there was one other noteworthy item; the Soviet spy organization TASS (they called it a news agency), was obvious by the presence of its two representatives, Rogoff and Yakshamin. We had more than one heated argument with the latter. Spencer Moosa was always amused by those bouts which, one time, almost came to blows when Yakshamin crashed his drinking glass to the tile floor after Lil called him a "Bloody Soviet." We thought he was going to have apoplexy.

NOTE: When Shanghai fell to the communists, who was in front of the victory parade? Of course, Rogoff and Yakshamin; and, remember, that was supposed to have been a Chinese affair!

CAT set up its maintenance and operations base at Canton. An LST was purchased and all the engineering shops were organized on it, then it was sailed to Hong Kong. By the month of May, 1949, our last evacuation flight left Shanghai. That beautiful City was never to be the same gay place again.

Most of us lived in the village of Tungshan, on the outskirts of Canton. It was hot but things went along smoothly until we began to hear the communist guns booming in the mountains to the north of the City. There was in effect an all-night curfew.

After the middle of May, each afternoon, I would take Lil in one of our cars, and bounce along the rough roads to Hackett Hospital on the other side of town. We could not take the chance that labor pains would start during the night leaving us trapped at home with no way to get through the curfew to the hospital. Every morning, Lil bounced back over the rough road to our house, because the hospital was so hot and the amenities were not all that great, anyway.

That went on for two weeks. Then, one morning, when I went to pick up Lil, the doctor told me that she had been in labor all night. By coincidence, it was in the same room where Anna Chennault had given birth to daughter, Claire Anna, a few months before. If nothing happened within the next few hours, he would have to operate because the baby was in a breech position, probably caused by the daily rough rides. I overheard Lil's lady-doctor Liang conferring with the hospital surgeon.

"We may have to make a decision," he was saying, "whether to save the mother or the baby."

I blurted out, "Save the mother, I don't know the baby!"

The operation was inevitable and, after seventeen hours of labor and a two-hour surgery bout, Dr. Cochran came to the room where I was nervously waiting and announced that we had a son! Imagine! After all those years of nothing, there was a family. It sure was a miracle for me; and Lil, too. That miracle occurred on June 2, 1949, weighing a resounding 10 lbs. 6 oz.

During that same period, our dearest friend, Sue Pollack, who was General Chennault's executive secretary, took leave and was married to Bob Buol, another one of our former Marine pilots. He was working with me in operations in what we called "Matchstick Village" because of the flimsy wooden structures that made up our complex at the airport outside Canton. The temporary appearance was a reflection of the tenuous position in which we found ourselves.

If things had been hectic up to that point, they became rip-roaring. The noise of the communists' guns was getting dangerously close. The General had word from his friend, Lu Han, the Governor of Yunnan Province, that things were quiet there; so, it was decided that operations would be moved to Kunming. However, as we all packed for the move, the Old Man and Whitey made the decision to transfer the Head Office to Hong Kong. That was much more significant than it appeared at the time.

The situation became unstable in the Kunming area; whereas, communist activity around Canton quieted down. Chennault sent me instructions to move Operations back to Canton! A skeleton crew was left in Kunming as we completed the evacuation flights and reoccupied "Matchstick Village."

Believe it or not . . . the seesaw continued! Maybe the communists were following our moves because they stepped up their activity around Canton to the point where the city was in its final death throes.

"Joe," the General was on the phone from Hong Kong, "the Governor has assured me that the Kunming area is quiet."

"Does that mean we go back?"

"You know how important the shipments of Wolfram ore from Mengtze are. Yes, the operation goes back to Kunming!"

Even at the time of the AVG, the mining of the strategic tungsten-tin ore was well-known. Shortly after, in CNAC, we flew the ore to India to be transshipped to the States. Then, in CAT, we were preserving that same supply line, via the port of Haiphong, Indochina.

The Mahjong game at Var Green's house was going along very well for Lew Burridge and me. The two experts, Lil and Sophie Green, could not understand how we were winning consistently. Just as I was passing another tile under the table to Lew, we heard the car outside that we had been waiting for.

"Here are the instructions from the General." Bob Buol began after greeting all of us. "There is secret information from the Governor that all of the military in the Kunming area is going to turn over to the communists. If we evacuate first thing in the morning, the Governor promises safe exit."

"Let's hope this is the last part of the seesaw ride!" I remarked.

Each family was allowed only 150 pounds of personal belongings. That meant that everybody would lose some of his possessions. Our biggest personal loss was a collection of National Geographic Magazines that went back to the original issues saved by Lil's father. Well, it was not to be the only big loss in our lives as we were to learn from the future.

At dawn, we all looked like a bunch of refugees, getting into the planes with paper-wrapped bundles and luggage beaten up from numerous evacuations. It had been only a few months, but seemed like years since the start of our odyssey in Shanghai earlier that year.

Safely on the ground at Kaitak Airport in Hong Kong, we all heaved a big sigh of relief at having returned to a certain semblance of civilization in the British Colony.

But, that was not "all." Shortly we received word that Captain "Big" Bigony, of Big Spring, Texas, along with the remnants of the operation, had been surprised by the guards at the Kunming Airport when they came onto the field with their hats turned over, a signal that they had turned communist. The Old Man sent an urgent message to the Governor requesting his aid, one more time, as a personal favor. The Governor, after much negotiation with the guards, was able to persuade them to release the plane. One more lucky break for "the CAT with nine lives!"

While the LST was being moved to anchor near Sanya on the southern part of Hainan Island where the Nationalists were to make their last stand, events were taking place that led to a clearer picture only much later. For example, that purchase of the LST which, at first seemed logical, was an unusual move for an airline. With the appointment of Jim Brennan as Treasurer and the announcement that he had provided finances to keep the Company going seemed strange. Then, the arrival of Al Cox, a former OSS Officer-parachutist, added to the mystery.

With the invasion of the north coast of Hainan Island by the communists, came the order to put everything on the LST and sail for the southern Taiwan port of Kaoshiung. The maintenance headquarters were set up not far away in Tainan. It was early January, 1950, when Lil and I took our new son, Jody, on the boat from Hong Kong and sailed into the northern Taiwan port of Keelung.

Then came that stroke of luck which guaranteed the future of CAT forever . . . almost forever, that is. All of our facilities were concentrated on Taiwan; but CNAC and CATC made their worst miscalculation by taking all of their aircraft and personnel to Hong Kong which really was an affront to the Nationalist Government. Not only that but a movement was being planned to defect to the communists.

Whitey Willauer contacted me for ideas I might have about any action we could take to keep the approximate one hundred planes in Hong Kong.

"Yes, I sure do." Was my answer. "George Yeh is the Minister of Communications and he has control over the registration of the planes. If he cancels all the registrations, the Hong Kong Government will be obliged by international law to keep the planes on the ground."

"Get a plane ready and we'll take George Yeh to Hong Kong." He ordered. "Be sure we have a typewriter on board."

During the flight, George prepared the order for the cancellation of all the aircraft registration certificates. Upon landing, it was immediately delivered to the Governor with the demand, in the name of the Nationalist Government, that the planes be grounded indefinitely. The request was honored and the planes remained grounded . . . for several years, until a number of court cases going all the way up to the Privy Council in London settled the matter and "Chennault and Company" were allowed to purchase them. The only proviso was that they could not be taken to Taiwan. The British tried to "save face" by salving the feelings of the communists.

Chapter 9

CAT — ARM OF THE CIA

Things began to happen very fast. Al Cox was made President, representing new financial blood transfused by a group called the Pacific Corporation in the States. At the time, no one could find out anything substantial about that company.

"Come up to room 206," Willauer said over the phone. "I have something to discuss."

I was sitting in the lounge of the Friends of China Club having a drink with Spencer Moosa and a few other correspondents.

Room 206 belonged to Roger Shreffler and Bob Rousselot and they were both there when I walked in.

"What I'm going to tell you is secret," Willauer began, very seriously. "If you ever disclose this information, you will be fired and other dire consequences will result."

"Whitey, you know that you and the General have always had my confidence."

"Anyway, I have to put it to you that strongly. We could not divulge this sooner because it took a fair amount of time to get Lil's clearance. We have that now and you are included in a very small group in the Company to know that the US Government is now behind us; but, in a covert way. No one is to know and that goes for wives. We will be doing many strange things but CAT is well suited for carrying them out. It means not only our survival but also that of many of the programs of US Intelligence in this entire area."

I was to learn that the "area" was far-flung, from Korea to Indonesia and as far as Tibet and other westernmost regions of China. Some of our pilots even went off to Central America and assisted in the Bay of Pigs operation, among others. The missions were complicated and often dangerous. Pilots and planes would be lost under mysterious circumstances that had to be explained overtly as routine. Sobering thoughts filled my mind as I returned home that night.

The summer of 1950 found Lew Burridge and myself in Hong Kong for an important conference with Whitey and the General. We were just on the verge of taking a nap when the radio in our hotel room blared out the news that war had broken out in Korea! Immediately, I was on the phone with the Old Man; and, a few minutes later, Lew and I were in a taxi to his house to review our situation, especially what role we would play in that new earth-shaking episode in history.

In accordance with orders from Chennault, Rousselot and I arrived at Tachikawa Airbase outside Tokyo for an urgent conference with General Tunner of the Combat Cargo Command.

"How many cargo planes do you have available?" He demanded, at the outset.

"With thirty-six C-46s from the Chinese Air Force, we can probably provide about fifty; when do you need them?"

"Yesterday!"

The Air Force was in sad shape when it came to availability of cargo planes. It seemed that Congress had whittled the Far East area down to almost nothing in that category, among others. Bob and I were quickly on our way back to Taiwan to discuss the situation with Hugh Grundy, head of our Maintenance Department. He laid out a long, meticulous plan to put the CAF planes into near-perfect condition. I had to tell Whitey that we would have to forego some of the polish and stick to the bare essentials in order to get the planes going. Grundy was irritated but had to go along with the elimination of some of the niceties.

Even then, General Tunner blew up and hit the ceiling when he heard how long he would have to wait. He forgot that CAT did not create the sad situation that existed, but the Air Force and the powers back home were responsible. In any case, within the next couple of weeks, we managed to get more than thirty planes into the fray. The Air Force cargo capability was far outshone by little, civilian CAT. Shades of the AVG!

In order to support the Wolfram operation, Bob Buol took some communications equipment, and a technician to set it up, to Mengtze. They had some difficulty in getting it operating. In order to see his mission through, Bob decided to stay over night in spite of warnings about communists in the area of the airstrip.

Sure enough, during the night, a big push was made and Mengtze, the last Nationalist foothold on the Mainland, fell to enemy forces. Bob was taken to a prison in Kunming where he languished for four long years.

In the meantime, I was in Haiphong with Rousselot to coordinate the shipments of Wolfram. That was the transshipment point for the ore to go by ship to a refining plant in Texas. All that stopped with the fall of Mengtze. We started moving our center of operation for the area to Saigon.

The French were losing their taste for war in Indochina and the situation was deteriorating rapidly. Our number of planes was inadequate for the ground support that was needed. So, Al Cox went to Clark Field in the Philippines and arranged for a quantity of C-119 "Flying Boxcars" from the US Air Force. All identifying marks were removed and CAT pilots flew them until the last stand of the northern Indochina area at Dienbienphu.

There, we almost lost Paul Holden. His C-119 was shot up and his arm was shattered badly by shrapnel. Fortunately, he was flown to Clark Field in time to save the limb. But, our world-famous "Earthquake Magoon" was not so lucky. He had survived an earlier ordeal in prison when he was captured by the communists in South China. They let him go because, according to one widely-held opinion, he was so fierce . . . and ate too much!

One day, his C-119 was crippled by ground fire over Dienbienphu. As he headed for home, he was followed by a C-119 flown by Steve Kusak who urged him to bail out.

"Bullsh--!" He responded over the radio. "I'm not going to be a prisoner again . . . either I get this crate home, or else - - -."

The wounded plane gradually lost altitude and went into a jungle-covered mountain ridge. That was the final exit for "Earthquake." His memory was immortalized by the depictions of famous cartoonist, Al Capp, and the last pictures taken by Kusak as he went down which later appeared in LIFE Magazine. We hear Earthquake's thunder whenever there is an especially fierce storm rumbling above!

Chapter 10

THEN CAME PINEAPPLE

Some time during that period, a most unsavory event took place; at least to my taste and that of many other key CAT personnel. A "wheel" from the Washington head office arrived at the Taipei Airport. A chubby figure stepped out of the door of the plane. His apple-cheeks, disarming smile and round face with a homburg hat perched on top presented an almost comic appearance. Especially when he waved the golf putter he was brandishing!

That's George Doole." Al Cox whispered in my ear. "He's the protege of General Cabell. And, don't let the smile fool you; he's a very ruthless guy."

That was my introduction to the "Pineapple" and thus began one of the most distasteful periods of my life.

The "ruthless guy" began unostentatiously, covertly if you will, to consolidate his position as the number one representative of CAT and go-between of the Agency.

"The way you maintain control," he confided in me, on a rare occasion, "is to control communications. For example, I get messages sent to ambassadors out here before they do."

That was done through NACC (Naval Auxiliary Communications Center). He took me there in Taipei to read the incoming and outgoing message file because from then on that was one of my duties, when the President was out-of-town. It turned out to be rather boring stuff except for an occasional "juicy" item.

Cox let me in on more of the background. It turned out that Doole, formerly a Panam pilot, was befriended by General Cabell, a very powerful, high-ranking CIA officer.

"As long as Cabell is there," Al said, "Doole has a guaranteed position."

Unfortunately, he was there long enough for Doole to survive all opposition and see the demise of CAT, as we knew it. In the meantime, he manuevered another nasty tactical move to consolidate and solidify his own situation.

Al was an excellent tactician himself; but, he had one weakness and the Pineapple harped on that with the powers on the "Board" back in the States.

Al called me over to Sue Buol's house one morning shortly after Doole arrived from the States, without warning. John Mason, from the Agency's Atsugi operation in Japan, was there with us.

"I'm here as one of Al's old friends." He began very solemnly. "Doole has finally gotten to Al."

"What are you saying, is he out?" I demanded.

"I'm afraid so."

"But why . . . how?" I couldn't believe it.

"Frankly, I think it's Al's drinking."

I looked over at Al and he had tears in his eyes. In spite of his habit, we all had to have a drink . . . but even that was not good enough to hold back the tears. For three grown men, it was just too much!

"Doole has arranged for the Old Man to call a meeting at his house and we are due there within a few minutes."

Even then, Pineapple had to use the General as the goat to do the dastardly deed.

All of our key people were gathered in the General's living room; among others, Bob Rousselot and Ward French were present.

"I have an announcement to make that affects all of you," Chennault began. "The 'Board' has arranged for Al to go away and take a much-needed rest. They have appointed Grundy to take his place as President!"

Both things struck me a deadening blow.

"General," I interrupted. "Neither you nor the 'Board' has arranged this; the one responsible for this is the SOB sitting right there." I pointed directly at Doole.

"Now, Joe," The General was almost smiling, knowingly.

Doole became as white as a sheet. I also noticed that Grundy looked very sheepish. But, the whole thing was a *fait accompli*. Doole not only got Al out but he got his man in. By coincidence(!), Grundy was a former Panam maintenance man having been hired by CAT from the defected CNAC, subsidiary of Panam. He was just the kind of "Yes-man" that the Pineapple needed to consolidate and make complete his control.

There was no way that I was going to take the whole thing sitting down. Taking a page from "Doole's book," I wrote a very strong personal letter to the head of the Agency, Allen Dulles. There was absolutely no way that such a letter could get through channels to the top man; so, I sent it, with a personal plea, to an old OSS friend of Al's, Dick Stilwell, asking him the big favor of effecting delivery.

It worked! Not only that, I received a personal answer from Dulles, ending with the invitation to contact him in the future if I felt the need. That infuriated Doole; I had penetrated his communications net. He accused me of "going out of channels." That was a ridiculous charge; my letter had not a hope in hell of being delivered if it had been sent through channels.

Of course, Pineapple was inclined to twist facts whenever it suited his purpose. For example, he claimed that Chennault and Willauer knew nothing about business and finance; and that CAT was in such a horrible state when he took over it required years of his effort to get it back to "normal." He neglected to point out that after setting up more than fifty stations all over the vast area of China, under the worst of circumstances, and then evacuating them all just in front of the communists, CAT survived. CATC and CNAC, Panam subsidiary, died in the face of such adversity. I hated to think what would have happened to CAT, and all of us, if Pineapple, with no General Cabell behind him, had been sitting in charge in Shanghai when the world came tumbling down!

It is to be pointed out that the Doole-Grundy "Pineapple Factory" did not need too many brains to carry on an airline operation which had no competition but did have the support of a Cabell and the influence and backing of the United States Government. I have to differ strongly with the statement on Page 173 of Bill Leary's PERILOUS MISSIONS:

"Doole . . . was a superbly talented airline executive and skilled bureaucratic infighter who merits a place in aeronautical history alongside Eddie Rickenbacker of Eastern, Juan Trippe of Pan American, William Patterson of United, C.R. Smith of American, and other giant figures of the industry."

In my opinion, and that of many others involved in the whole picture, Doole never came close to the stature of those giants of the airline industry and he could never command the respect of the CAT pilots (the core of the operation) performing dangerous CIA missions. On the other hand, Chennault was that kind of giant; the *esprit de corps* that he instilled in all his personnel, down to the lowest level, could never be approached by a Pineapple.

As a politician and negotiator with top Chinese, Doole was a failure; the Chinese never trusted him. Chennault could always be counted upon to solve the large problems which required consultation with, and the essential assistance of, both the Generalissimo and Madame Chiang Kai-Shek. Doole could not develop that kind of contact. He even told me on one of my visits to Washington that the son, Chiang Ching-Kuo, could never take over the reins of the Government because the United States was backing a democratic approach to succession. He did not even know that Chiang already had taken over and was in fact running the Government; that lack of knowledge, for a CIA representative, was pretty sad.

Trips to Washington were not unusual. On one of those occasions, I happened to be in a meeting in my suite in the Willard Hotel when the phone rang.

"It's for you, Connie."

Connie LeGueux was one of the agency people who served as a CAT executive in the Hong Kong office.

"Oh, No!" His face dropped as he listened to the other end.

As he hung up, he motioned me to the bedroom.

"What is it?" I asked anxiously.

"One of our planes went down over the Mainland."

"You mean in China? Who were the pilots?"

"Yes, I'm afraid so," Connie went on, "Schwartz and Snoddy were the pilots. We have to release a story out of Taipei."

After looking over the map and sending a message to NACC in Taipei, the press had a news item that a CAT C-47 had gone down in the sea of Japan on a routine flight to Korea. Although the Chinese communists had the wreckage of the plane and put pictures of it in the newspapers, the CAT story was believed. It was a case of the communists press, having cried "wolf" so often, not being able to be trusted even when it had the evidence. They also had the two agents who had gone along to see the pickup of the Chinese operatives they had trained. Schwartz and Snoddy had a special sling apparatus in their plane to pick up agents. Unfortunately, when the plane crashed at a very critical point, Fecteau and Downey of the CIA spent many horrible years as prisoners of the communists, after surviving the accident.

I had asked Al Cox, sometime before, "What do they get from trained agents when they're captured?"

"If they live through the ordeal," he replied, grimly, "they tell everything because the commies have methods to extract info that do not fail...unless they kill the captives in the process."

So, in the case at hand, the prisoners told everything; they were not going to hurt anyone because Schwartz and Snoddy were no longer of this world. From above, they must have agreed; especially later on when the two long-suffering agents were released through Hong Kong. At least, they got away.

There were many other hair raising incidents, too numerous to mention in this book. But, the escapades of the famous DC-6 are noteworthy. Rousselot, and others, took that unmarked plane on agency missions from Clark Field or Okinawa to the far westernmost parts of China, dropping supplies and personnel to beleagured resistance groups. The aircraft performed missions that taxed its capabilities way beyond those ever envisioned by the Douglas Company when they designed it. The "CAT with nine lives" got away with those adventurous operations without a scratch.

With the Vietnam War developing from the Indochinese war when the French lost all taste for pursuing the conflict, CAT's participation reached military proportions for which the airline had never been organized. Air American, which had been set up mainly to handle contracts with the Air Force in Japan, expanded to a full-size air force. It eventually grew to over five hundred pilots flying everything that the Air Force had to offer.

The ultimate was reached when an unmarked chopper landed in a remote area to take on fuel to go on into enemy territory. A tough Air Force sergeant stood with his chin hanging down to his chest when a strange figure climbed into the pilot's seat.

"What the hell is that?" He gasped.

There clad in one of those black, shiny, Chinese coolie outfits, straw sandals, scrawny beard, blond hair topped by a pointed hat, was CAT pilot Art Wilson. Maybe the outlandish garb helped him to survive many dangerous covert operations, because survive he did!

During those frantic times, it appeared that there was never time for home. But, nature was wonderful and so was Lil...we had two more children. First, there was Marie, born in Los Angeles after our wonderful trip across the Pacific on the luxury liner, President Cleveland. Just before leaving Tokyo, we attended the beautiful wedding of Ann and Lew Burridge. On that ocean voyage were Lil's mother and grandmother whom we had rescued from the UN refugee camp at Samar Island in the Philippines.

During the trip, Lil and I would visit them in another section of the ship. Sometimes, Lil would go alone. We found out later, in Honolulu, that there was some dope smuggling going on and Lil was one of the suspected characters, because of her condition. It seemed like a "tip" disclosed the information that the culprit was traveling "under false pretenses." The guilty party was arrested when the agents on board our ship found out that she was carrying dope in her falsies!

Then, there was Robert, born in Hong Kong. For that reason, he had dual citizenship of a sort in that he could choose to be British or American. We had so many Russian friends that he was often called "Bobka" just as Jody was known by the diminutive "Joshka."

That completed our brood. We not only loved and enjoyed them, but they traveled with us all over the world to many far-flung lands that most children only dream about. They took in stride the inconveniences, like our escapades camping across the States; or, the luxuries that were enjoyed on many cruise liners.

There was a most memorable trip to Europe with Sue Buol. All six of us arrived at Rome Airport during the Easter holidays of 1954. The Eternal City was impressive from the very first when we drove up to the stately, old Grand Hotel and checked into two huge, high-ceilinged rooms that were more like apartments.

Early Easter Sunday morning, I walked around the block to a florist shop that I had spotted looking down from the window of our room. There I found two pretty little corsages and a bouquet of lilacs.

Back at the room, two waiters were setting up a long table. We ordered everything imaginable; all kinds of Italian salamis and cheeses, and giant loaves of crusty country bread. The poached eggs, of a different texture and taste than those in the Far East, were served more like Eggs Benedict than just plain old eggs. At the auspicious moment, when the cold champagne was being served, I pinned the corsages on Lil and Sue. The kids each had a beautiful Italian chocolate Easter Egg with candies and a prize inside. The lights shone in our eyes like stars that unforgettable morning.

After a week of doing Rome, I ordered a car from the concierge to take us on a tour of Italy, Switzerland and southern France. We had no idea what was in store for us. Arriving outside the entrance of our hotel, after checking out, we were greeted by our uniformed chauffeur standing in front of a very impressive Lancia Limousine!

"I am Leopold," he announced in his proud Italian manner.

And Leopold turned out to be a jewel. He loaded and unloaded the vehicle, drove in a very professional way, found out-of-the-way typical restaurants and located the best of hotels for us. And, as if that were not enough, he acted as tour guide, especially for me. Lil and Sue were in the back with the three kids. When they made too much noise, Leopold just rolled up the separating window and we enjoyed a bottle of wine and some cheese, while he explained all the interesting sights we were passing!

Country bumpkins that we were, we said that we wanted to see Florence; Leopold nodded in assent. After a late lunch in the centuries-old town of Siena, I became anxious because I had seen no signs of Florence. As we came over a hill, Leopold pointed in the distance.

"Firenze," he announced.

My heart dropped...I was sure that we had missed Florence and were going to spend the night in another place. It was not until we had checked into the Excelsior Hotel, one of the grand hotels of Europe, that I discovered that "Firenze" was the Italian name for the great city of Florence, located on the Arno River at the foot of the Apennine Mountains!

After a lovely visit in that city, we passed through northern Italy into Switzerland, arriving at the Lausanne Palace Hotel in the city of that name just about thirty-five miles short of Geneva. Sue wanted to contact John Foster Dulles who was scheduled at that time to have a conference with Soviet Foreign Minister Molotov to see what could be done about getting Bob released from the Chinese communist prison in Kunming.

Something happened that might have changed Sue's luck. Lil convinced her to cut her long hair which she had for years. That changed her appearance completely and, except for one brief period, she maintained the short cut from then on.

That night, dinner in the main dining room was an experience. The headwaiter, in formal tails, hovered over the table and the serving waiters like a mother hen. We savored everything from "soup to nuts." The fish course was Sole Marguery with a smooth cream sauce of mushrooms, oysters and little shrimp. It was shown to us at the table, bubbling and lightly browned on top, before it was served individually. Then, there was Gigot d'Agneau, roasted crusty brown outside. When it was skillfully carved at the serving table, each perfect slice was pink inside; the accompanying little vegetables were glistening.

As we sipped our wine, and listened to the violin player beside our table, we were in heaven! What more fitting culmination than a flaming platter of Crepes Suzettes and a snifter of Cognac with our coffee.

After a night at the casino on the French side of the Lake of Geneva, we had to take our leave of Lausanne. The trip down the Rhone Valley was intriguing, especially when we arrived at the City of the Popes, Avignon. We passed the Pont d'Avignon, inspiration for the children's song, on the way to our hotel which was converted from a Marquis' mansion of centuries before. The doors and the ceilings were high, the stairs slanted, and creaked with each step. . .we felt like we were in a museum, particularly when we rode the birdcage elevator which stopped two or three times between the only two floors.

Incidentally, I took Lil and Sue to the Pont we had passed on our way in, to dance like the kids in the song. We certainly did play the part of country hick tourists; a woman, laughing so hard she could barely explain, did manage to get the words out- - -we had the wrong bridge!

A few days later, in Cannes, we were enjoying dinner at the Drap d'Or Restaurant which was done inside like a sheik's tent. After talking the owner out of two huge heart-shaped ashtrays, we headed for Maxim's Nightclub.

Lil and Sue were both radiant in new outfits and hairdos. An afternoon shopping spree also produced French perfume which added to the atmosphere. I felt exhilarated that they were having such a good time. Of course, the wine at dinner and the drinks afterward played a part in the euphoria; and the show girls I had invited to the table had a lot to do with the exuberance!

The next day, after an exploration of the Riviera, we were in the Hotel de Paris in Monaco. The Hotel fascinated us for many reasons. First of all, it was the most esteemed establishment in the entire area. Then, it was connected to the world-famous Casino next door by an underground passage, so that patrons did not even have to go outside to cross the street.

The highlight of that part of the trip was a night at the Casino. After a delectable dinner at the Hotel with unsurpassed European-style service, I took the ladies, one on each arm, to see how the millionaires did it. Well, they did it in great style; the jewels and the furs, not to mention the big piles of large chips on the gaming tables, were dazzling.

We each took fifty dollars of our money and separated to our own favorite gambling activity to see who could do the best. A while later, I saw Lil and Sue sitting in the cocktail lounge looking a little grim; they had lost their capital.

"It's OK," I said cheerfully. "I won, let's have some champagne."

My ladies smiled and I added a thought.

"We may not be millionaires, but we certainly are living as though we were!"

Lil and Sue laughed, and it was one more occasion when the lights sparkled in their eyes like stars.

It was almost painful to reach the point of having to say "Farewell" to Leopold in Genoa, the birthplace of *Cristoforo Colombo*. We all had a drink together in the lobby of the Hotel bearing the name of the famous explorer. Then, we waved "Goodbye" to our faithful friend as he headed his Lancia Limousine back towards Rome.

The next morning we boarded the brand new Italian luxury liner, the *Andrea Doria*, and continued our voyage to the States, by sea.

An interesting note: Later, Sue talked to Senator Richard Nixon when we were at a cocktail party at Ambassador Rankin's house in Taipei. We never knew if it was that conversation and Nixon's further efforts, but Sue got her Bob back from the communists not too long after.

The cruise to New York was luxury to the nth degree. We never had seen so many diamonds and minks before, nor after. The opulent dining room served the best the Italian cuisine had to offer. Our redheaded waiter had been on the *Conte Verde* when it was sunk by the Japanese at dockside in Shanghai. For awhile, after the War, he worked in the Italian Club across the street from the York Hotel, our abode during the early days of CAT.

When Camilo (equivalent to my first name) found out about our experiences in Shanghai, at the same time he was there, he could not do enough for us. We got all the best dishes, recommended by the Head Chef; and Camilo, of course. The pastas, the veal, the beef, the everything, could not be bettered in the finest restaurants in Rome.

One night, I sent Lil and Sue to the dining room without me; I just could not eat another bite that day. Camilo waited until long past closing; and, finally sent someone to my cabin to see if I were sick! He was crushed that I could not partake of the specialty he had saved for me that evening.

In New York, we attended the four-day Reunion of the Flying Tigers. We were headquartered in the Belmont Plaza Hotel and had many a party in the Waldorf Astoria.

One of the highlights of the festivities was a party in the private dining room of the Stork Club given by Tex and Jinx (nee Falkenberg) McCrary. With us were; Bill Bridgeman and Chuck Yaeger, Air Force heroes, Ed Rector (my Pensacola classmate) and Sue Buol, Stella and Jason Myers, owners of the St. Regis Hotel. Jason, not to be outdone, had us all over, the next day, for a sumptuous lunch at his prestigious hotel.

It was almost painful to leave all that fun and diversion and start thinking about a return to the Far East.

Two years later, the CAT that we old-timers knew was dealt yet another blow with the news that the General had lung cancer. Willauer had since departed to take up his ambassadorship in Central America. So, our mighty old warrior was stricken with the ultimate disease. Oh, yes, he returned to Taipei one more time after the diagnosis; but, it was not too long before he was back in Monroe, Louisiana, hoping for some kind of miracle cure.

During the fall of 1957, Lil and I met Sue at the Monroe Airport to visit Anna and the General, and to cheer him up. Up to that point, after the removal of one lung, every monthly check had been negative. If that could only continue for twelve months, the doctors felt he had a chance for a reasonable period of longevity. It was during that visit that the Old Man showed us how to make his famous squirrel stew (Page 243). We also visited his riverside camp a few hours drive away where Anna prepared catfish fried in cornmeal batter.

Upon our return to Taiwan, we received the terrible news that the report for the twelfth month was positive; the Old Man lasted only a short time after that. CAT, as we knew it, ceased to exist; the last of his founding and guiding spirit had expired with our leader. It then became completely an impersonal arm of the CIA. Within a comparatively short time, old key personnel began to leave. Lew Burridge had already gone; he stayed in the Far East with a well-known drug company.

"Bob, I wanted you to know before anyone else."

Rousselot had a couple of visitors in the living room, so I was sitting on the bed in the back room, telling him of my latest plans.

"What's that?"

"Well, you probably have guessed that, ever since Al was booted out,

I have been making my own plans."

He just nodded his head.

"Lil and I have made our home on the Island of Majorca," I went on. "Today I'm handing Grundy my resignation."

"That is news," he reacted. "I always knew that you had that kind of thing in mind, but didn't know it was coming so soon."

"Actually, I wanted to do this right after Al left but I had to get my ducks in a row and be sure."

"Yeh, well we'll all miss you and Lil. Now, I'll tell you that I won't be far behind."

I appreciated that he was up to his neck with the Doole-Grundy combination which a lot of us called "The Trans-Pacific Farce" because of the hours-long telephone conversations they had between Washington and Taipei. We saw each other often during my "notice period" but then I was not to see Bob and Ann again until many years later at their Gray Oaks Ranch in Wagoner, Oklahoma.

I told Rouss, "Doole has got to be something of a coward. It's been four years since that meeting where I called him an SOB to his face, in front of Chennault and the whole meeting. A ruthless guy like him certainly should have been able to think of some scheme to get me fired during that time."

Bob could only comment that he guessed that I was right.

It was not too long after that that Bob Rousselot joined Slick Airways in California and was later wooed away to Continental Airlines by Bob Six. Henry Yuan, senior Chinese Vice-President, passed away. Along with the General and Whitey, most of the original Civil Air Transport people were then gone.

Left was a conglomeration of various entities set up by the Agency possibly to confuse the public, or which just grew like "Topsy." In the picture were: CAT Incorporated, CATI, Civil Air Transport (Chinese Company), Civil Air Transport Inc., CATSA, Asiatic Aeronautical Co., Air America, Southern Air Transport and God know what all. There was even a SOP (Standard Operating Procedure) circulated which attempted to explain the various identities of "CAT."

The original CAT of General Chennault and Whitey Willauer, the "CAT with nine lives," had finally run out of luck and taken its last breath. And, it was not too many years later that all semblance of "CAT" had disappeared. It was replaced with China Airlines by the Chinese Government which saw no further need for such an impersonal organization

There would never be another airline like Chennault's Civil Air Transport. He began with the AVG (Flying Tigers)...and CAT was the end. Those two stars will certainly shine brightly, forever!

RECIPES

Grand Hotel, Taipei, Taiwan

In the early 1950 s, when the CAT contingent started to arrive on the Island of Taiwan, there was very little in the way of living accommodations. Everyone had to locate his own, with the help of Chinese friends of course. Then, too, visitors started to flock to the area. There were correspondents and diplomats of many foreign countries, and military brass mostly from the United States. The Government provided a 2-story building in the center of town, principally for the correspondents; but many CAT personnel stayed there from time to time, and most of us locals were members. It became known as the Friends of China Club.

The only other place to speak of was the Grand Hotel, situated on a hill, a few minutes from downtown, across the Tamsui River and overlooking the entire city. It was a sleepy, rundown building. Occasionally, one would see a rat or two running around. Upon entering, it did not appear to be a hotel at all because you could hardly ever find anyone at what was supposed to be a reception desk. Recognizing the need for better facilities for foreign visitors, Madame Chiang Kai-Shek asked Sue Buol, General Chennault's Secretary, to take on the job of organizing, refurbishing and decorating the place. She conceived the idea of forming a club with a board of directors to assist and advise her in accomplishing the task. Joe Brent, who was the head of the American aid program, served as Chairman and I pitched in as Treasurer to handle the financial accounting.

In order to whet the interest of Club members, Sue worked with the new Manager, Eddie Zee, to start a Chinese cooking school right in the main kitchen. There were about a dozen persons in each class and it was so successful that it was continued for three years. Every Saturday morning, with recipe notes under arm and Chinese cooking utensils in each hand, off we went to the lessons. Later, during worldwide travels, my recipes were lost. Recently, Eddie Zee, kind man that he is, sent us a beautiful, silk-covered box in bright Chinese Red with Chinese characters in gold thread. Inside: What did we find? A recipe book with all the dishes we had learned to make in the school! There were also four pairs of ivory chopsticks and brochures describing all of the present day amenities of the now world-famous Grand Hotel.

Before beginning this section of Chinese cooking, here are some hints, especially for foreigners; that is, non-Chinese.

There are three basic steps in the preparation of Chinese food.

1. Cutting and Chopping

Generally, all food, vegetables and meat, is cut into bite-size pieces prior to cooking. This has a practical aspect which goes with the use of chopsticks. But, no less important, the Chinese consider barbaric the employment of knife and fork to cut food at the dining table.

Meat is sliced thinly, slivered or cut into pieces. Vegetables are slivered, cut at an angle (stem vegetables, green onions, etc.) or cut into triangular and square pieces.

When fish is to be cooked whole; it is slashed at intervals, almost to the bone, for quick and even cooking and ease in eating with chopsticks at the table.

Fowl is often cooked whole; steamed, deep-fried, roasted or a combination. Then it is chopped through the bones into portions easily manipulated with chopsticks.

Vegetables. Almost any kind can be used; such as, broccoli, cauliflower, carrots, green and red peppers, zucchini, squash, cucumbers, turnips, etc. However, it is always nice to use Chinese vegetables when you can get them; Bok Choy, Chinese Cabbage, "Celery Cabbage," snow peas, etc. "Chinese Parsley" is cilantro grown from coriander seed; very pungent, used in small quantities.

Remember; in China there is no celery as we have in the States. Chinese restaurants use it here as a filler. In China, there is a small, green variety that is something between parsley and celery.

Also, the Chinese do not use dairy products in cooking and therefore do not have cheese. Tofu, a soy bean curd, is sometimes fermented; when finished it is similar to Gorgonzola cheese.

There is a dish made with whole pieces of pork or beef cooked with anise seed (or star anise), ginger and soy sauce. The cutting is done after the cooking.

2. Sauces

Sauces are made almost exclusively with chicken stock, regardless of the dish being prepared. Some sauces are used to marinate; others are added to the cooking pan at the end just before serving. Cornstarch mixed with water is usually added to thicken the sauce when the cooking is finished. But, this is only to eliminate the watery quality; never make the sauce too thick.

Make chicken stock from the bones and odd pieces; necks, wings, etc. Keep in the refrigerator; boil 5 to 10 minutes every three or four days to prevent spoiling.

3. Cooking

Frying is done; either in a small quantity of oil (so-called "stir frying"), or deep-fried in a large amount. In the latter case, a vessel should be kept handy to drain and strain the oil so that it can be reused. This is necessary when using a wok because it will be used to continue with the cooking process.

Steaming is employed with fish and fowl. An oblong steamer is useful for this purpose, although any large pot can be used with a plate in the bottom to keep the food above the liquid. Steaming and frying can be done ahead of time; then, the cooking of the meal can be accomplished in a matter of minutes.

Now, some useful items for Chinese cooking.

Wok, with cover. These come with a ring to place over the burner of a conventional stove both to hold the heat and to keep the wok level. However, lacking a Chinese type burner which enables heating the wok to a high temperature, I find that a large frying pan will do just as well, especially if you have an electric stove.

Spatula for stir-frying

Slotted spoon for removing food when deep-frying. The Chinese use a flat, net-like (metal) utensil about 6 inches in diameter.

Vessel for straining and holding oil

Large, sharp knife for cutting and chopping; the Chinese use a very sharp cleaver

The following ingredients are recommended:

Cooking oil; peanut or other vegetable oil

Soy sauce

Hoisin sauce, generally for vegetable and fowl dishes

Oyster sauce, usually for meat dishes

Sesame oil; must be Oriental, not the refined kind found in super-markets or health stores

Chinese Five Spices

Anise seed or star anise

Bamboo shoots and water chestnuts

Rice and noodles

Regular kitchen items; vinegar, sugar, salt, baking soda, cornstarch, peas, etc.

Beverages with Chinese food

The chinese are not great drinkers of alcoholic beverages. Tea is drunk with all meals; but, it is green tea, not the black type used here. However, they do have a yellow rice wine called Shiao Shing which is served warm. In the States the two favorites are beer and wine. Use a Chablis. Try it warm first. If that is not appealing, serve it chilled.

Among the recipes you will find almost no desserts because the Chinese seldom indulge in sweets after a meal. However, they do enjoy fresh fruit or sometimes ice cream.

The Chinese do not consume great quantities of sugar as is done in the States; but, you will note that most recipes have a small amount of it to bring out flavors. If you are dieting or are diabetic, use artificial sweetener in place of sugar. Be careful with the quantity; the dish is not supposed to taste sweet.

Be ADVENTUROUS! Almost any food can be prepared Chinese style. And, there are as many variations as you have the imagination and courage to try. Use recipes as a start and a guide. Go on from there.

The following recipes are a result of the schooling received in the Grand Hotel way back in the early 1950 s.

NOTE: The measurement cup used in the Grand Hotel kitchen was a teacup which is a little smaller than the usual measurement cup.

SWEET AND SOUR PORK

This is a Cantonese dish from south China. Assemble the following:
1 cup pork loin in one-inch squares
1 green pepper cut into diamond-shaped pieces
1 green onion cut into one-inch pieces
2 tbsp ginger, thinly sliced
1 tbsp cornstarch in 1 tbsp water
Sufficient cornstarch to coat the meat
Oil for frying

SWEET AND SOUR SAUCE

4 tbsp each of vinegar and sugar
1 tsp salt
2 tbsp each of hot water and Worcestershire sauce
3 tbsp catsup and 1 tsp cornstarch
It is better if the pork loin is a little thicker than one inch, then you can pound it with back end of cleaver or large knife to make it more tender. Also, the meat will be much more tender and juicy if the part with a little fat in it is purchased. After cutting it into one-inch pieces, sprinkle it with a little salt. Make a paste of 1 tbsp of cornstarch with 1 tbsp water and work it into the pieces of pork with the fingers; set aside while cutting the vegetables and mixing the sauce (at least 15 minutes). Roll the pork

squares in cornstarch until thoroughly coated.

Deep fry the pork pieces until brown; about five minutes, then drain. Heat the wok or frying pan with 1 tbsp of oil. Stir fry the vegetables about three minutes. Stir the sauce well and add to the vegetables, mix. Add the pork and toss quickly. Serve at once while it is still bubbling.

NOTE: For most cooking in the Grand Hotel, peanut oil was used. Now the recipe book says "crisco." I recommend the oil. Many people like the outside of the pork to be crisp. If it is mixed in the wok with the vegetables and the sauce, the outside coating will start to turn soft. I always put the meat on a hot platter and, at the last moment, pour the vegetables and the sauce over it, without mixing. Also, not traditional, pineapple pieces are sometimes added to the sauce.

Suggestion: An old friend of ours from CAT, Nina Wilson, had the idea of shaking the pork pieces in a bag with Shake n' Bake and cooking them in the oven until brown, instead of deep frying.

DICED CHICKEN WITH WALNUTS

Assemble:
1 cup Chicken, boneless and cut into one-inch pieces
½ cup toasted walnuts
1 Black mushroom cut into strips
1 tbsp ginger cut into thin strips (julienne)
2 tbsp bamboo shoots, chopped
1 green onion cut in one-inch pieces
1 tbsp green pepper cut in small diamonds
Oil to cook
Marinade:
2 tbsp chicken broth
½ tsp each baking powder and salt
1 tsp cornstarch
½ egg white slightly beaten
Frying Sauce:
Mix: 2 tbsp chicken broth, 1 tsp each soy sauce, wine, cornstarch, and half tsp salt.

Mix chicken pieces with the marinade. Cut vegetables. Drain the meat and deep fry only until the color changes, about 1 minute; drain. Heat wok with 1 tbsp oil, stir fry vegetables about 3 minutes. Add the sauce until bubbling, then the chicken; toss and, last, add the walnuts

The recipe recommends that, before toasting the walnuts, they be blanched in boiling water with a little salt. Then the thin skins can easily be removed. When toasting the walnuts, I add a tsp of white or brown sugar and about half tsp ground ginger. Be sure to stir constantly so as not to burn. Also, if the nuts are put on the top of the dish instead of mixing them, they will be crisper. Another suggestion: If the short deep frying operation is bothersome, just stir fry the chicken pieces in a little oil over high heat; once again, only until the color changes to opaque white. Set the meat aside while doing the vegetables.

CHICKEN CORN SOUP

Assemble:
1 can (about 2 cups) creamed corn
4 egg whites, slightly beaten
2 tbsp evaporated milk
4 cups chicken broth
1 tbsp salt
3 tbsp cornstarch in 3 tbsp chicken broth
3 tbsp melted lard
Mix beaten egg whites and milk thoroughly. Heat chicken broth in pan with creamed corn and salt, bring to a boil while stirring constantly. Remove the pan from the fire, stir the egg and milk mixture well and add slowly to the soup, stirring all the while. Finally add the lard and serve.

NOTE: You may not like the idea of the lard. It can be reduced in quantity or eliminated.

FRIED SHRIMPS WITH TOMATO SAUCE

Prepare:
1 cup shrimps, shelled and cleaned
Half cup onions cut in half-inch pieces
1 tsp ginger, chopped fine
Oil for frying
Marinade:
Half egg white, slightly beaten
Half tsp salt
1 tsp cornstarch
Frying Sauce:
2 Tbsp each of chicken broth and catsup
1 Tbsp sugar
Half tsp salt
1 tsp cornstarch
Mix shrimps with the marinade very thoroughly with the fingers. Deep

fry the shrimps for one to two minutes, depending upon the size. Do not overcook. Stir fry the onions and ginger in 1 Tbsp oil over high heat for about two minutes. Add the Frying Sauce and stir until bubbling. Add the shrimp and toss quickly. Serve.

BEEF WITH GREEN PEPPER

Prepare:
1 cup beef tenderloin sliced paper thin
Half cup green pepper cut in thin strips, ½" long
1 tbsp ginger cut in thin strips (julienne)
2 green onions cut in 1 inch long pieces
Oil for frying
Marinade:
3 Tbsp chicken broth
1 tsp baking soda
1 Tbsp soy sauce
Half tsp salt
1 tsp cornstarch
Frying sauce:
2 Tbsp chicken broth
Half tsp each of salt and cornstarch
1 Tbsp sesame oil
1 tsp sugar

The beef will be easier to cut thin if it is half frozen. Add it to the marinating sauce and work it in with the fingers; set aside for at least 15 minutes. Deep fry the beef for only one minute. Stir fry the vegetables in 1 Tbsp oil over high heat. Mix in the beef and then the frying sauce; cook about two minutes more. I prefer to eliminate the deep frying operation: When stir frying the vegetables, push them to the side of the pan and stir fry the beef in the other half until the red color has disappeared, then mix all together, following with the sauce. I find tenderloin a little too soft for this dish. Any other kind of steak, including chuck, is more satisfactory; and easier on the pocketbook.

For Beef and Oyster Sauce, use the same recipe and, at the end, add about 2 Tbsp Oyster Sauce.

SPRING ROLLS

Assemble and Prepare:
1 cup pork sliced into thin strips about 1½" long
1 cup shrimps shelled and cleaned, cut in ½" pieces

3 cups bamboo shoots sliced, the size of a match
Half cup black mushrooms sliced in thin strips
2 cups chicken broth
4 Tbsp cornstarch
1 Tbsp each salt and sugar
Oil to fry and 1 lb spring roll wrappers

Mix the pork with 1 Tbsp chicken broth and 1 tsp cornstarch. Mix remaining cornstarch, salt and sugar. To this add four Tbsp chicken broth to make a sauce. Heat the pork with four Tbsp oil; add pork, shrimps, mushrooms and bamboo shoots; stir, add the 2 cups chicken broth, stir again. To this, add the well mixed sauce. Cook 4 minutes, stirring constantly. Remove from the heat and spread out on a large platter to cool.

Spring roll wrappers are very thin, unlike egg roll wrappers which are too thick. One brand which I found was made in the Philippines. It's worth tracking them down; because, once you have had a genuine spring roll, you will never have an egg roll again. They are crisp and delicate on the outside and melt in your mouth. By the way, the recipe from the Grand Hotel in Taipei, Taiwan, poduces the best spring rolls I have ever tasted.

The wrapping operation is fairly simple but takes a little time and care. Besides the wrappers, have a small bowl of paste handy, made from flour and water. Place one wrapper on the working surface in front of you. Put 2 Tbsp of filling on the wrapper in the one-third nearest you. Lift the part of the wrapper closest to you and roll it over the filling. Fold the two sides toward the center. With the finger, put a little paste on the remaining part of the wrapper and complete the roll being sure that the part with the paste adheres well to the rest of the roll. Deep fry several at a time in hot oil until they are brown, about five minutes.

SWEET AND SOUR FISH

This is one of the many spectacular dishes in Chinese cuisine. The Chinese like to use what they call a "Yellow Fish". If this is unobtainable, use a salt water fish of mild flavor and tender flesh with as few bones as possible. It should be scaled and gutted but with the head and tail left on.

Assemble:
1 tbsp green peas
3 tbsp chopped onions
2 tbsp chopped ginger
1 Tomato, cut in wedges and seeds removed
1 tbsp cornstarch

3 egg yolks
6 tbsp flour
¾ cup water

SWEET AND SOUR SAUCE

4 tbsp each of catsup, water, Worcestershire sauce
8 tbsp each of sugar and vinegar
1 tbsp each of salt and cornstarch

Wash the fish and remove the back bone by cutting along each side of it and pulling it out. Make cross slits on each side almost down to the main center bone and about two inches apart. In a large bowl mix the egg yolks, flour and water to make a batter. Dip the fish, turning it over and moving it back and forth until it is completely covered. Leave it in the bowl until you make the sauce. To deep fry the fish, heat 6 cups of oil in the wok to very hot. Put the fish in and fry for 2 minutes. If the fish cannot be completely submerged, keep pouring the hot oil over it with a ladle. Remove the pan from the heat and let it stand for 5 minutes. Now put the pan back on the burner for 3 more minutes. Drain and place the fish on a hot serving platter. Now stir fry the peas, chopped onion, ginger and tomato in 1 tbsp of oil for about 2 minutes. Add the sweet and sour sauce and fry until it is bubbling and thickened. Pour over the fish and serve.

FRIED MINCED PIGEON

Minced Meat Mixture:
2 Pigeons: if not available, 4 oz chicken meat
3 chicken livers
1 egg yolk
1 tsp soy sauce
½ tsp salt
Vegetables:
1st group: 1 tbsp chopped green onion
    1 tsp chopped ginger
2nd group: 1 tbsp chopped green pepper
    1 tbsp chopped mushroom
3rd group: ½ cup chopped bamboo shoots
Frying Sauce:
2 tbsp chicken broth
1 tsp each soy sauce and cornstarch

½ tsp each salt and sesame oil
Garnish:
½ cup rice noodles
15 lettuce leaves

Mince the pigeon meat(or chicken meat) together with the chicken livers. After it is finely chopped, mix with the egg yolk, soy sauce and salt.

Prepare the vegetables and have ready on three separate plates. Prepare the Frying Sauce. Deep fry the rice noodles; they will puff up and turn slightly brown in just a few seconds. Place on serving platter.

In a hot wok with 3 tbsp oil, put the 1st group of vegetables, stir and add the 2nd group of vegetables. Stir and add the minced meat mixture and stir fry for about 1 minute, then add the 3rd group. Fry for about 2 minutes more. Lastly, add the Frying Sauce; stir quickly and remove from the stove. Place the Fried Minced Pigeon on top of the noodles and serve with the lettuce leaves. This dish is eaten by placing a portion of the meat mixture and noodles on a leaf and rolling it up.

ASSORTED VEGETABLE DISH

1 cup Chinese cabbage, cut into 1" pieces
¼ cup black mushrooms, sliced wedge-shaped
½ cup bamboo shoots, thinly sliced
1 green pepper, cut in diamond-shape
1 cup chicken broth
1 tsp each salt and cornstarch
¼ tsp sugar
2 tsp soy sauce

Place 2 tbsp oil in wok over high heat. Add cabbage, mushrooms, bamboo shoots and green pepper. Fry for 2 minutes, then add chicken broth, salt, sugar and soy sauce. Stir well and cook for 5 minutes. Finally, add the cornstarch diluted with 1 tbsp chicken broth. Stir well and serve.

NOTE: You can improve the flavor of the sauce by adding one tbsp Hoisin Sauce however it will be darker in color.

SMOKED POMFRET

Use one whole Pomfret, about 1 ½ to 2 lbs., with the head and tail but scaled and gutted. If this fish is not available, use a Flounder. The difference between the two fish is: the Pomfret is the same dark color on both sides and swims in a vertical position; the Flounder is dark on one side and almost white on the other, and swims in a flat-horizontal attitude. The taste and texture of the Pomfret is the better of the two.

Marinade:

1 tbsp each of salt and chopped ginger
1 tsp each of sugar and sesame paste
2 green onions, chopped
2 tbsp Chinese rice wine (or sherry)
6 tbsp soy sauce

Make 7 or 8 cross cuts in each side of the fish almost to the center bone. Place in the marinating sauce for 30 minutes, turning occasionally. Drain and deep fry in hot oil for 2 minutes. The fish is then smoked for 20 minutes spraying or basting with the marinade. If you do not have a smoker, use a pan or charcoal briquets which have burned down to the coals. Place damp sawdust on top and put the pan in the bottom rack of the oven. Place the fish on a wire net on the rack above the charcoal. Turn after 10 minutes and do the other side for about the same amount of time. NOTE: Use sawdust from any hard wood.

MIXED FRIED RICE CANTONESE STYLE

Prepare:

5 cups cooked rice
4 eggs, beaten
¾ cup shrimps, shelled and cleaned
½ cup diced ham
⅓ cup peas, cooked or canned
1 tbsp salt

In a wok over high heat place 8 tbsp (½ cup) of oil. First fry the shrimps for about 1 minute, only until they have changed color. Add the beaten eggs and stir for 1 minute. Add the rice and mix well. Finally add the ham, peas and salt. Stir constantly while cooking for 2 or 3 minutes more. You can add all kinds of goodies to this dish; sliced onions, green onions, left over meats, etc.

NOTE: This type of fried rice was served in Tiger Joe's Restaurant. One evening, a man called me to his table.

"This is not genuine Chinese Fried Rice," he chided.

"Why not?" I asked him.

"It's not brown like it's supposed to be."

"Well, that's the way it's made in China," I informed him. "If you want it brown, just add soy sauce; that's what they do in American Chinese kitchens."

So, if you want the Fried Rice brown, add soy sauce.

SLICED DUCK WITH PINEAPPLE

Prepare:
1 cup sliced raw duck meat
2 slices pineapple cut into 8 pieces
1 green pepper cut into diamond shape
¼ cup sliced ginger
1 tbsp sliced green onion
Marinade:
½ tsp each salt, soy sauce and baking soda
1 tsp cornstarch
Frying Sauce:
1 tbsp each chicken broth and Worcesterhsire sauce
2 tbsp catsup
1 tsp each salt, vinegar and cornstarch
Using your fingers, mix well the duck slices with the marinade. Deep fry the meat for 2 minutes. Add the green pepper and pineapple and fry for not more than 1 minute; drain. Stir fry the onion and ginger, then add the pre-cooked duck, green pepper and pineapple and fry for about 2 minutes. Last, add the Frying Sauce and stir quickly until bubbling and thickened.

ROAST CHICKEN CANTONESE

Immerse a whole chicken in boiling water for 2 minutes. Drain. Rub the inside of chicken with 1 tbsp "roasted salt". This is made by stir frying in a dry pan; 3 tbsp salt, ¾ tsp each of cinnamon and black pepper for 5 minutes over low heat. Rub the outside of the chicken with 1 tbsp molasses in 1 tbsp boiling water. The Chinese hang the chicken to dry and one sees them hanging in the food shops and restaurants in Canton. You can put it on a cake rack for at least four hours.

Deep fry the chicken in hot oil for about ½ hour until it is a nice golden brown. As suggested in the recipe for cooking a whole fish, use a ladle to pour the hot oil on top of the chicken, in case it is not completely covered. The traditonal way of cutting the chicken is right through the bone, cross-wise, in bite-size pieces, and then placing it on the serving platter in its original shape. The skin should be crisp and the inside juicy. Serve the rest of the "roasted salt" on the side to dip the pieces in.

STEWED SHRIMPS ON CRISPY RICE

Prepare:
½ cup shrimps, shelled and cleaned
1 tbsp ham, sliced in very thin diamond shapes
½ cup fresh mushrooms, sliced
2 green onions, sliced very thin
2 tbsp bamboo shoots, sliced in very thin diamonds
Sauce:
4 tbsp catsup
1 tbsp salt
4 cups chicken broth
1 tsp cornstarch
1 cup pieces of dried crispy rice.

Deep fry the shrimps in hot oil until color changes, but no more than 1 minute; drain and set aside. In the empty wok, mix the catsup, salt and chicken broth. Add the shrimp and allow to boil for 2 minutes. Mix the cornstarch with a little water and stir into the soup until thickened. Pour into a serving soup bowl.

Now return the cooking oil to the pan and bring to high heat. Add the crispy rice and fry until brown, only a few seconds. Drain and put pieces of crispy rice into a serving bowl large enough to hold also the soup. Place both bowls in the middle of the table. With a flair, quickly pour the soup over the crispy rice. If this is done immediately after frying the rice, there should be a loud crackling sound; and when we were in Taiwan, we used to call this: "Bombing Tokyo"!

NOTE: Crispy rice can be made at home but that is difficult; best purchase it in an oriental food store.

GLAZED BANANAS

Although it was mentioned in the initial notes on Chinese cooking that the Chinese do not make many desserts, the following recipe which we learned in the Grand Hotel is an excellent one to try. Experiment with family first before trying it on guests; it takes a while to become proficient making the syrup come out to the right consistency. However, if you have made candy, you should have little difficulty.

Assemble:
3 bananas, peeled and cut into 1 ½" diagonal pieces
1 cup flour
1 egg
9 tbsp (about ⅔ cup) water

Syrup:

7 tbsp (almost ½ cup) each water and sugar

½ tsp sesame seeds

1 tsp sesame oil

Mix with the fingers, 1 tbsp of the flour with the bananas coating each piece. In another bowl, beat the egg, add the remaining flour and beat again. Add the water and stir to obtain a smooth batter. Add the bananas and coat each piece. For deep frying bring the oil to a very high temperature, remove from the heat. Add the bananas, one piece at a time. When all are in the oil put the pan back on the heat and fry until the bananas are a light brown color; drain. Dissolve the sugar in the water on the stove, stirring until it is boiling. Add the sesame seeds and stir while continuing to cook the liquid until a sticky syrup results. Add the sesame oil and then the bananas. Stir and cook for about one minute. Then pour onto a serving platter that has been brushed with sesame oil. If the syrup has reached the right consistency during the cooking; when the diner picks up a piece of banana with his chopsticks, the syrup adhering to it will "spin a hair". A bowl of cold water is put on the table for the diner to dip in his piece of banana to harden the glaze before eating it.

SLICED CUTTLEFISH IN HOT PEPPER SAUCE

This is probably a Hunan (or, maybe Szechuan) dish because of the hot pepper sauce. It is unlikely that you will find cuttlefish in the market; use squid which, although not the same animal, is similar. Clean 2 large squid and take off the thin outer skin. Cut in 2 inch squares. Score the outside diagonally in both directions about every ¼ inch about half way through the flesh. This should result in diamond design which will open up when cooked.

Assembles:

4 dried red peppers (hot)

2 cloves garlic, one sliced, one chopped

2 green onions cut in 1 inch pieces

3 tbsp chopped parsley

2 tbsp hot pepper sauce

2 tbsp wine

1 tsp each cornstarsh, salt, vinegar, sugar, pepper

1 tbsp soy sauce

In hot oil, deep fry the squid for 3 minutes; drain. In 1 tbsp oil in a wok over high heat, stir the dried peppers for a few seconds. Add the green onion, wine, sugar, salt and a little cold water (about 2 tbsp) and stir quickly. Add the squid and cornstarch (in 1 tbsp water) and quickly mix well. Serve immediately with hot seasoning sauce on the side for dipping the squid: chopped garlic, chopped green onion, parsley, soy sauce, red pepper sauce, sugar, vinegar and pepper (white or black). The red pepper sauce is sold in Oriental food markets. This is a HOT dish; have plenty of cold beer to ease the pain.

There are three other dishes that we learned to make in the Grand Hotel cooking class which are not in the pretty little red and gold book sent to us by Eddie Zee, the Manager of the Hotel: Crab, Corn and Eggs; Roasted Chicken Livers, and Szechuan Duck. The latter is in the group of recipes sent by Priscilla and Moon Chen. Here are the other two.

CRAB, CORN AND EGGS

Assemble:
8 egg whites, lightly beaten
1 cup crab meat
½ can creamed corn
1 green onion, chopped
4 tbsp chopped bamboo shoots
1 tsp cornstarch
1 tsp salt
2 tbsp evaporated milk

Mix all the ingredients in a large bowl. Heat 1 tbsp oil in a wok and add the mixture. Stir constantly until it has just solidified but is still moist. Immediately put on serving platter.

ROASTED CHICKEN LIVERS

I have tried these on many skeptics who said they would never eat chicken livers but they devoured this dish. Use about 2 livers per person. Cut them into 2 or 3 bite-sized pieces. Cover with a little soy sauce and put aside.

Make a sweet and sour sauce with: juice of 1 lemon (save the skin of ½), equal amount of sugar, 1 tbsp soy sauce, 1 tbsp Worcestershire sauce, 1 tbsp catsup and ½ cup chicken broth.

Drain the livers and roll in whole wheat flour covering each piece well. Deep fry until brown, about 2 minutes. Drain and put on a hot serving plate with the reserved half lemon (cut side down) in the center. Stir fry 1 green onion cut in 1 inch pieces, ½ green pepper cut in diamonds and 1 tbsp ginger cut in thin strips (julienne). Add the sweet and sour sauce. When it is bubbling stir in 1 tsp cornstarch which has been mixed with water. Pour over the chicken livers and serve.

Moon Chen joined the CAT organization in the early days in Shanghai managing the Traffic and Sales Department. He and wife, Priscilla, are both excellent cooks. Since returning to the States after the CAT episode she has given cooking lessons in many parts of the country.

"What's this?" I asked Moon of a strange dish served during the course of a dinner at their house in the French Settlement in Shanghai. One could always expect something unique and exotic when dining with them.

"Duck tongues!" He replied succinctly, smiling mysteriously with that twinkle in his eyes.

"I didn't know a duck had edible tongues," I remarked dubiously. "It always seemed to me that they had some kind of a hard, reed-like 'tongue' to make those quacking sounds."

That inscrutable smile was his only answer.

Only recently, when Moon parted with the recipe, did I learn that there are also duck brains and duck webs in the dish! Duck feet, and chicken feet, also, are not unusual in Chinese cuisine. After holding them over a flame, the skin comes off and they are ready for use as directed. Here's the recipe.

DUCK TONGUES MOON CHEN

Assemble:
8 duck tongues
8 duck webs (feet)
8 duck brains (cook the heads separately; when cold, remove the brains with a spoon)
2 duck breasts, without bones, cut into 1-inch pieces
8 water chestnuts sliced
1 cup bamboo shoots
1 cup yellow Chinese wine (can use sherry)
3 cups chicken stock
3 tbsp soy sauce
1 green onion
1 tsp chopped ginger
cornstarch

Pan fry in 1 tbsp oil the duck pieces on high heat, only until lightly brown; then add the tongues and webs and stir fry 3 or 4 minutes.

Put all the ingredients, except the cornstarch, in a pot and bring to a boil. Simmer on low heat for 45 minutes. Thicken with cornstarch when ready to serve.

If you happen to be in a place where ducks are raised, you can experience the adventure of preparing and dining on this unusual dish. However, since the ingredients cannot be purchased in a store, Priscilla and Moon have most kindly given some of their other favorite recipes to try.

DRUNKEN CHICKEN (the Chinese are very descriptive)
Assemble:

1 whole chicken
1 slice ginger
1 green onion, cut in half
1 tbsp salt
1 ½ cups yellow Chinese wine (can use sherry)

Put chicken in a pot with green onion, ginger and salt; cover with water. Bring to a boil with the back down. Turn the heat to low and simmer for ten minutes. Turn on one side for ten minutes and the other side for ten. Remove chicken to cool. Put it in a container of a size where it just fits. Pour wine over it. Refrigerate and brush with wine every four hours. One day will result in a slightly inebriated chicken and two or more days will result in a very drunken bird! Chop the chicken into serving pieces and place on a platter in its original shape. Garnish with parsley and slivered green onion, two inches long.

That is the Shanghai version. The Cantonese serve it as "White Chicken," eliminating the last part with the wine; serving it with a dip of hot, sesame oil and soy sauce. It is common to see this chicken hanging in food shops in Canton.

POM POM CHICKEN

Use left over Drunken Chicken or White Chicken Cantonese. Remove the bones and shred the meat. Mix it with slightly blanched bean sprouts or broccoli, or both. Toss in a large salad bowl with:

1 tbsp soy sauce
2 tsp wine
½ tsp crushed pepper corn
1 clove chopped garlic
salt to taste
1 tbsp sesame oil
1 tbsp salad oil
1 tsp sugar
1 chopped green onion

Julienne of celery two inches long can be added if desired. If you like it hot, add red pepper and pepper oil, found in Oriental shops. Or, make your own by frying broken or crushed dried red hot peppers in oil. This throws off very acrid fumes; keep ventilator on and do not breathe the *vapors.*

KUNG PAO CHI TING (Diced Chicken with Cashews, Szechuan Style...that means HOT!)

Cut deboned chicken into ¾ inch pieces and marinate in; 1 tbsp soy sauce, 1 tbsp water and 1 tbsp sugar.

Prepare sauce of: 1 tbsp sugar, 1 tbsp cornstarch, 2 tbsp soy sauce, 1 tbsp sherry, 1 tbsp water, 1 tbsp white vinegar and 1 tbsp sesame oil.

Cut 1 green pepper or red, or a combination of both, into 1-inch pieces. Add 1 tsp chopped ginger, 1 chopped garlic clove and hot pepper; quantity to be determined by how adventurous you are. Add these ingredients to the chicken and let stand for at least 20 minutes.

Heat pan or wok with 1 tbsp oil over medium heat. Stir fry chicken mixture, with the marinating sauce, for 3 or 4 minutes until the meat just turns white; do not over cook. Add cashews, which have previously been browned in oil, and stir until well mixed.

Add the sauce and cook only until thick and bubbly. Can substitute peanuts, almonds or walnuts.

GREEN ONION PIE (Chung You Ping)
2 cups all-purpose flour
6 strips bacon; fried crisp and crumbled, reserve fat
6 green onions, sliced very thinly
¾ cup lukewarm water
salt
cooking oil

In a mixing bowl, gradually add the warm water to the flour and mix until it is dampened. Turn onto a well-floured board and knead until smooth, about 2 or 3 minutes. Divide into five balls. Roll them into pancakes about 1/8 inch thick. Brush with bacon fat on one side, sprinkle with salt, spread 1/5 of the onions and crumbled bacon on each one. Roll them up and fold over the two ends to meet in the middle. Flatten and roll out again to the pancake size. At this point you can put wax paper between them and refrigerate or freeze depending upon the time they are to be kept.

When ready to serve, fry in 2 tbsp oil, pressing them with a spatula, until brown on each side. Cut each into six wedges and serve at once.

VARIATION: Eliminate the bacon. Brush each pancake with sesame oil. After rolling up with the green onion, press sesame seeds into each side and roll into the finished pancake as before. These "pies" are a tasty item with Oriental roast chicken or duck.

EGGPLANT IN SPICY SAUCE

1 eggplant
2 tbsp green onion
1 tbsp minced ginger
1 tsp minced garlic
Sauce, mix:
¼ cup soy
1 tsp each white pepper, sugar, sherry, cornstarch in 1 tsp water
2 tsp hot bean sauce; available in Oriental food shops

Cut eggplant into 3 x 1 inch slices, soak in cold water for 15 minutes, dry with paper towel. Heat pan with 6 tbsp oil; add eggplant and cook quickly for 2 or 3 minutes. Add the green onions, ginger, garlic and cook another minute, or until the eggplant is tender. Pour in sauce, heat until bubbling. If you prefer a more pepperish taste, add more hot bean paste or crushed red pepper. This dish is very good, hot or cold.

SZECHUAN DUCK

1 duck, 4 or 5 lbs
2 tbsp salt
8 slices ginger
4 green onions cut into 2-inch pieces
1 tbsp anise seed
1 tbsp Szechuan pepper corns or Chinese Five Spices

After cleaning the duck inside and out, wipe dry with paper towels. Place in a steamer and cover with all the above ingredients. Steam for 1½ hours. Drain, cool and let dry. Rub duck all over with honey. Heat enough oil to cover the duck. deep fry until brown and crispy. Serve with Chinese Onion Pie (Chung You Ping).

BROCCOLI A LA CHEN

1 bunch broccoli
1 tbsp soy sauce
1½ tbsp sesame oil

1 tsp salt

Cut off flowerettes from the broccoli, reserve them. Peel the stems and cut into diagonal pieces, blanch in boiling water for one minute. Drain and dry with paper towel. Add salt and cover for 30 minutes, drain off any liquid. Toss with soy sauce and sesame oil. Very good served cold.

NOTE: I like to add the flowerettes at the end of the blanching operation and include them in the dish.

STUFFED CHINESE MUSHROOMS

20 medium size black Chinese mushrooms
1 lb Pork, chopped fine
6 water chestnuts, chopped fine
1 tsp each sherry and sugar
4 tbsp soy sauce
½ tsp salt

Rinse the mushrooms, cover with water in a pan and bring to a boil. Cover and let stand at least half an hour so that they will be tender. Cut off the stems being sure to remove all the hard parts. Combine the meat with all the other ingredients and mix thoroughly. Stuff each mushroom and steam them for 20 minutes.

PAPER-PACKED CHICKEN

Breast of chicken
3 tbsp soy sauce
1 tsp sherry
½ tsp sugar
1 tbsp green onion, chopped
Wax paper

Slice the chicken into pieces about 1" by 2". Let it marinate for one hour in the mixture of the other ingredients (except the wax paper). Cut the wax paper into 5"x 5" squares; spread with oil and wrap the chicken into little packets. Have oil hot in a pan. Slide the packets in and turn quickly. Since the oil is hot and the chicken thin it will be ready almost immediately. Suggestion; put a few drops of sesame oil when wrapping the chicken pieces

CHICKEN CORN SOUP

1 can cream of sweet corn

¾ cup raw chicken meat, cut into slivers or small pieces
1 tbsp shredded ham
1 egg, beaten
Chicken stock

Heat the corn on low fire; when hot, stir in the chicken meat adding salt to taste. If it is too thick add some chicken stock. When the mixture boils, add the beaten egg, slowly, stirring at the same time. Top the soup with the shredded ham

PORK OMELET OR PORK FOO YUNG

5 eggs beaten until fluffy
½ lb bean sprouts
5 black Chinese mushrooms, softened and shredded
¼ lb pork, shredded
2 or 3 tbsp shredded bamboo shoot
Seasoning: sherry, salt, sugar, soy sauce

Fry the pork and add all the other ingredients except the eggs. Stir quickly. Pour in the eggs to finish the omelet; goes well with a sweet and sour sauce.

STEWED PORK ANISE

This dish was first enjoyed at the home of Cora Tsai, one of the CAT secretaries, who is now married to a doctor and lives in Canada. The shank part of the pork leg is used; do not remove the skin. Select a pot that just barely holds the meat. Cover with equal parts of soy sauce and chicken stock. Add:
1 tsp sugar
2 tbsp sherry
4 slices ginger, unpeeled, flattened with knife
1 tbsp anise seed, or 4 pieces star anise

Cover, bring to a boil, then simmer on the lowest heat for 3 hours. After 1½ hours, turn the meat. Place the meat in a large serving bowl; pour the liquid over it after removing the fat. The meat is so tender, it can be taken with chopsticks without slicing it. After the leftovers have been in the refrigerator, you will be able to remove more of the fat, if so desired.

The following two recipes were provided by Nadia Boring. One of the CAT wives, Nadia has become a painter of some note, traveling around the country giving exhibitions. She also teaches Chinese and other types of cooking. Her husband, Jim, was head of the Ground Transportation Department from the Shanghai era until the final days of CAT on Taiwan. They now reside in Naples, New York, not far from Buffalo. Jim dabbles in golf and relaxation.

NADIA'S DOUBLE COOKED PORK SLICES

This recipe comes from North China. Assemble:
½ lb boneless pork
1 green onion
2 slices ginger
2 green peppers, cut into 1" pieces
3 red peppers, cut into 1" pieces
3 cloves of garlic, sliced
2 tbsp sweet soy bean paste
1 tbsp hot bean paste
1 tbsp soy sauce
2 tsp sugar
1 tbsp dry sherry
½ tsp anise seed(optional)

Stew the whole piece of pork, with the green onion, in the one tbsp sherry and water to cover, for 20 minutes. Remove the meat and slice it.

Mix in a bowl: the sweet paste, hot paste, soy sauce and sugar. If you cannot find the 2 pastes, use Hoi Sin sauce, sesame oil and hot pepper sauce.

Fry the pork slices in 2 tbsp oil for one minute. Add the garlic and the green and red peppers; stir for 1 minute. Return the pork and vegetables to the pan; stir well and serve.

NADIA'S DUCK, OR CHICKEN, MANCINI

A dish similar to this was one of the specialties of the Grand Hotel in Taipei. Let's try Nadia's version.

Assemble:
6-lb duck or 3-lb chicken
3 tsp salt
¾ tsp pepper
1 tsp (½ tsp for chicken) paprika
½ tsp garlic powder

Reserve 1 tsp of salt and ¼ of pepper for later. Except for this, rub all of the above ingredients inside and outside the fowl.

Prepare:

¾ cup chopped onions
½ lb chopped mushrooms
4 tbsp half butter and half oil
2 tbsp chopped parsley
3 cups cooked medium noodles
2 eggs, beaten

Saute the onions and mushrooms in the butter and oil, (suggestion: during the cooking, add a pinch of marjoram). Chop the giblets and add to the pan and saute for about 5 minutes more. Remove from the heat; add the parsley, noodles, eggs and adjust salt and pepper to taste. Toss lightly and stuff the bird with the mixture. Sew or skewer the opening. Extra noodles can be heated in the oven about ½ hour before the roasting is completed (mix with a cup of sour cream, if desired). Place the bird on a rack in a pan in a 375 degree oven; about 2 hours for the duck, 1 ¼ hours, or until brown and tender, for the chicken. If the duck browns too fast, place a piece of foil on top and turn oven down to 350 degrees. Flavor is enhanced if some white wine is put in the bottom of the pan during the last half hour of roasting. If you like the duck less fatty, place it in a pot of boiling water for 5 to 10 minutes before starting the preparation, drying it first.

CHINESE STEAMED FISH

Any kind of fish can be steamed; so, choose one to your liking, of a size that will fit into, with head and tail, the vessel that will be used in the cooking. If the pot will not take entire fish, you can cheat a little by cutting the fish in half and, after cooking, join it together on the serving platter with some decoration over the wound!

The fish is scaled and gutted, but with the head and tail left on. Cut into the fish crosswise, almost down to the center bone, at 1½" intervals. Also, take the back fin out by running the knife down each side of it. Rub the fish all over, inside included, with sherry. Salt lightly. In each slit, and in the inside, place one or two slivers of ginger and green onion. Sprinkle each side with a little sesame oil. Place in the steamer on a plate above the boiling water. Cover and steam about 5 to 12 minutes depending upon the thickness of the fish. Check with a fork in the thickest part of the fish. It should be just barely opaque. Do not overcook! At the point of serving, sprinkle with a little soy sauce and decorate with Chinese parsley (fresh coriander, also known as "cilantro"). You may like fish fried but, once you have tried Chinese steamed fish, you will have to admit that it is the most delicate of all.

Ura Tschen (Chen) is the brother of Peter, husband of Kira Chen (Page 238). We were friends for many years on Taiwan. Now that he and his wife, Lily, live and work near Raleigh, we have more opportunity to follow our mutual culinary pursuits. Ura is especially good at making the dumpling called "Chiao tze". This and other dumplings are from north China where wheat is used for the coverings and for steamed bread. Many varieties of fillings are used: shrimp, chicken, vegetables, beans, etc., and they may be boiled, steamed or fried. Cooks outdo themselves in devising artistic forms for the finished product. Chiao tze is one of the simplest. Recently, Ura and Lily were visiting us here in the Great Smokies and, together, we made well over one hundred. Some were devoured then and the remainder frozen to be savored later. The wrappers for Chiao tze are very thin and therefore quite difficult to make. So, you should find a source for the definitive ones which are round. If this is not possible, use Won Ton wrappers which are square but can be adapted.

CHIAO TZE
Prepare

1 lb pork, shredded

Chop: 3 green onions, 3 tbsp bamboo, 1 tbsp ginger, 1 cup Chinese cabbage

1 tbsp cornstarch, 1 tbsp soy sauce, 1 tbsp sesame oil

1 tsp sugar

Mix all ingredients. Use a floured working surface and have a bowl of water with a little flour to stick the edges of the wrappers together. Put about one heaping tsp of the mixture in the center of the wrapper. With the finger, spread the water-flour paste around the exposed border, fold over and pinch the edges securely together. Boil some of them in salted water for soup. Drain and serve in chicken broth with fresh chopped green onion on top.

Chiao tze can be steamed, but the way we like them best is fried. Cover the bottom of a frying pan with oil and heat. Place the Chiao tze, separated, in the pan and fry until the bottom is starting to turn brown. Sprinkle with a water-cornstarch mixture and cover for a minute or two to complete the browning. Turn over and repeat the process with the cornstarch to brown the other side. Serve with soy sauce, hot mustard and hot pepper oil. You will find yourself eating them like peanuts.

NOTE: Leftover boiled Chiao tze is also very good fried.

NOODLES

Noodle-making is an art in China. We used to have noodle parties in Taipei where the maker would twirl and slap the dough on a long table, doubling it several times.He would then cut off the two ends and: Lo and Behold! What had been a long roll of dough had miraculously turned into a large bundle of noodles which were immediately dropped into a large pot of boiling water.

Noodles are eaten at any meal in China, even for breakfast. In a hearty soup, they are accompanied by slivers of cooked chicken or ham with chopped green onions and garlic on top. And, of course, they can be fried just like *Chiao tze*. However, use just enough noodles to cover the bottom of the pan about ½" thick. They are kept intact during the turning so as to come out on the serving plate like a large pancake. Do not forget to use the cornstarch mixture on each side to facilitate browning. Top with any stir fried dish; such as, pork, shrimp or chicken.

Francis Tong was a very ardent CAT employee on the Mainland and later in the Tokyo area. He came to the States about the same time we were migrating from Spain, and settled in the Santa Cruz area of California. During the ensuing period he has been more than enthusiastic about culinary matters, especially his two restaurants in Capitola and Aptos; and, of course, the pride of his life, "Oriental Ketchup." That is Bon Bon which he invented to be used in a variety of Chinese dishes. It is now being bottled and Francis expends a large portion of his time promoting its future. His 1983 Christmas card had a great picture of his very nice family with a news write-up about the sauce; and, on the other side, a tantalizing recipe for Red Snapper Szechuan. Here it is.

RED SNAPPER SZECHUAN FRANCIS TONG

Marinate ¾ lb Red Snapper fillets, cut into 1 x 1½ inch pieces, in:
1 tbsp Chinese wine, or sherry
1 egg, lightly beaten
¼ tsp salt
Dash of pepper
Combine in a bowl:
1½ tbsp chopped green onion
4 tsp fermented black beans, mashed
1 tbsp chopped ginger
1½ tsp Szechuan chile paste (this is HOT!)
In another bowl, mix:
¾ cup chicken stock

⅓ cup soy sauce
3 tbsp Chinese wine, or sherry
2½ tbsp sugar
2 tbsp vinegar
1 tsp salt
In another bowl, mix 1 tbsp cornstarch with 1 tbsp water. Then prepare:
¼ head Chinese cabbage, cut into 1-inch pieces
1 small onion, cut into 1-inch cubes
1 green pepper, cut into 1-inch diamonds
Shake fish pieces in a bag with cornstarch being sure that each piece is well coated; shake off excess. Deep fry in hot oil until lightly browned, but no more than one minute, drain. In a wok with a little oil, stir fry cabbage, onion and green pepper; remove and wipe wok. Use 2 tbsp oil and stir fry black bean mixture for a few seconds. Add stock mixture and bring to a boil; add cornstarch and water to thicken. Add fish and vegetables, stir quickly and serve with rice. Have lots of cold beer, or chilled wine, for this one; it's HOT! Thanks, Francis, for many a good time enjoying the food served in your restaurants in the Santa Cruz area.

Millie Yuan, born in the United States, was married to Henry Yuan, the son of Yuan Shih-Kai, the first President of the Republic of China. For several years, Henry was a Vice-President in CAT and was responsible for all official correspondence and relations with Chinese organizations including the Government itself. Not only was he well versed in Chinese art and the classics but also spoke perfect English, better than all of us. His widow, Millie, now lives in Hong Kong and has provided us with the recipe for steamed Chinese cake. Try to get the red dates in an Oriental food shop, they make it typically Chinese.

CHINESE DATE CAKE MILLIE YUAN

6 large eggs
3 tbsp shortening (Millie uses lard)
3 tsp baking powder
Dash of salt
½ lb sugar
½ lb flour
½ lb red dates
½ lb walnuts, chopped
Sift flour with baking powder and salt. Bring the dates to a boil in water; remove the skins and stones. Add half the sugar and all the

shortening to the dates and mix. Beat the eggs until very fluffy and slowly add the other half of the sugar, continuing to beat. Blend in the date mixture and the flour. Add the walnuts and mix well. Pour into a 9-inch cake pan and steam for 30 minutes.

ODDS AND ENDS

Chinese Pickling

The Chinese pickle all kinds of things: ginger, cucumbers, turnips, carrots, cauliflower, garlic, etc. It is very simple to do. For ginger: peel and slice it thinly, lengthwise. Boil equal parts vinegar and sugar and pour over the ginger. After 24 hours put it in the refrigerator; keeps for months. To pickle cucumbers and other vegetables; cut in diagonal pieces. Add some sliced ginger, garlic and hot pepper if you like. Use a mixture of equal parts water, vinegar and sugar; boil and pour over the vegetables. Vary the amount of sugar depending upon the desired sweetness or tartness. Leave outside one or two days to "ripen" then refrigerate.

DIPPING SAUCE FOR STEAMED OR BOILED CRAB

½ cup Chinese vinegar (can use wine vinegar)
3 tbsp minced ginger
3 tbsp sugar

Rae Rahf was a CAT Secretary in Taipei and then lived in Hong Kong before passing away recently. This is her recipe for Lobo Salad. Lobo is a giant white radish over a foot long and 2 to 3 inches in diameter. It can now be found in the markets in the States.

LOBO SALAD RAE RAHF

About 20 minutes before eating, peel and grate the Lobo. Salt it and let stand about 15 minutes. Squeeze out the water; there will be a distinctive odor but do not mind that. Have ready chopped onion and green pepper. You may add chopped green onion and hot pepper. Put all into your favorite oil and vinegar dressing with a little sugar and pour over the grated Lobo. Once you acquire the taste, you will not be able to stop eating it.

Charles Beauregard Davenport was a CAT communications expert in Taipei during the Fifties. Many a good time was had cooking and eating together. The area was noted for snails which could be found by the hundreds, especially after a rain and there was plenty of that. Beauregard loved to make them. But first it was necessary to clean them of sand and other debris. This was done by putting them in a container with cornmeal and a little water. That did the cleaning job plus fattening them up a bit. Then they went into a container with water, vinegar and a little salt. They spit out a lot of slimey stuff which was washed away. After cooking 10 to 15 minutes in a salted bouillon, they were taken out of the shells. Beauregard made a beautiful butter sauce loaded with lots of chopped garlic, parsley and freshly ground pepper. When the sauce was heated in a pan, the snails were added to absorb the flavors. Stuffed back into the shells, the sauce poured on top and popped under the broiler until bubbling; Abra Kadabra, out came Escargots! Served with wine and crisp French bread: Mon dieu!

NOTE: The Parisien Grille in Hong Kong placed the Escargots on a bed of mashed potatoes which took the overflow of any of the precious sauce and was eaten as an accompaniment. Incidentally, you can buy snails in the can with a separate container of shells so that it is not necessary to go through all the initial preparations.

We have so many recipes from Beauregard, it was difficult to choose the ones for the book. So, we put them all in except for those which duplicate others. Here are a few that belong in this Oriental section. Look for others starting on Page 256.

BEAUREGARD'S SHRIMP FOO YUNG

1 lb raw shrimp, peeled and cleaned
¼ lb ground pork
3 slices ginger, slivered
1 tsp salt
2 tbsp sherry and 1 tbsp soy sauce
NOTE: A handful of bean sprouts goes well.
Stir fry the pork with the ginger (I like to add some chopped green onions); add the shrimp and cook for one minute. Mix in the other ingredients. This quantity should serve 4 persons. Beat 8 eggs and pour in the pan with the hot mixture. When the eggs are brown on one side, flip over for a very short time, only enough to set the other side. Place on a hot serving plate and top with a sweet and sour sauce. If a wok was employed, the Foo Yung will have a rounded top. If done in a frying pan, the same effect can be accomplished by first fitting the finished product into a bowl and then inverting it on the plate.

Beauregard had another recipe for Cauliflower Foo Yung which is similar and will not be repeated here. You can make Foo Yung with almost anything; crab is especially good.

PORK AND SHRIMP FRIED NOODLES

Boil 1 lb Chinese noodles in 5 cups of water to which a little oil has been added. Drain and rinse in cold water. Divide into 6 portions and roll up "like a shredded wheat biscuit." Fry in oil until brown on both sides. To help in the browning, sprinkle with a cornstarch-water mixture during the frying. Keep warm in the oven while preparing:

1 lb pork, shredded
½ lb raw shrimp, shelled and cleaned
½ bunch Chinese celery cabbage, shredded
½ lb fresh mushrooms, whole or sliced
1 or 2 green onions, chopped
1 tbsp cornstarch
4 tbsp soy sauce

Stir fry the pork; add cabbage, mushrooms and green onion. Stir quickly and add the shrimp, cook 1 minute. Mix in the soy with the cornstarch. If too thick, add a little chicken stock. Serve on top of the noodle portions

TEA EGGS

Beauregard reports that this is one of the ways to cook hard-boiled eggs so that they become soft again!

2 dozen eggs
2 tsp each salt and black tea leaves
1 orange rind

Boil eggs for one hour; cool in cold water and crack the shells but do not remove them. Cover with water to which has been added the salt, tea and orange rind. Simmer for 2 hours. Take off the heat but leave in the liquid. Serve hot or cold, shelled and cut in wedges.

BEAUREGARD'S SWEET AND SOUR SPARERIBS

These are similar to Tex Hill's recipe on Page 93 . However, the ribs are first simmered in salted water to cover for one hour, drained and simmered in sweet and sour sauce for about 10 minutes. If a crisp outside is desired; the ribs, after being cooked in the water, can be roasted in a

450-degree oven for 10 minutes, brushing with the sauce during the cooking.

BEAUREGARD'S ALMOND JUNKET

    1 cup evaporated milk
    3 cups water
    1 tbsp almond extract
    2 tbsp unflavored gelatine
    5 tbsp sugar
    ½ cup almonds, chopped and roasted

Heat milk, sugar and water together to scalding temperature. Soften gelatine in 3 tbsp cold water; add to hot liquid and stir until dissolved. Cool and stir in the almond extract. Pour into a container to set. When ready to serve, Beauregard instructs: "Cut into small rhombohedrons; serve with almonds on the top or on the side. PS...I don't like it but the ladies do." The Chinese do like it and often serve it after a meal with hot lotus seeds in syrup on top.

Eastie Hicks was the wife of Commander John Hicks, Naval Attache in the American Embassy, Taipei during the fifties. Since giving us the next two recipes she has gone to the big kitchen in the great beyond. If there is such a place, hope she looks down favorably upon our culinary efforts here.

EASTIE'S PORK TENDERLOIN FOR COCKTAILS

Use 1 or 2 tenderloins. This is not the loin but the fillet, a long, tapered piece on the other side of it, usually about 2" in diameter at the thick end. It is very tender with almost no fat. It is best barbecued over coals but can be done in a hot oven. Marinate in soy sauce and sesame oil with a little sugar for several hours or overnight. In the cooking, it should get almost black on the outside; brush with the marinade several times. Cool and slice thinly. Serve with hot mustard and a sauce made with sesame paste (or ground sesame seeds), sesame oil, soy sauce and hot pepper; also, some toasted sesame seeds. The meat is taken with toothpicks, dipped in one of the sauces and then the seeds.

PICKLED SHRIMP A LA EASTIE HICKS

In a dish with a cover, place in a couple of alternate layers: about 2 dozen large shrimp, cleaned and cooked; and 2 large onions, thinly sliced. In a pot, bring to a boil:

½ cup salad oil
½ cup vinegar
¼ cup tarragon vinegar
Juice of one lemon plus some of the peel
2 oz brandy
2 bay leaves
1 tbsp sugar (I would put at least 2 or 3)
1 tbsp crushed peppercorns
¼ tsp dill seed
3 or 4 dashes tabasco
Celery salt to taste
2 sticks cinnamon
5 cloves

Pour boiling liquid over the shrimp and onions. Cover and let cool. Store in the refrigerator. Will keep 8 to 10 days. Serve on toothpicks, with the onions on pumpernickel. Use the juice for salads. We like this shrimp in the following Chinese salad.

TIGER JOE'S CHINESE SALAD WITH PLASTIC NOODLES

This traditional salad is best made with Agar Agar. This is a gelatinous substance extracted from red alga. It comes in dried shreds and can be purchased in Oriental food shops. For the salad, it is softened in warm water. If not available, use "plastic noodles". Actually these are clear noodles made from rice. To use, stir into boiling water for about 2 minutes; check for doneness, they get tender in a short time. Drain and cool. Make the sauce.

1 tsp hot mustard powder in 1 tsp sherry
2 tbsp vinegar, Chinese type, if possible
1 tbsp sugar
1 tbsp sesame oil
1 tbsp soy sauce

Mix well and set aside. In a salad bowl, place the cooled agar or noodles, 3 chopped green onions, 2 tbsp shredded bamboo, 1 tbsp shredded ginger and one cucumber. This is peeled, cut lengthwise, the seeds removed and sliced crosswise. On top put shredded chicken and ham. If using the pickled shrimp, put that on top with, or in place of, the chicken. At the table, stir the sauce and pour over the salad. Toss well. NOTE: If you can get sesame paste, mix 1 tsp when making the sauce.

Shanghai Lil has a saying: "There's no "tea" (t) in *Borsch*!" That is true, at least in Russian. The "t" got in there somewhere, probably in Germany after leaving Russia, and emerged in the Yiddish as *"Borscht"*. That grates on Lil's Russian mind: so, we always stick to the Russian spelling. By the way, there are dozens of ways to make this hearty soup, both cold and hot. The next recipe is only one example.

NINA'S *BORSCH*

Use the cheapest cut of beef, such as chuck. Boil it with water to cover adding: onion, carrot, bay leaf and pepper corn. When the meat is completely tender, remove to a plate and let cool. Strain the stock and put it in a large soup pot. Add one head of cabbage, tomatoes, green pepper, celery, carrots, all cut up. When the cabbage is tender, add quartered potatoes. Towards the end, add a couple of tbsp of tomato paste, some cut up cooked beets, juice of a lemon and sufficient sugar to take away the bite of the tomatoes and lemon juice. Serve with a dollop of sour cream in each bowl. The cold meat is sliced and presented with hot mustard, horseradish and, of course, sour cream.

Nina proclaims: "For that Russian effect, add or pour sour cream on anything and it won't be bad; even common old stew turns up glamorous!"

Nina Wilson's mother, Elizaveta Petrovna Varpula, has provided us with a recipe for a kind of Russian dumpling.

VARENIKY

Make a dough with one egg well mixed with one cup of water. Add enough flour to make the dough workable but not hard. Roll it thin and cut circles with a large glass. Put filling in the center and pinch the edges together. Simmer in salted water for about 5 to 8 minutes. Serve with sour cream. The filling can be meat, left over casserole, or different kinds of jam. Elizaveta P. likes to use seasoned mashed potatoes to which a little sauteed onion and some of the frying oil has been added. The next day, serve cold or deep fry in oil.

The next three recipes; stuffed peppers (two kinds), and cabbage rolls are from Lil's repertoire. Later, they were very popular in our restaurant operation in Majorca and, after that, in Tiger Joe's Gourmet Restaurant in North Carolina.

SHANGHAI LIL'S CABBAGE ROLLS

Select cabbage that has good-size leaves with no blemishes. Cut part of the core out. Bring a large pot of water to a boil; add 2 tbsp sugar. Put the head in for 5 minutes. Remove and take off the first few leaves that come off easily, cutting into the thick stem near the core. Return the head to the boiling water and repeat the process until you have a sufficient supply of leaves. Depending upon the quantity to be made, it may be necesssary to use a second head. The smaller part of each head can be saved for soup or cole slaw. With a sharp knife remove the thick part of the stem by cutting it off parallel to the leaf. Save these pieces to be put in the sauce.

Meat and Rice Filling (use also for stuffed peppers)
Mix 2 parts uncooked ground beef with 1 part cooked rice. Add sufficient tomato sauce to make a soft mixture; salt and pepper to taste. Work with the stem part of the cabbage leaf away from you. Put 2 or 3 tbsp filling in the middle and fold the leaf over it, towards you, until it is only half rolled up. Fold over each side towards the center. Lift the thin part of the leaf nearest you; fold it up and over. There should be a little excess which is then tucked under the two sides which were previously folded toward the center. Tie with thread or stick a toothpick in each side. These are removed before serving. Place the rolls in a pot and cover with sauce; simmer for 1½ to 2 hours until cabbage is tender. Serve with mashed potatoes and peas.
Sauce (use also for stuffed peppers):
Saute chopped onion until soft and put in a large pot in which the cabbage rolls will be cooked. Add:
Juice of 5 lemons
½ cup sugar
½ tsp Italian seasoning
Salt and pepper
Tomato sauce sufficient to cover cabbage rolls
2 chicken cubes
Sliced mushrooms, sauteed (wine optional)
If, because of the lemon juice and tomato sauce, it still tastes a little sour, add more sugar. Add the stems previously cut off the cabbage leaves.

SHANGHAI LIL'S STUFFED PEPPERS

Use unblemished peppers. Cut the stem part out and remove the seeds and white membrane. Blanch for five minutes in boiling water as for the Cabbage Rolls (above); drain. Stuff and cook, in the same Sauce as for Cabbage Rolls, until the peppers are tender. They will keep in the refrigerator for a week to 10 days; in fact, they are better the day after cooking.

SHANGHAI LIL'S STUFFED PEPPERS FOR *ZAKUSKA*

Prepare the peppers the same as for Stuffed Peppers (above). The sauce and stuffing are made together as follows:

Saute 1 chopped onion until soft. Coarsely grate half pound carrots; this will do 6 to 8 peppers. Add to the onion and saute until not quite done. Add 2 large cans tomato sauce, parsley stems finely chopped, salt and pepper, ¼ tsp Italian seasoning, 1 Bay leaf and 1 tbsp sugar. Simmer for one hour. Add ½ cup chopped parsley leaves. Take off the heat; cool and strain. Stuff the peppers with the carrot mixture; place in a pot, cover with the drained sauce and simmer until the peppers are soft, about 1 hour. Let cool in the sauce. Serve cold with some of the sauce. The same system is used to stuff tomatoes.

The next recipes are for two kinds of patties.

SYRNIKY

These cottage cheese patties are light and delicious. Prepare the following, mixed into a dough:

1 lb cottage cheese, put through strainer or mashed
1 egg, beaten
1 tbsp sour cream
½ tsp sugar and a little salt
½ cup flour

On a floured pan or cookie sheet, make the patties, about 2 ½ inches in diameter. Refrigerate 2 hours or overnight. Brown on both sides in butter in a frying pan. Serve with sour cream and powdered sugar. You may like jam with these.

KASHA PATTIES

Kasha is any whole grain; but, this recipe uses the traditional buckwheat. The one sold in supermarkets is already toasted; but, if you get it in a health store, you may have to toast it in an oiled frying pan. Cook as with rice. Make the pattie mix:

2 cups cooked *kasha*
½ cup finely chopped onion, sauteed
¼ cup minced green onion
1 clove garlic, minced
½ cup finely minced mushrooms
2 eggs, beaten
Seasoning: basil, salt and pepper
Form into 2 ½ inch patties and refrigerate at least one hour. Dip in beaten egg, roll in bread crumbs and brown on both sides in butter. Serve in place of potatoes or rice.

Lil recommends that you try the next few, old Russian recipes.

QUICK LIVER PASTE

Remove the tendons and other hard parts from one lb beef or calf's liver. In a heavy pot, brown it on both sides together with one onion, sliced (take care not to burn the onion). Add one carrot, sliced, one bay leaf, salt, about 20 peppercorns and sufficient chicken stock to cover. Boil until the carrot is tender. Take the liver out and put it in a blender or food processor with ½ lb butter. Blend, add one shot of brandy and blend again until smooth. Refrigerate.

CUCUMBERS WITH SOUR CREAM AND DILL

Put 4 cucumbers, peeled and sliced, in a bowl with 2 tbsp salt. Mix well and let stand for ½ hour. Pour the liquid off and dry the cucumbers on paper towels; then wrap them in paper towels and refrigerate until ready to serve. At that point, put them in a serving dish and top with about 5 tbsp sour cream; mix well and sprinkle generously with dill, fresh if possible.

SHANGHAI LIL'S EGGPLANT CAVIAR

Also known as, "Poor Man's Caviar", it is made in many ways; this is one of them. Bake two large eggplants at 325 degrees until they start to collapse and are tender, about 2 hours. When cool, cut in pieces, lengthwise, to remove the inside. In the process, be sure to scrape all of the molasses-like substance near the skin; this gives the finished product a distinctive taste. Chop fine and set aside.

In a large frying pan, saute' in oil one large onion and one green pepper, both chopped. When soft, add the chopped eggplant; cook 10 minutes, stirring constantly (careful, burns easily). Add: 1 tbsp tomato paste, salt, lots of freshly ground pepper, ½ cup tomato sauce, ¼ tsp Italian seasoning and enough sugar to take away the sour taste, about 2 tbsp. Cook on low heat for 15 minutes, stirring so as not to burn. Cool and refrigerate; keeps well for 2 or 3 weeks.

PELMENI

Prepare dough as for *Vareniky* (Page 232). Use the same technique for putting them together but, after the edges are sealed, pull the two pointed ends back and pinch them together, thus forming a moon shape.
Filling: One lb ground beef, mixed well with one minced onion, salt, pepper and a pinch of sugar. If the mixture is not soft enough, add some chicken stock or water. Serve, boiled in chicken or beef stock. They freeze well; place individually on a flat pan in the freezer, then store in bags to be taken out as needed. They can be cooked from the frozen state.

KOTLETKI

Lil gave this recipe to the Grand Hotel in Taipei for their hamburgers. Also, we served them in our restaurant operation in Majorca and, later, in Tiger Joe's in North Carolina as Russian Burgers. They were always a great hit.

Fry one large onion, chopped, until golden brown; cool. Mix the fried onions with one lb ground beef, one egg, 2 tbsp soy sauce, 1 tsp sugar, 2 slices of French or Italian bread (soaked in water or milk), salt and pepper to taste. Add enough chicken stock or water to make a soft mixture. Form into oval patties, roll in bread crumbs and fry. Can also be baked in the oven but are not quite as tasty. Serve with macaroni; spinkle with a little of the frying oil. Also try a white sour cream sauce to which has been added sliced sauteed mushrooms. Ice cold vodka is a must.

Beef Stroganoff has its origin concealed in the murky legends of Old Russia; here's at least one of them!
On a battlefield, during one of the wars, a Russian Officer asked his Dienschick (Aide) to order something to eat. He could find nothing but a piece of meat (some say it was horse meat) that had frozen in the subzero temperature. With difficulty, he shredded the meat, fried it with onions and served it with fried potatoes. He called it "Stroganoff" which means "shredded". Count Stroganoff could not complain about it because, you

see, there never was a "Count Stroganoff"! Although there have been variations since that propitious occasion, the following is the traditional method of preparation.

LIL'S BEEF STROGANOFF

Saute' ½ lb sliced mushrooms until golden brown; transfer them to a cooking pot. In the same oil, saute one onion, sliced, until soft; put with the mushrooms.

Cut one lb beef fillet (tenderloin) into strips 2¾" long, ¾" wide and ¼" thick; roll in seasoned flour. Fry quickly in the oil previously used, adding more if needed. Sprinkle generously with some of the flour that was left from coating the meat. Add 3 tbsp tomato sauce, salt, pepper, the sauteed onions and mushrooms and some milk, stirring constantly until you have a smooth sauce. Adjust the consistency with more milk; when it is bubbling, remove from the heat. Fillet should not be cooked too long. Stir in ½ cup sour cream. Keeps well in the refrigerator. When reheating, do not boil. The same sauce may be used for meat balls or Kotletki (Page 236)

The "Old Russian Way" to serve Stroganoff is with homemade French fried potatoes, but it also goes well with rice or wide noodles.

For "Chicken Stroganoff", employ the same procedure using the white meat of the chicken and a little white wine in the sauce.

Served in many of the best restaurants in Shanghai was a spectacular dessert. In the "Towers Room" on the tenth floor of Sir Victor Sasoon's Cathay Hotel on the Bund, the lights were turned down as it was ceremoniously presented in a blaze of glory on a silver serving platter. Here's Lil's version.

BAKED ALASKA

Assemble:
1 lb pound cake, cut lengthwise into 4 slices about ¾" thick
1 quart Neapolitan ice cream
4 egg whites
½ tsp lemon juice
1 cup confectioner's sugar
1 tsp vanilla
Salt

Make the meringue: Beat the 4 egg whites with a pinch of salt until frothy. Add ½ tsp lemon juice and continue to beat until the whites are stiff. While still beating, gradually add the vanilla and the cup of confectioner's sugar until the meringue is glossy and thick and stands in peaks. Preheat the oven to 425 degrees.

On an ovenproof serving dish, place one slab of cake. On top put the ice cream; it must not be larger than the cake. Put a slab of cake on each side and one on top. If you have sufficient cake, cover the ends. Cover completely with the meringue, piling any excess on top. Brown in the hot oven. This should take a very short time, so watch closely that it does not burn. Have a cup of warm brandy ready. When the dish comes out of the oven, immediately slosh the brandy over it and light it. Put it on the table flaming. You can insure that the ice cream will not even start to melt in the oven if you plan the timing so that you can freeze the dish for at least an hour after assembling the cake and the ice cream.

Piroshky (accent on the last syllable) is a Russian, doughnut-like turnover filled with either tasty meat or vegetable mixtures. *Pirog* is a large pie with similar fillings, cut into serving size squares. We have two recipes; one from Nina Wilson and the other from Kira Chen. Both of these ladies were born in Harbin, Manchuria. This was the beginning of a lifetime friendship during which we shared many good times and interesting recipes. Features of the two Piroshky recipes have been combined here, along with several of Lil's refinements and additions.

Piroshky

First, the dough. Nina's hand is quicker than the eye; she uses one box of hot roll mix and makes the dough according to the directions! Kira gives the old-fashioned recipe.

½ cup lukewarm water

1 tbsp dry yeast; add to water and let stand

When yeast proofs (bubbles: this can be facilitated by adding 1 tsp of sugar), mix with 1 cup each of milk and water, lukewarm. Stir in:

2 tbsp sugar

4 tbsp melted lard or other shortening

1 tsp salt

2 eggs, well beaten

Mix well and gradually add flour (will take about 5 to 6 cups), kneading until the dough no longer sticks to the hands. Do not add too much flour; the dough should not be hard. Put in a warm place in a large pan covered with a cloth and let rise for about 1 to 2 hours until double in bulk. The time can be lessened by placing a pan of hot water on top.

Meat Filling:
1 lb ground beef
½ lb ground pork
1 medium onion, minced
Fry together until the meat is brown; cool and mix in 3 chopped hard-boiled eggs, salt and pepper to taste.

Cabbage Filling:
1 head of cabbage (about 3 lbs), sliced thinly
1 onion, sliced thinly
Better start with a big heavy pot as the volume will be large, initially. Saute the onion in half butter half oil until soft; add the cabbage and continue cooking until it is tender, stirring frequently as this can burn easily. Halfway through this cooking process, add about 4 tbsp each of chicken stock and white wine, 1 tsp sugar. When complete, if there is any juice, it is necessary to let the cabbage drain in a sieve. Then add 4 chopped hard-boiled eggs and salt and pepper to taste.

Carrot Filling:
1lb carrots, shredded
Saute in butter with a pinch of salt and 1 tbsp sugar until tender.
Mushroom Filling:
2 lbs mushrooms, cleaned and chopped
1 small onion, minced
Saute in butter with salt to taste until lightly browned.
Roll the dough on a floured board and form it into long rolls about 2" in diameter. Cut off 1 ½" pieces and roll into balls. Flatten each into 5"pancakes about ¼" thick. Be sure the fillings are completely cooled down. Place about 2 tbsp filling in an oblong shape in the middle of each pancake. Bring the edges up over the filling and pinch together firmly to insure that none leaks out during the frying. Use a pan large enough to hold oil that will come up almost to the top of the Piroshky when frying. Bring the oil to about 375 degrees (will brown a cube of bread in about 60 seconds). Put each Piroshky in the pan with the seam side down. When they are golden brown on the down side, turn over to finish the cooking. Drain on platter with paper towels. Mark each platter so as to distinguish the fillings. Serve with beef bouillon. Good cold, or hot (a microwave oven does an especially good job of reheating). For tea, try filling the Piroshky with jam or cooked apple filling.

Cabbage is a versatile vegetable. The Chinese pickle it with ginger; the Germans with salt, hence sauerkraut (in German, sauer is sour and kraut, cabbage). The French have their *Choucroute Alsacienne* and the Irish their ham and cabbage. But, you have never had cabbage unless you have tried *Solyanka*. Here is the recipe from Shanghai Lil's kitchen

RUSSIAN *SOLYANKA*

1 head cabbage, shredded
1 large onion, sliced
1 lb pork, blade chops
3 slices bacon, diced
1 can sauerkraut, drained
4 tbsp oil, 1 tbsp butter
1 tbsp sugar
3 or 4 medium potatoes
    cut in quarters
3 cups chicken stock
1 large bay leaf
2 cloves garlic
1 tsp pepper corns
Salt to taste
Cayenne, if you like it hot
2 thick smoked sausages, or Bratwurst, or 4 hot dogs; cut into ½ inch pieces

Cut pork off the bone and into 1-inch pieces. Fry the bones in oil until very brown; then, the meat until just tender, set aside. Fry bacon and transfer to a large, heavy pot. Saute' the onions in the same oil until translucent; put in the pot with the bacon. Add butter and the shredded cabbage. Saute' the mixture over high heat for a few minutes, stirring constantly. The cabbage will brown but do not let it burn. Reduce heat to low, add some of the chicken stock, cover and let stew, stirring occasionally. Add sauerkraut and sugar. Repeat the high heat treatment 5 or 6 times, adding some chicken stock each time until all three cups have been used. Then simmer on low heat for about an hour until the cabbage is soft. Add the potatoes and the meat and bones. When the potatoes are about half done, add the sausage, or hot dog pieces, and salt to taste. Serve when the potatoes are done. This dish is better the next day.

VARIATION: During the simmering, add beer or white wine; half in the pot and half in the chef, the effect is euphoric!

PASHA

Pronounced PAHS-hah, this is a traditional Russian Easter dessert very similar to cheese cake, made in a pyramid-shaped mold which has the inscription: "Christ has risen". It has been speculated that almost all cheese cakes and tarts have developed from *Pasha*. Although we are not going into detail about making the mold, it can easily be constructed out of 4 pieces of plywood cut into a tringular shape. If the points of the triangles are cut off, the mold will stand with a little support.

The night before, put 3 lbs of cottage cheese in cheesecloth bag and hang to drain (put a container underneath to catch the liquid).

The next day: mix 3 cups of sugar with 15 egg yolks (Use the whites for a cake or decoration of Kulich—see next recipe). Melt 1½ lbs butter and let cool. Mix with cottage cheese and combine with egg yolk mixture. Add:

2 tsp vanilla

½ cup each raisins and slivered almonds.

Finely chopped glazed fruits can be added, if desired. A half cup heavy cream is also optional. Line the form with cheesecloth; pour the mixture in and fold the cloth over it. Put a weight on top and refrigerate overnight, with a container underneath (there will be drainage). The next day, take the weight off, unfold the cloth, put a serving plate on top and invert. Carefully remove the cheesecloth, decorate around the base with colored eggs. Serve with slices of Kulich.

KULICH

Pronounced koo-leech, this is the traditional cylindrical-shaped Russian Easter semi-sweet bread served with Pasha. It is baked in varied-sized cans to give it the classic form. It is usually made the night before Easter Sunday. The recipe can be cut in half if you just want to make a trial run.

Proof 2 tbsp dry yeast by mixing it in ¾ cup warm water with 1 tsp sugar. Assemble:

½ cup sugar
8 cups flour
2 cups melted butter, cooled
2 tsp salt
15 eggs
1 cup milk, scalded and cooled

With an electric beater, mix all the ingredients (except half the flour) including the bubbling yeast, for 10 minutes. Gradually add the rest of the flour. When it becomes too stiff for the beater, add and mix by hand. This will be a sticky dough until it has been worked a while, including slapping it hard in the bowl. When it no longer clings to the sides of the bowl and the hands, place it in a large greased bowl in a warm spot, with a cloth cover. When it has doubled in bulk (about one hour), punch down and stir in:

1 cup raisins
1 cup chopped glazed fruit
1 tsp each nutmeg and cardamon   Prepare the cans for baking using oiled waxpaper. A circular piece goes in the bottom. A rectangular piece should be cut a little longer than the diameter and wide enough to be half again as high as the can. Fit this piece against the sides and carefully put in sufficient dough to come up only half way in each container. It will rise in the baking higher than the can and into the wax paper part. Place the cans in a warm spot for ¾ hour and then bake in a 350 degree oven with the rack at its lowest level. Baking time will vary with the size of the containers. So, it is necessary to start checking after one hour. Use a thin wooden skewer; it should come out dry. As the smaller ones are taken

out of the oven, they should be placed on their sides on a blanket and rolled occasionaly. This keeps the cake from falling, until it has cooled considerably when it will come out of the can easily. It will still be hot, so roll it some more.

When all are done and cooled, they can be stood on plates and decorated. Lil cooks the egg whites and sugar into an icing then makes different colors, principally blue and pink, with vegetable dye. The plain white is spread on a square piece of cloth to be draped over the largest *Kulich* which is then sprinkled with multi-colored *non pareils* (also known as sprinkles). All the others are decorated with the colored icing. To serve with the Pasha, slice circular pieces and cut in two or in four, if large. *Kulich* will keep several days. Any leftover should be sliced and browned in the oven. Place in jars for later use.

General Chennault had a great appreciation for good food but it had to be well spiced. The center of the table in his home was always adorned with a group of at least six or seven different kinds of hot pepper concoctions, of which he partook liberally. He was a great hunter and, in China, always taught his cooks how to prepare the game which he brought home. There was duck and, among other things, rabbit. You have heard the nursery rhyme: "Four and twenty blackbirds baked in a pie..." Well, the General had a spectacualr presentation of his own, Dove Pie, which was large and contained all kinds of game birds.

But his favorite was Squirrel Stew. Shortly before he was taken by the Big C, he escorted us to the market down by the river in Monroe, Louisiana. A large squirrel was selected. Fortunately, it had been skinned but the head was intact. At home, he showed us how to remove the eyes and cut up the animal.

SQUIRREL STEW A LA CHENNAULT

Marinate the cut up squirrel overnight in:
1 clove garlic
1 bay leaf
1 cup vinegar
2 tbsp sugar
1 tsp salt
¼ tsp cayenne
½ tsp pepper
Drained and dried with paper towels, the meat was then browned on all sides in oil. In a stew pot, the following was sauteed until soft:
2 onions, 2 green onions and 1 green pepper, chopped

The pieces of squirrel were added with:
2 cloves garlic and 2 tomatoes, chopped
1 bay leaf
1 dried hot pepper
1 tbsp worcestershire sauce
1 cup red wine

The stew was cooked over low heat until the meat was tender. (It is necessary to put more water to maintain the consistency of stew). 2 or 3 potatoes, peeled and diced were added; when done, 2 tbsp sherry were added with seasoning to taste. (If the stew is too thin, add flour mixed with a little water). When serving, the head is given to the guest of honor; that time, the General presented it to Lil!

When entertaining, the General loved to serve, after dinner, Cafe Brulot.

The recipe was for 150 demitasse which would take care of 80 to 100 guests. I have reduced it to 15 demitasse.

CAFE BRULOT GENERAL CHENNAULT

Peel from one lemon and one orange
10 allspice corns
10 whole cloves
8 small sugar cubes each rubbed on the lemon skin
8 small sugar cubes each rubbed on the orange skin

For effect, the citrus skins should be peeled in one continuous strip. Place all the ingredients in a chafing dish with the flame going underneath. Add one pint of brandy. Place a little brandy in a metal ladle and ignite it (will light more easily if warmed first). Pour into the chafing dish. As the brandy burns, slowly add 5 cups of strong hot coffee. Serve in demitasse cups.
Salute to the General!

No story (culinary or otherwise) about CAT would be complete without something from the Willauers. As the partner of General Chennault, Whitey's contribution to the history of the airline was immeasurable. Fortunately, Sue (Buol) Hacker had a recipe in her files in Honolulu from the early Fifties which Louise Willauer (now Jackson) said was "Whitey's favorite breakfast dish."

WHITEY'S CREAMED KIDNEYS ON TOAST

NOTE: Kidneys tend to have a strong taste. To eliminate this, soak them in water with a little vinegar for about an hour; then rinse with cold water. Slice the kidneys, removing all tough connecting tissue. Shake with seasoned flour and brown quickly in butter. Add milk and stir until the sauce thickens. Do not cook more than 10 minutes, altogether, otherwise the kidneys will turn tough. Stir in 1 tbsp each of sour cream and sherry. Serve on triangles of toast and sprinkle with a little chopped parsley.

Lil Chu was Whitey Willauer's Executive Secretary, first in the early days of CAT in Shanghai, then in Hong Kong. Later, she married Bob Finnerty, Pan American Airways pilot and they now live, retired, in Santa Cruz on Monterey Bay, California. She is a great gourmet cook and often invents her own dishes. Also makes one of the best French breads outside of France. Here are three of her recipes, all different; interesting to make and savorous to eat.

CREAM OF TOFU AND ZUCCHINI SOUP

2 tbsp butter or your favorite shortening
4 cups thinly sliced zucchini
2 cloves garlic, sliced or chopped
2 cups chicken broth
1 tsp salt and pepper to taste
½ lb tofu cake
1 cup buttermilk, optional

In saucepan large enough to hold all the ingredients, saute garlic in the shortening until golden. Add zucchini and stir until coated with shortening. Add chicken broth, salt and pepper. Bring to a boil, cover and simmer 4 to 5 minutes until zucchini is tender. In blender or food processor place the tofu, and zucchini mixture and blend until mixed and thick. Pour back into the pan and add the buttermilk; stir. Serve hot or chilled. Top with: garlic croutons, bacon bits, chopped chives or green onions.

DUCK WITH PANCAKES

Lil's recipe calls for duck which could be purchased, already roasted, in any Cantonese food shop in China or in Chinatown in any one of our big cities. Use roast duck or the meat from almost any duck recipe. But, first the "pancakes". Actually, they are most like crepes or flour tortillas. The dough is the same as for Onion Pie (Page 218) and is made with flour and sufficient warm water to make a soft mixture. Knead until smooth and make long rolls 1" in diameter. Cut into ¾" pieces and cover with a damp cloth. Use two pieces at a time. Flatten each and brush one with sesame oil and place the other piece on top. Roll into a thin pancake about 5-6" in diameter. Try to keep them round (it's not easy but with practice you can do it). Put into a hot frying pan with no oil. When it starts to bubble, turn until the other side does the same. At that point the pancakes should pull apart into two very thin ones. Stack them, wrapped in a damp towel.

Now, the meat. Shred the duck meat with the skin on. Saute with bean sprouts and, if you can get them, garlic sprouts. Have ready green onions cut in 1" strips, sweet bean paste or hoi sin sauce. This dish is eaten by placing some duck meat in the middle of the pancake with green onion and some of the bean paste or sauce. Roll and devour with gusto. Lil says: "Good luck!" I think she means with the pancake making operation.

LIL FINNERTY'S SHRIMP CURRY AND RICE

    1 ½ lbs shelled raw shrimp, or prawns
    1 tbsp curry powder
    2 tbsp curry paste, best if both items are imported
    1 chopped onion
    2 or 3 potatoes, peeled and cut in chunks
    ½ cup grated coconut
    2 tbsp chopped roasted almonds
    Cooked rice for 4 to 6 persons

Fry onion in shortening until just starts to turn brown; add potato chunks and cook for 5 minutes. Add curry paste and powder (add more to taste, if not hot enough) and coconut. Stir the mixture well so that it does not burn. Add 3 cups chicken stock and mix well. Simmer for one hour, stirring occasionally. Have the rice ready, adding a little grated coconut right after cooking. Add the shrimp to the curry mixture and cook for 3 minutes (if using the larger prawns, cook for 5 minutes). Serve with the chopped almonds on top, accompanied by Chutney and other various condiments; browned onions, raisins, chopped tomatoes, peppers, bananas, apples, browned coconut, etc.

The next recipe was presented by the Rousselots who live on their cattle ranch, Gray Oaks Ranch, near Wagoner in the northeastern part of Oklahoma. Besides heading the Operations Department of Civil Air Transport, Bob was the Best Man at our wedding in Shanghai in 1948. His wife, Ann, was with John Mason's operation in Atsugi, Japan before being transferred to NACC (Page 189) in Taipei.

ROUSSELOT'S SOURDOUGH PANCAKES AND WAFFLES

The recipe requires a sourdough starter. For those who do not keep one in the refrigerator, see page 588 for the formula. The quantities used by Ann must be for the Gray Oaks Ranch entire family, friends and help! So, if you are only three or four, use about one half the recipe.

The night before, put one cup of starter in a large bowl; add 2 cups warm water, 2 ½ cups flour, ¼ cup sugar. Cover and set in a warm place.

The next morning, add:

¼ cup instant dry milk

4 tbsp melted butter (for pancakes)

3 egg yolks (2 extra for waffles)

Beat thoroughly, then mix in:

1 tsp salt, 1 tsp baking soda and 2 tbsp sugar. Fold in the white of the eggs which have first been beaten. Allow the batter to rest a few minutes while making the griddle or waffle iron very hot. Make pancakes big or little as you like. For thin ones, add milk or water, a small quantity at a time, until the desired consistency is obtained.

Rest awhile before engaging in any strenuous work or exercise!

Weldon "Big" Bigony from Big Spring, Texas, was a Naval Aviator who joined CAT in the very first days of its formation. We flew and worked together and he and Muschi and Lil and I have been good friends through all these years. Big is retired, jogging and playing golf; while they live the good life in the Country Club of Miami Estates in south Florida. Muschi parted with one of her favorite recipes.

MUSCHI'S SWEET AND SOUR RED CABBAGE

Since this dish takes some time to make, you might want to double the recipe and freeze the excess for future use.

1 medium size head red cabbage, finely sliced

1 large onion, sliced

1 large apple, chopped

2 tbsp sugar (or more, to taste)
1 tsp salt
1 bay leaf
½ cup white vinegar
½ to ¾ cup water
1 cup red wine (Burgundy goes very well)

Saute onion in your favorite shortening until transluscent; then add the cabbage. After about 15 minutes of stir frying, start adding the liquids, a little at a time throughout the cooking. Add the spices. At this point, we always put in a couple of chicken cubes. Cook slowly for 2 to 3 hours, stirring occasionally and adding more of the liquids as needed. Towards the end, add the apple and ½ tsp white pepper (optional). Before serving, check for seasoning and consistency. If too watery, add flour and water thickening; this is not done to make the dish thick but only to eliminate the excess liquid. Use instead of sauerkraut.

CAT pilot, Don Teeters, had some of the most intriguing experiences with the airline because he flew, among other types of planes, my old standby the PBY. That provided the opportunity for missions that other equipment could not perform. He lives in Tawas City on the northeast coast of Michigan with his wife, Stella, who has provided this Philippine recipe.

CHICKEN AND PORK *ADOBO*

1 Chicken, cut into serving pieces
1 lb pork, cut into 1-inch pieces
½ cup vinegar
1 cup chicken stock
1 cup soy sauce
1 bay leaf
2 cloves garlic, mashed
½ tsp anise
4 slices ginger
1 green onion cut in pieces
pepper to taste
1 tbsp sugar

Mix all ingredients together in a heavy pot or large skillet. Bring to a boil, cover and simmer on the lowest heat until meat is tender. Pour off almost all the sauce, reserve. Brown the meat, then return sauce and bring to a boil. Serve over rice.

NOTE: The original recipe did not have the following items: chicken stock, sugar, anise, ginger and green onions. They were added to give a Chinese flavor. The dish can be made to Stella's recipe by eliminating them and increasing the vinegar to 1½ cups.

The Chinese recipe can be used for beef. Use one thick piece like boneless chuck steak. Serve, cut in strips, hot or cold, sprinkled with 1 tbsp oriental sesame oil.

Stella also provided us with a second recipe.

STELLA'S MEXICAN LIVER

Cut liver into 1-inch pieces; shake with seasoned flour and brown in bacon fat. Remove the liver from the pan and saute chopped onion and green pepper in the fat. Return the liver to the pan and add one can of tomatoes with the liquid. Add 1 tbsp chili powder, or to taste. Simmer about 10 minutes only until the liver is tender but not hard. Put in 1 cup cooked rice, ½ cup peas and ½ cup corn. Stir until well heated and serve over rounds of crisp cornbread.

SUGGESTION: Sprinkle with grated cheese and chopped green onion, or chopped fresh tomatoes, or both.

Pat Hildreth was one of the first doctors with Western Enterprises, adjunct of the CIA, which was set up in Taiwan in 1950 when CAT started its establishment there. He had his clinic in the WE compound in Yang Ming Shan just a couple hundred yards from where we built our house. We developed a great friendship with him and his wife, Dee. They live in a beautifully decorated old farm house in Mohnton, Pennsylvania not far from Pat's work as head of the Reading Hospital. Dee was kind enough to let us have these recipes.

ELEGANT CHICKEN

4 whole, boned chicken breasts
8 slices bacon
4 oz chipped beef
1 can mushroom soup
½ pint sour cream
paprika

Cut each chicken breast in half and wrap with bacon slices.

Cover the bottom of a greased 8 x 12 baking dish with chipped beef (you may like sliced onion on the beef). Arrange the chicken on top; cover with the soup mixed with sour cream, sprinkle with paprika. Bake at 275 degrees, uncovered, until done; recipe says 3 hours but I find that less time gives a more moist savory chicken.

CURRIED FRUIT BAKE

Dee says this goes very well with Elegant Chicken.

5 tbsp butter
¾ cup brown sugar
4 tsp curry powder
1 can pear halves
1 can peaches (apricots can be used)
1 can pineapple chunks
5 Maraschino cherries

This dish is much better when made the day before and reheated at serving time. Heat oven to 325 degrees. Melt butter; mix in sugar and curry powder. Drain and dry fruit. Place in 1 ½ quart casserole. Add butter mixture. Bake one hour; refrigerate when cool. Reheat at 350 degrees.

Aristides "Artie" Lazarus was legal counsel for NACC (Naval Auxiliary Communications Center) in Taipei during the fifties. He and his pretty wife, "My Mary", have traveled extensively and when they claim that their recipe for *Baklava* (pronounced bahk lah VAH) is the best, we have to believe it. Artie says: "I have eaten *Baklava* in Athens, Istanbul, Cairo, Amman, Bagdad, Damascus and many other places; but, NO ONE ANYWHERE makes it so well ...or even comes close. She has the benefit of America's plentiful supply of the finest ingredients, of course, but she has that 'certain touch' with Baklava." He refers to Mary's sister, Mrs. Helen Saridakis of Rockville, Maryland, who provided Mary with this jewel of a recipe.

BAKLAVA SARIDAKIS

1 lb finely chopped walnuts
1 cup sugar
1 tbsp cinnamon
1 lb phyllo pastry sheets
1 lb butter, melted
Syrup (instructions below)
Whole cloves

Phyllo pastry comes in very thin sheets and can be purchased in the frozen food specialty section of supermarkets in large cities. It is essential to this recipe. It can be made but the process is very tedious and long. Combine the walnuts, sugar and cinnamon. Use a pan 8x14x2 inches. Brush the bottom with butter; add 8 sheets of phyllo, brushing each lightly with butter. Sprinkle the top generously with the nut mixture and place 2 buttered phyllo sheets on top of that; sprinkle with the nut mixture. Continue adding buttered phyllo sheets, sprinkling every second sheet with the nut mixture until the latter is used. Place the remaining phyllo on top, buttering each sheet. With a sharp knife, make diagonal cuts from the upper left to bottom right; and then, from upper right to lower left. Thus, the entire *Baklava* is cut into diamond-shaped portions. Stud each piece with a whole clove.

Mary instructs: The secret to good, flaky *Baklava* is to bake it the day it is to be served. So, do all of the above 1 to 4 days in advance; cover well and refrigerate (it may be frozen). On the big day, bake at 350 degrees for about an hour, until it is a nice, deep golden color. Remove from the oven and pour cool syrup over the hot Baklava.

Syrup: In a saucepan, combine ¾ cup each of sugar and honey, 2 cups water and the juice of half a lemon; bring to a boil. Boil for 20 minutes. Cool. The gods of Olympus move nervously whenever you savor this delicacy!

Peppi Paunzen was one of the most colorful persons who ever worked for CAT. His family escaped from Austria where they were in the business of raising geese for making *Pate de Foie Gras*. They were refugees in Shanghai. Everyone knows of his fame as photographer and writer for the CAT Bulletin. Later, while awaiting visas for the family to go to the United States, he operated the Foreign Correspondents Club which was situated on top of a hill overlooking Hong Kong harbor. During that time, the spot became famous as the site of the film: "A Many Splendored Thing" with William Holden and Jennifer Jones.

Soon, good fortune came in the form of permission to enter the States.

They settled in southern California where Peppi married Gladys and they opened a restaurant which was very successful in the way of cuisine and entertainment (Peppi on the piano) but short on financial results. They had to close down the operation. But, Peppi provided us with some of the evidence of the brighter side of the business, the food.

PEPPI'S GOULASH

2 lbs shin meat (use any cheap cut of beef)
3 large onions, sliced
1 tsp marjoram
4 tbsp paprika
1 tbsp caraway seeds

Fry the onion in oil until just turning golden; add the paprika, marjoram and caraway seeds. Reduce the heat and add the meat, cut into 2" to 3" chunks. Simmer, covered, for 3 to 4 hours. Towards the end, add 1 tbsp vinegar and a pinch of sugar, and season to taste. If more sauce is desired, add the desired amount of water with a little flour to thicken. Serve with boiled or mashed potatoes and Peppi's cabbage. NOTE: Peppi had a similar dish made with brisket of beef. The caraway seeds and marjoram are omitted. The meat is spread on all sides with mustard and puree of garlic, then browned with the onions. It is cooked as for Goulash until the meat is tender.

PEPPI'S VIENNESE CABBAGE

1 medium head of cabbage, shredded
2 medium potatoes, peeled and diced
1 small clove garlic, pureed in squeezer
Salt and pepper

Put all the ingredients in a pot and cover with water. Let boil about one hour until the water almost disappears. Make some thickening with about 2 tbsp flour mixed with water. Add to the cabbage, slowly, while stirring until the desired consistency is obtained.

Mama made all the special cakes in the restaurant and they were famous. Here's one to try.

MAMA PAUNZEN'S PANAMA TORTE

7 egg yolks
1 cup sugar
3 oz semi-sweet chocolate, melted

Mix together and add:

6 oz almonds, ground with the skin
7 egg whites, beaten

Butter spring-form pan and dust with flour. Bake 45 minutes at 350 degrees. Test with toothpick.

CREAM ICING

6 oz sweet butter
2 whole eggs
1 cup sugar
3 oz semi-sweet chocolate, melted
Dash of vanilla

Mix all together. Cut torte in half and put icing between layers and on top.

While savoring all these goodies, remember to: "Be happy like Peppi!"

Eve Myers spent many years with CAT before going to Majorca to live. We did some work together there which had to do with the Son Vida Hotel and Urbanization project. Since then she has lived in Hawaii working as Editor of the CAT Association Bulletin. All CATer's and friends look forward every two months to the results of her efforts. The next recipe is a classic Mexican dish.

EVE MYERS' *CHILES RELLEÑOS*

Cut the stem part out of the top of six green peppers, remove seeds and white membrane. Blanch in boiling water for 2 or 3 minutes; let cool.

Prepare tomato sauce: 1 can tomatoes, squeezed into pieces with the hands. Add one can tomato sauce, a little water, one onion and 2 garlic cloves, minced,cumin, oregano and salt; simmer until onion is tender.

Prepare batter: Separate 2 or 3 eggs; beat both yolks and whites until fluffy. For each yolk, blend in one tbsp flour; fold this and the beaten whites together.

Frying: Heat ¼" oil in a pan. Put pieces of sharp cheddar cheese and a little minced onion in each pepper. Dip in the batter and fry to a light golden brown. Serve topped with the tomato sauce, beans and rice.

NOTE: Ground beef, browned, can be added to the cheese for the filling. Also, after dipping the peppers in the batter, try rolling them in a mixture of bread crumbs and grated cheese, then in the batter, again.

Sam Tweedie, staid (!) British accountant, had a twinkle in his eyes and a devilish smile. He kept us CATer's entertained for many an hour relating tales of his travels with fellow accountants and their escapades in such interesting places as the hot baths in Tokyo. We lost track of him when he retired to England but his memory lingers on with this recipe from his wife's collection.

EDIE TWEEDIE'S BEEFSTEAK AND KIDNEY PUDDING

Prepare about half pound of suet dough: Finely shred ¼ lb beef suet; mix in ½ lb flour, ¼ tsp salt, ½ tsp baking powder and sufficient cold water to make a soft dough. Roll out on a floured board to about ¼" thick. Cut one piece for the bottom and sides of a deep pie pan (Edie stated, "a deep pudding basin.") and a circular piece for the top.
Assemble:
1 ½ lb beefsteak, cut in 1" x 2" strips
1 ½ lb lamb kidneys, cut in pieces
2 large onions, chopped
1 cup beef or chicken stock
Salt and pepper
Mix the flour, salt and pepper on a plate and roll the pieces of meat in the mixture. Fry the chopped onions until nicely browned. Grease the pie pan and cover the bottom and sides with the suet dough. Place the meat and the onions on top of the dough and add the stock. Wet the edges of the dough and place the circular piece on top, pinching the edges all around to seal well. Cover with buttered paper and steam for 3 hours.
NOTE: We did not try this dish using the steaming method, but it looks like the recipe would lend itself well to baking. If you are going to try the latter method, be sure to brown the steak and kidney pieces before putting them in the pie. Also, a couple tbsp sherry will add to the flavor. Cut slits in the top of the dough and brush with egg wash before baking. Voila! You have Steak and Kidney Pie.

When the weather got a little chilly, for a couple of weeks (!), in the winter in Taipei, we served two dishes that are worth recording here.

MANHATTAN CLAM CHOWDER

2 dozen hard-shelled clams, shucked; save the juice
2 oz salt pork, diced
½ cup each onion and leeks, thinly sliced
1 garlic clove, minced

½ cup each chopped green pepper and diced carrot
¼ cup chopped celery
3 cups potatoes, peeled and diced
1 can tomatoes, chopped
¼ cup catsup
¼ cup chopped parsley
1 ½ tsp thyme
1 bay leaf
4 whole cloves
2 tsp salt and freshly ground pepper to taste

Grind one half the clams and chop the other half. Saute the salt pork until the pieces are browned; add the ground clams, green peppers, carrots, celery, potatoes, salt and 6 cups of water. Bring to a boil and simmer for 10 minutes. Add the chopped clams with their liquid (a small bottle of clam juice can be added) plus enough water to make 3 cups, the tomatoes, catsup, parsley, thyme, bay leaf, cloves and pepper. Simmer 20 minutes. Remove the bay leaf and the cloves before serving. Goes well with hard Baltimore oyster crackers. If you are from New England and will not settle for anything but Boston Clam Chowder: leave out the tomatoes and the catsup; at the end, add milk and thicken with cornstarch, if desired.

ROSBERTINI BARBECUED PORK CHOPS

Prepare 5 lbs pork chops cut one inch thick. Mix the following marinade:
1 cup soy sauce
1 cup Cointreau, or other orange-flavored liqueur
1 cup honey
2 cups canned crushed pineapple
2 lemons, thinly sliced
4 tsp powdered ginger
1 cup white wine vinegar
8 cloves garlic, finely chopped

Marinate the meat for at least ½ hour. Grill for one hour over coals that have burned down to just hot embers, or use a gas charbroiler. The meat should be 8" to 10" from the coals and brushed with the marinade sauce, and turned often so as not to burn it. When finished, the meat should be white and juicy on the inside and a deep, rich brown on the outside. Spareribs can be used in place of the chops. When we cooked on the beautiful, handmade stone barbecue in the garden of our Yang Ming Shan home, it became a gathering spot for all the guests to enjoy their drinks and become famished by the tantalizing aromas rising from the fire.

In answer to my question about his favorite recipe, Beauregard had this to say: "Now that, Chum, is a tough one. I think of lots and lots of favorite recipes but one of my really favorite favorites is a good, homemade Reuben sandwich. Now hold on there! I don't mean the kind where you go down to the delicatessen and pick up some kosher corned beef, a loaf of colored rye bread at the supermarket, a can of Libby's sauerkraut, French's prepared mustard and a swiss-style plastic cheese. No Sir! I mean HOMEMADE. You make your own corned beef (or pastrami) from scratch, your own sauerkraut from scratch, your own rye bread and you prepare your own hot mustard. About the only principal item you buy is a good Swiss cheese; stay away from the processed stuff which I call 'plastic cheese'." So, with that dissertation, here are the recipes.

BEAUREGARD'S CORNED BEEF OR PASTRAMI

1 ½ cups salt
1 tbsp sugar
2 tbsp pickling spice
½ oz saltpeter (potassium nitrate)
8 bay leaves
5 lbs brisket of beef
8 cloves garlic

NOTE: It is not necessary to use saltpeter but it gives the meat a nice, rich, red color, especially if you corn pork; if not used, the meat will have a grey cast.

Beauregards's recipe calls for water to make a brine in which the meat is pickled. The dry-cure method is simpler and takes up less space. Use a plastic bag which will hold the meat. By the way, any cut of meat can be cured; experiment with different kinds, lamb for instance, and you will find the result quite interesting. Rub the ingredients into the meat; it is necessary to mince the garlic in a press. Place in a bag; and then in a shallow pan which will just hold it. Turn the bag every couple of days for about two weeks. Remove from the bag, rinse under cold water, cover with water in a pot; simmer until tender, about 2 or 3 hours depending upon the cut and kind of meat.

The difference between corned beef and pastrami is that the latter is highly spiced. With the dry-cure method, you can make the pastrami from the beginninng of the process. Just add the following and rub into the meat along with the other ingredients; freshly ground black pepper, some crushed red pepper and ground ginger.

But, you may want some corned beef, too. Make it according to the instructions. Remove a portion that you want as corned beef. Rinse the portion that you want for pastrami. Cover with water and boil 4 or 5 minutes; place under cold water to cool it. Rub in the aforementioned spices. Place in a baking pan, cover with aluminum foil and bake at 350 degrees until tender, about 3 hours. Allow to cool for at least 20 minutes before slicing. The meat can be frozen whole or sliced, if you do not want to devour it all in one sitting. It will also keep in the fridge for 3 or 4 weeks.

BEAUREGARD'S YOGURT RYE BREAD

Here, we will not go into the details of making the bread; refer to the recipe on Page 316 for Tiger Joe's Rye Bread.The major difference in Beauregard's ingredients is two cups of yogurt which is mixed in before the flour is added. Also, before placing the loaves in the oven, they are brushed with cold water. He gives another hint: for an even crisper, crusty top, remove the baked bread from the pans and return to the oven for about 8 to 10 minutes until crisp.

BEAUREGARD'S HOMEMADE SAUERKRAUT

Shred one head of cabbage with a sharp knife or in a food processor. Mix with a tbsp salt; plain free-running not iodized. Pack into a large jar or crock. Fill with lukewarm water. Place a shallow vessel unnderneath. Cover loosely to allow the fermentation liquid to run over; check everyday to see if it is necessary to empty the vessel. When the cabbage has stopped fermenting, in about 9 days, it can be eaten or stored in the fridge in covered jars. See the recipe on Page 318 for preparing Tiger Joe's Sauerkraut for the Reuben and the way the Sandwich is put together.

HOT MUSTARD

Mix equal amounts of Coleman's dry mustard and rich cream, adding a little salt and sugar; let stand about 20 minutes before using.

NOTE: You can use wine or beer instead of cream.

BEAUREGARD'S SOUTHERN STYLE HASH

This dish utilizes the homemade corned beef or pastrami that you have just made.

    ½ cup each diced onion and green pepper
    2 tbsp butter
    1 cup uncooked potatoes, diced
    2 cups diced corned beef or pastrami (can use any leftover meat; roast beef, pork, lamb, chicken, turkey, etc.)
    1 cup meat stock, chicken or beef

Saute pepper and onions over low heat in a covered skillet until soft, about 5 to 10 minutes. Add all the other ingredients and cook slowly for 30 minutes. Add more stock if necessary, but all of the liquid should be absorbed at the completion of the cooking which is at the point that the potatoes are tender. Fold in some chopped parsley reserving a sprinkle for the top when serving.

SOUTHERN STYLE BISCUITS

These biscuits go well with the Hash. Sift together: 5 cups flour, 1 tsp baking soda, 1 tsp salt, 3 tbsp baking powder and 2 tbsp plus 2 tsp sugar; cut in ¾ cup shortening. Proof 1 tbsp yeast in ½ cup warm water to which 1 tsp sugar has been added; mix with the other ingredients. Work in 2 cups buttermilk. Roll out on a floured board to ½ inch thick. Cut into biscuits and bake at 400 degrees until golden brown; should take only about 8 to 10 minutes. Save unused dough in a plastic bag in the fridge until the next morning when you can cover with sugar and cinnamon and bake into shortbreads. Beauregard says modestly: "These are quite different!"

Pat Stone's husband, Jim, was one of our excellent maintenance technicians in CAT. She was another of my executive secretaries in Taipei. We have here one of her dessert recipes.

PAT'S GRASSHOPPER PIE

    1 ¼ cups crushed chocolate wafers
    4 tbsp butter, melted
    Mix together and pat into a 9" pie plate; chill.
    25 large marshmallows
    ¼ cup green creme de menthe
    ¼ cup white creme de menthe
    ⅔ cup milk
    1 tbsp plain gelatine softened in ¼ cup water
    1 cup heavy cream, whipped

2 tbsp shaved chocolate

Melt marshmallows in milk and mix in the softened gelatine, stirring until dissolved; cool.Fold in the liqueurs and the whipped cream.If it does not have enough color, add a few drops of green food coloring. Turn into crumb crust and freeze. Remove from the freezer about 20 minutes before serving.

Ann Rousselot, who has the recipe for Sourdough Pancakes on Page 247, submitted this one for an interesting cake.

ANN'S OLD-FASHIONED PRUNE CAKE

Sift together:
2 cups flour
1 tsp baking soda
½ tsp salt
1 tsp each cinnamon and nutmeg
1 ½ cups sugar
Mix in:
¾ cup oil
1 cup buttermilk
3 eggs, lightly beaten
1 cup cooked prunes, pitted
1 cup chopped nuts
You can bake this in one round pan or a 9 x 13 pan; however, Ann bakes it in 3 layers at 350 degrees for about 30 minutes.

OLD-FASHIONED COOKED ICING:

In a saucepan, mix:
½ cup each buttermilk and margarine
1 cup sugar
1 tbsp syrup (plain sugar, or corn)
½ tsp baking soda
Cook, stirring to prevent burning, to a "soft ball stage"; that means a ball will form when a small quantity is dropped into a glass of cold water (you can use a candy thermometer). Add 1 tsp vanilla and beat until it loses   gloss. If the icing seems too thick, add a little cream. Ice the cake when it has cooled, putting it between the layers besides the top and sides.

Ann Bagnell, also one of our CAT executive secretaries, recently passed away after being retired for a number of years in the Westwood area of Los Angeles. Her cake recipe dates back to 1917 (the year I was born!). Dividing the batter between two loaf pans, she made Christmas gifts for her friends. Baking the cakes in this manner, it is necessary to reduce the time in the oven.

ANN BAGNELL'S 1917 NUT AND DATE CAKE

1 lb pitted dates, cut up
1 lb nuts, chopped
1 cup flour, sifted before measuring
3 tsp baking powder, sifted with the flour
1 cup sugar
5 eggs, separated and beaten
1 tsp vanilla

Mix the nuts and dates with the flour and baking powder; add the sugar and mix. While stirring, slowly add the yolks; then the vanilla and fold in the beaten egg whites. Line the bottom of a cake pan, or loaf pans, with oiled wax paper. Cover with foil and place in a lower level of the oven. On the top level, put a pan of water. Bake for 2 hours and 15 minutes: first hour at 250 degrees, second hour at 275 degrees and last 15 minutes at 325 degrees. Using two pans, you can probably decrease the total time by 20 to 30 minutes.

The next recipes are for three mixed drinks that will be interesting to many.

Joe Alsop was in General Chennault's headquarters of the AVG, original Flying Tigers. However, he is in this section because, as a well-known columnist, he made many trips to Taiwan and other parts of the Far East, flying the line with CAT. His visits were always preceeded by solicitations to Lil Chu in Hong Kong, or to me in Taipei, for special gourmet meals to be arranged at the appropriate places to obtain the best of those requested items. On one occasion, there was a sumptuous banquet arranged by Lil in the best Chinese restaurant in Hong Kong. On another, I flew to Tokyo to join him for a luncheon of Japanese raw fish which had everything; three different kinds of fish, raw shrimp and squid, among other things.

Joe was also particular about his drinks. Although, on one occasion in the Grand Hotel in Taipei, a mutual friend, Frank Shor, a writer for National Geographic Magazine, and I shared with Joe his magnum of warm champagne poured over ice in large water glasses! The following two drink recipes are his.

JOE ALSOP'S REAL WHISKEY SOUR

4 parts Bourbon
1 part lemon juice
Just a little sugar, to taste
Shake hard with ice until it foams then serve

JOE ALSOP'S MILK PUNCH

1 pint brandy
2 quarts milk
Just a little sugar, to taste
Shake hard with ice until it foams; serve in Old Fashioned glass. Joe informs us, "I float a tsp of dark rum on top with a dash of nutmeg." If you suffer from insomnia, this is a sure cure. Of course, you might need a little champagne (better chilled) in the morning to clear your head!

Uncle Elephant Chow, former Mayor of the beautiful city of Hangchow south of Shanghai, was a Yang Ming Shan neighbor and great friend of ours. Besides enjoying his great hospitality at home, we made trips to different parts of the Island with him. One of the most memorable was to Alishan in the highest (over thirteen thousand feet) mountain region of central Taiwan. From the main terminal of Chiayi, he had arranged a private car (often used by Generalissimo Chiang Kai-Shek) on the ancient little steam train which wound its way most of the day through the mountain tunnels and around steep curves to reach the quaint village of Alishan. The area reminded one of the giant tree country of California. We were all a little worn out,...and thirsty, too. Upon opening our bag of alcoholic goodies, inspiration came in the form of a new drink; we call it,

UNCLE ELEPHANT'S ALI SHAN SEAFOAMER

1 ½ oz vodka, or gin
½ oz lemon juice
1 oz syrup
1 tsp Cointreau, or other orange-flavored liqueur
½ cup milk
Shake well with ice. Pour half a glass and fill with ice cold soda water. Long may the Elephant trumpet!

Lin Arison was in charge of the Armed Forces Radio Station in Taipei. But there were other accomplishments; such as, teaching the Chinese Military Band how to play. In that task he had to start from scratch. Within a comparatively short time Lin was giving concerts leading the band. It was most impressive especially when the Chinese National Anthem was played. The official Government arrangement was done by Lin. For an American to be accepted in that manner was outstanding to say the least. Often, he and his wife, Janie, along with Lil and myself would be entertained by Chiang Ching-Kuo and his wife, Fania. They were intimate, family affairs which we shall remember for the rest of our lives.

In the early days of 1950 in Taipei it was difficult to obtain chocolate unless someone happened to bring it from Hong Kong. So, it was something to remember when, one day, Janie brought us a copy of Good Housekeeping Magazine with a recipe for "Chewies" which can be described as a Brownie without chocolate. It is curious that one recalls such a small thing as a recipe for that sweet thing; but, that's one of the ways we think of Janie, especially at holiday time.

CHEWIES

1 egg
1 cup brown sugar
1 tsp vanilla
1 cup walnuts, coarsely chopped
½ cup flour
¼ tsp baking soda
¼ tsp salt

Mix egg, sugar and vanilla. Stir in flour, soda and salt. Add walnuts. Spread in greased 8-inch square pan. Bake at 350 degrees (325, if using a glass pan) 18 to 20 minutes. Should be soft in the center when done. Cut into 2-inch squares; makes sixteen.

Memories! Memories!

PART V: Majorca

Chapter 11

ORIENT TO MAJORCA

"You have to take a look at Majorca," Steve advised.

We were having a party in our house in Yang Ming Shan. Kusak had just returned from a vacation in Europe with another CAT pilot, Gene Bable, and had been relating the story of their travels.

He continued, "It's a sleeping place and is sure to develop into something big in the next few years."

When he finished, I commented, "Sounds great to me, I'll arrange to go over this winter and have a visit; that way it can be seen at the worst time of the year. If I like it then, I imagine I'll like it anytime."

The CAT passenger service was in its infancy; so, I decided to set up a visit to SAS (Scandanavian Airlines) in Stockholm to go through their food department. That way I could return, with a little detour to Majorca.

February was not the best time of the year to be in Stockholm; and, certainly not during one of the worst winters in recent history. Except for a couple of hours during the middle of the day, it was perpetual nighttime. And I nearly froze to death the entire time, until the converted cargo Bristol twin-engine plane of Iberia Airlines from Barcelona finally touched down on the small airport of Son Bonet on the Island of Majorca. The diminutive, Spanish style structure seemed more like a restaurant-motel rather than an airport administration building, and I liked it right away.

The 1930's vintage taxi passed through a few miles of rolling rural countryside with hundreds of windmills turning in the breeze. Shortly, we were passing down the center of Palma, along a broad, tree-lined boulevard, on one side of a Paseo, known as the Borne. We came out on the shore of the beautiful Bay of Palma, dominated by a 13th century Gothic Cathedral, which seemed much too huge for the size of the capital city of Palma.

The Bahia Palace Hotel was less than a half mile around the half-moon shore, overlooking the Port and the Yacht Club. The balcony of my suite took in the entire view. I was deeply impressed, except for one thing. The next morning, I was awakened by the early sun shining through the window; but, when I stepped out onto terrace, I put my hands on a balcony that had an inch of SNOW!

But, an hour of Majorcan sun saw the quick disappearance of the snow and the next few days could not have been more beautiful. I loved the Island and the surrounding turquoise sea. It was about forty miles across and 1,300 square miles in area, making it just one-tenth the size of Taiwan. Barcelona was only one hundred miles across the Sea to the north.

Restaurants, bars and sidewalk cafes abounded everywhere. And churches were on almost every block. I enjoyed visiting the bodegas where all kinds of wine were dispensed from huge wooden casks, the size of a small house. Many of them served the specialty of the Island, suckling pig, roasted all day on a spit until the skin was crisp and golden.

I could hardly wait to get back to Taipei to tell Lil all about the newfound paradise. Almost immediately we started to make plans for our three-months' vacation coming up that summer.

Lil's mother, Olga, accompanied us and the three kids on the Air France Constellation out of Hong Kong to Bangkok and on to Teheran. On takeoff from there, I noticed a strange noise in one of the engines but said nothing to Lil knowing how frightened she was of flying. Imagine, an airline executive married to a wife who hated to fly! Twenty minutes out, there was the voice of the Captain.

"We are returning to Teheran because of engine trouble."

"I knew it." Lil said, nervously, but she did not add much more. She had noticed the rough engine some time before the pilot made his announcement.

It turned out that a replacement engine had to be flown in; so, we were guests of Air France for a couple of days while the work was completed.

In the meantime, we busied ourselves seeing the area and enjoying the food, especially the Caspian Beluga caviar which was served in large bowls at dinnertime in the garden of our hotel. And we had the opportunity to visit Ed Overend, Flying Tiger buddy, who was with the U.S. Embassy and resided in a beautiful home north of the city.

On to Paris, where we piled the kids and Grandma into a taxi and went sightseeing like a bunch of tourists while waiting for our plane to Majorca.

Steve was at Son Bonet Airport waiting for us when we landed. As soon as we got on the ground Lil made an announcement.

"That's the last time I ever fly!" There was finality in her words and I knew then we were in for a long stay in Majorca.

Steve had arranged a house for us for three months in Genova which was situated in the mountains about ten miles northwest of Palma. On the way, I told him about Lil's decision not to fly.

"What does that mean?" He asked, hopefully.

"You can guess that we probably will leave the Far East and settle here, as we speculated many times."

"I thought the same about leaving Swissair." He commented, overjoyed at the turn of events where we might finally find a project to develop on the Island. He had been looking at many prospective places and, during the next few days, we went together to evaluate them. We got pretty weary in the process.

"There's a large place just north of Palma." He finally suggested. "It has a castle and about twelve hundred acres of land. It's no doubt too large for us to handle, but you can take a look at it."

About two miles on a narrow paved road, with a "Toonerville Trolley" running on one side, we passed through the small, sleeping village of Son Rapiña. Then a mile of dusty, dirt road took us up a curve to an impressive stone gate with two immense, ornate wooden doors. The "mayoral" (caretaker) swung the doors open and we entered the courtyard of the castle. The granite structure had a fairy tale tower on one side, topped with a turret all around.

The interior was unbelievable. There were paintings and statues everywhere, including suits of knights' armor. One room had a treasure of all kinds of guns and rifles, another a collection of swords. There was a complete library with interesting old books. The main dining room had huge crystal chandeliers and a mural oil painting around all four walls. Off the central, glass-covered atrium was a family chapel.

The crowning feature presented itself when we were shown out onto the terrace which ran the entire front length of the building. There in front of us was the city of Palma with its moon-shaped bay extending on each side as far as the eye could see.

"This is it." I announced with finality.

"But, how can we handle a project so large." Steve was very doubtful.

"We have to raise the money, that's all there is to it. After our vacation, I'll go back to Taipei and promote it with our friends. In the meantime, can we set up a meeting with the owners to see what kind of a deal we can make?"

The meeting was held in the bodega of Juan Mora, one of Palma's sharp businessmen. Jose Ferrer, the biggest wine merchant on the Island half ownership which meant that we would have to raise the other half of the money needed. Steve and I calculated that, with our savings and if we liquidated our holdings in a Honolulu apartment house and a Tokyo property, we could handle more than half of the requirement. The rest would have to be raised; I would take on that responsibility. I knew it would be tough because, in addition to the purchase money, there would have to be working capital for construction and improvements.

That was the beginning of the plan for the Urbanization of Son Vida, which included the only super deluxe hotel on Majorca, and only one of four in all of Spain.

I made arrangements to go back to Taipei at the end of that summer, not only to raise money for the project, but also to sell our house and get everything ready to move permanently to Majorca. In the meantime, we took over a small construction company to work exclusively on Son Vida. That way, we had much more control than if we had contracted with an outside company.

Back in Taipei, it was September when I gave three-months notice of resignation from CAT. Hugh Grundy, the President, did not say a word at the time. I knew that that night there would be another two-hour transpacific telephone conversation with the Pineapple. From that time until three months later when I departed for good, I knew that they would hold their breath so as not to rock the boat. Such good fortune that they never had to face the problem of how to fire me. I learned, many years later from a CIA friend, that Samuel S. Walker, member of the Board set up by the Agency to handle CAT affairs, had recommended that I be given a bonus of One Hundred Thousand Dollars for outstanding services rendered. The other members mumbled some kind of assent but nothing further was ever done about it.

There were hundreds of good friends at the airport to see me off. Chiang Ching-Kuo had a private room arranged where most of us gathered to await takeoff time. It was enough to make a grown man cry but I bit my lip and managed a smile even when Ching-Kuo gave me a bear hug and wished me "bon voyage." It was very difficult leaving China with its many memories and friends of more than sixteen years time. As the plane flew away from the shores of Taiwan, I had to force myself to think of the future ahead in another far-off land.

Chapter 12

A PRINCESS CAME TO HOTEL SON VIDA

Lil had located an apartment in Son Armadans, a section not far from the foreign community known as Terreno. Sue Buol had been visiting and she pitched in to help in the moving. It seemed as though everytime she turned around a glass was broken. The Russians believe that means "Good Luck!" However, when the day came that she broke a glass in the door, Lil and the kids did not think that the belief was all that great.

Christmas was nigh and a festive spirit was everywhere. The kids especially enjoyed a second Christmas after the twenty-fifth, the Feast of the Three Kings on January fifth. The Kings, with full entourage, came across the lighted water of the port in the evening and rode in a parade through Palma on camels that had accompanied them on their boats. That night, the kids' shoes were placed outside the door to recieve gifts brought by the Three Kings. Bad behavior was rewarded with a piece of coal!

After the holidays, it was down to business in a serious way. I set up my office in the Son Vida castle and directed the construction which was moving along at a fair pace but not as quickly as I had hoped. Our initial target was to get the Hotel ready within one year; but that was not to be.

An arrangement was made with Alfonso Font and his partner, Salvador Palmada, to handle the operation of the Hotel. Alfonso managed the Palace and Ritz Hotels in Madrid and Salvador, the Hostal de la Gavina in S'Agaro on the Costa Brava. They had to have more kitchen and dining space which meant expanding the scope of construction. That included the addition of elevator facilities and the only logical place was where the family chapel was located. It broke our hearts to tear it out and install a mundane thing like an elevator in its place.

Towards the end of 1960, there were signs that a most unusual hotel was emerging. Two round honeymoon suites were constructed in the tower. Men with hand chisels had laboriously opened the slits in the 3-foot thick granite walls into windows. The mural oil paintings which had been stored away while the dining room was being redone, were installed again. The collection of swords and guns were hung on the walls of the main bar and cocktail lounge. The entire front terrace had been completely excavated and another dining room built underneath, overlooking the City, and a large pool was tucked into the side of the hill.

If that were not enough, we drilled and struck a large supply of water. On Majorca, that was like finding gold. An English golf architect was brought down from England and a golf course was laid out. Luck was with us. The cultivated area of the *"Finca"* was just sufficient for an

18-hole course. Construction of nine holes was begun at once. That encompassed the area around the castle.

Then, there was the opening to be planned.

"We are going to make this the biggest social event ever to hit Majorca," Alfonso announced at a meeting to arrange the affair. "Besides Generalissimo Franco's wife, there will be Indian princes, movie people and, to top it all off, Onassis will come on his yacht with Maria Callas, Prince Rainier and Princess Grace."

"And there will be plenty of publicity coverage," added Palmada. "We will have Hedda Hopper, Elsa Maxwell, Bob Considine, Gerry Zerbe and others."

"It will be a week-long gala affair." Alfonso said. "There will be worldwide coverage, especially in publications like Time Magazine. Also, I've got Charley Farrell to come over from the Racquet Club in Palm Springs to open the new tennis court."

It was a day in May of 1961 and what a gala occasion it was. As Onassis sailed his yacht "Cristina" into the Bay of Palma, there were thousands onshore to cheer him and his party. When Prince Rainier and his beautiful Princess Grace came ashore, the police had a difficult time keeping the crowd back.

The invited guests took over the Hotel for a week and even the luncheons assumed the air of a Hollywood set. The Prince of Baroda and his mother, the Maharani, were especially impressive in the colorful costumes of their native India. Also, ever-present during the day, was the tall figure of Charley Farrell of "Seventh Heaven" fame, clad in his white tennis outfit and sporting a tennis racket.

Hedda Hopper and Elsa Maxwell mingled with the guests, always managing not to encounter each other; they were not the best of friends. There was one anxious moment when they happened to find themselves together in the elevator, one day. Fortunately the other occupants acted as a buffer, preventing any confrontation.

Hedda was purported to have said of Elsa. "I launch movie stars, she launches ships."

The Hotel Son Vida was officially opened the first night by Madame Franco. After her nice words, the entire party was entertained at a gala dinner, in the open, on the front terrace overlooking the twinkling lights of the City below. The food was memorable, prepared by a Spanish Chef who was an expert in French cuisine. The fish course was *Loup de Mer au Fenouil* (Sea Bass cooked over fennel) and the main course, *Solomillo a la Bernesa* (Roasted whole fillet of beef with Bearnaise sauce). The latter was carved at the table. The charred outside contrasted with the red interior and, laced with the golden Bearnaise Sauce, was a sight to behold.

During dinner, there was Spanish entertainment provided by the nightclubs of Palma. The costumes and the dancing were outstanding. The singing of the famous group, Los Valldemosa from Tito's Nightclub, was great enough to bring tears to ones eyes.

After dinner, there was dancing. As the evening went on, some of our guests participated in the entertainment. Prince Rainier played the drums and Elsa Maxell joined in on the piano. It was such a terrific evening, that it was the small hours of the morning before the party broke up and our visitors reluctantly headed for their rooms.

For the rest of the week, the festivities continued and there was a diferent variety of food and entertainment every evening. After one cocktail party, Prince Rainier was honored with a gift of the most prized pair of pistols in the Son Vida collection (see photograph on Page 168).

During the day, our children swam with, and got to know, the Rainier daughter, Caroline. Princess Grace was always on hand to look after her. It was during that period that they became personally interested in Son Vida by actually purchasing a piece of land not far from where we had built our house. Son Vida wanted to make a gift of the land but they would not hear of it.

My sister, Marie, and her husband, Ben, came down from Stockholm to stay with us and join in the celebration. Our favorite friends, Jackie and Charles Lawrence, were with us on several occasions. He was one of the lawyers at the Tokyo military trials after World War II and Jackie was of the Rumanian family, Miclescu, related to the royal family (sister Lulu provided the Rumanian recipes on Page 288).

At the end of the merrymaking, when Onassis and the Rainiers sailed away on the yacht "Cristina", an enormous impression had been left, not only on the people of Majorca, but also on all who heard and read about the fairy tale Son Vida Hotel and the events that had transpired there during that fabulous opening week. It was almost like a "shot heard round the world."

Shortly afterward, our friend Ilia Tolstoy paid us a visit to see the hotel wonder of Majorca. He was the grandson of Leo Tostoy whose WAR AND PEACE and other literary works were world-famous.

We got to know Ilia from the time he first arrived in Taipei in 1955 with his friend, Babbie Holt. They had homes in New York and the Bahamas where we enjoyed many pleasant times together.

Ilia, knowing the CAT-CIA connection, confided that he was involved in covert operations in Tibet, out of northern India. He was well-suited for the job with his Russian background and former OSS experience.

One time, he took us for dinner at the Embassy Room of the Ambassador Hotel which was run by Sergei Obolensky. We were served a luscious Fillet Mignon a la Obolensky which was sauteed and then covered with a wine-mushroom sauce and served flaming at the table. The only disappointing point in the dinner came when Lil ordered canned peas and canned corn! Always the royal Russian gentleman, Sergei arranged to have the unusual request presented in a most elegant manner. To top the evening off, he performed the Georgian Sword Dance, to the delight of everyone!

Another visitor during that period was Major General Charles R. Bond and his pretty wife Doris. He was a Vice Squadron Commander in the Flying Tigers and an ace pilot. He also had the distinction of being only one of two Flying Tigers to make General.

NOTE: Charlie recently had his book: A FLYING TIGER'S DIARY, published by the Texas A & M University Press in College Station, Texas.

We settled down to a quiet, unhurried life on Majorca. The children were attending Spanish schools and, although discipline was tight, they thrived on the orderly and peaceful atmosphere. Marie did well in Inmaculada, the girl's school. Joe had to spend a year at the American School learning Spanish; but, soon, he and Bob were together in San Francisco, the school highly regarded by Majorcans.

It was fun exploring the Island with its beautiful coves and beaches. And, the northwestern area had spectacular mountains with steep cliffs descending straight down to the bluest water we had ever seen. The family of one of Marie's schoolmates had a second home in that area in the unique little village of Bañalbufar and we were guests there for family weekend gatherings. Just to watch the clear blue water pounding against the precipitous cliffs was a symphony in itself.

There were restaurants everywhere; so many, it would take many years to visit them all. Unusual, especially, were the many old *fincas* converted to food establishments. A half dozen of the larger ones could serve anywhere from five hundred to fifteen hundred in one seating. One of those belonged to our friend, Pepe of the distinguished Perelada family. He arranged the main banquet for the 1967 Reunion of the Flying Tigers. The meals consisted of chicken and pork done on large rotisseries which were a wonder to see in operation. The heavy red wine of the Island went well with that type of meal.

Down on the Port, there were seafood cantinas where an excellent meal could be had for one or two dollars. Then, in little corners, down narrow cobblestone streets, one could find full, economy meals for the unbelievable price of forty to seventy-five cents! A large *"jarro"* (pitcher) of good wine was always available for pennies.

The countries of Europe were easily accessible and every three to six months we would take the car on the Barcelona ferry and do a tour. Over a period of time, we visited all the Western nations. Nancy and Temple Fielding, who lived in Formentor on the eastern side of Majorca, had probably the best and most famous travel guide. We always consulted it before going anywhere. They often came to Hotel Son Vida and we remained friends during the many years of our sojourn on Majorca.

But, some of the best times were had just covering the different parts of Spain. Everything was cheap and we played a game of seeing where we could get the most for our money. Spain is a most varied country with mountains and plains; and, the sea was never very far, on most trips. One of the highest roads in Europe was in the Sierra Nevada, just up the mountains from Granada. There, we found a ski resort, and that in southern Spain!

The walled city of Avila and Segovia, with its tremendously impressive Roman aqueduct, offered some of the best veal and lamb in all of Europe. The latter was so tender that the serving waiter would cut it with a plate!

Salamanca, the University City was outstanding with one of the largest "Plazas" (square) we had ever seen in all of our travels. There was Santander with its nearby centuries-old village of Santillana, where we visited the caves of Altamira that had paintings over twenty-five thousand years old. In the fading light of the evening, herdsman would lead the cows through the dusty main street to their berths for the night. Then off we'd go to one of the charming outdoor restaurants and enjoy a meal of seafood and, perhaps, roast lamb laced with garlic, lots of crusty country bread, and all washed down with a pitcher of wine. That was paradise!

Peace and tranquility do not last forever. One of the guests that we met at the Hotel was Eddie Gold of Chicago. He had set up a chain of Wimpy Restaurants there and later in London. He convinced us that it would be a good idea to start a chain in Majorca. I went to London to study the setup and returned to help find our first outlet, a block down the street from Tito's Nightclub. We rearranged what formerly had been a bar and restaurant overlooking the Bay of Palma. The hamburgers were made in the kitchen downstairs and all went well with that initial operation.

At Son Vida, the weekly meetings turned into a boring recurrence of the previous ones. I told Kusak that there was no point in both of us wasting our time listening to all the BS so we agreed that he would be responsible for that end. Besides he loved to talk, especially in Spanish, the sole language of the meetings. As things happened, the arrangement turned out to be a disaster for me.

Another thing occurred which determined our final fate in Majorca. Mark Stevens, former movie actor, came to our second house in Son Vida. We had sold the first one and bought another from a friend who had retired to the States. Stevens had an idea for a Mexican restaurant and wanted a partner for the venture. Lil and I took the plunge. We located a patio-type restaurant that had been closed. It was just around the corner from Plaza Gomila, the gathering place for most of the foreign community.

With great enthusiasm, we redecorated the place and made it into a colorful Mexican hideaway. There were two bars and the open patio lent itself especially well to the decor and the summer outdoor dining so suited to the Majorcan climate.

It was that year, 1967, that the Flying Tigers decided to have their re-union in the Hotel Son Vida. The whole gang flew in on a Flying Tiger Line plane for the three-day festive affair. Bob Prescott and his pretty wife, Anne Marie, sailed into the harbor on an Italian millionaire's yacht. Ann Marie was joined by her parents in the Hotel to celebrate the reunion together.

Our restaurant served as a meeting place and helped to make our first year a resounding success.

The next year, we had a branch on the beach at Palma Nova and one in the mountains near Valldemosa. For two years, we worked our butts off in that expanded operation. We finally had to give it up, as far too strenuous and time-consuming.

But, there was still another world to be conquered. Stevens had always dreamed of having a racquet club, something along the lines of the famous one that Charley Farrell had built and developed in Palm Springs. I had several disscussions with Son Vida about the idea and, very reluctantly, they agreed to lease us a piece of land for the development. I went to Madrid and negotiated a government loan to finance the construction.

The Son Vida Racquet Club had a restaurant and hotel of fifty rooms which overlooked nine tennis courts and the Hotel Son Vida. The junior Olympic-size pool was especially attractive with its surrounding umbrella-covered tables where one could drink or dine. We catered to groups of fifty to one hundred and that part of it was a great success.

However, the bills for constructing and finishing the project were overwhelming. I had numerous discussions with Son Vida. They turned a deaf ear on my pleas for financial assistance. Especially vociferous against me was the corporation's lawyer, Damian Barcelo. I always had the feeling that he was against foreign participation in Son Vida from the beginning. He had Kusak convinced that this was no friendship matter, but a legal one.

I realized, of course, that any difficulty that forced me out of the Racquet Club would benefit Kusak up to fifty percent of anything Son Vida could take over. I was forced to sign my share of Son Vida over to Kusak who maneuvered the rest of the foreign ownership into the name of his wife, leaving him with a full fifty percent of Son Vida. The "story" was that I had signed off on the takeover; and, so Kusak "had to go along with it."

As evidence of how ridiculous that was, I was forced to declare a *"suspenso de pagos"* which is the equivalent of going into receivership. However, there is one big difference in Spain; I, being the one to make the declaration, would be sent to jail until such time as the court decided whether I had committed fraud! When I heard that shocking news, while sitting in a sidewalk cafe in downtown Palma, the day before the declaration was to be formalized, I sent our son, Joe, to the Club to get my bag and passport.

At the airport, I was afraid that, at any minute, the police would pick me up and cart me off to jail. But, the plane got off to London and I escaped that horrible fate. A few days later, Bob accompanied Lil on the train to London, thus ending a thirteen-year chapter in our lives on the Island of Majorca. We had a lot of wonderful memories but we left most of our worldly possessions there!

According to the report of certain sources, the upshot of the entire mess was that Son Vida, later, forced a bankruptcy proceeding that resulted in their takeover of the Racquet Club.   Thus Kusak, from any realistic viewpoint, wound up with fifty percent of my project.!

RECIPES

In ancient days, Spanish cuisine developed first from the Greeks and then the Romans. Later came the Arabs. By the time they were ejected from the country; the French, just across the Pyrenees, were exerting their influence. This coincided with that of the Italians. Hence, the widespread use of tomatoes, green peppers, garlic, olives (especially the oil), spices, herbs, rice, wheat and all kinds of beans. Many items were brought from the New World by the explorers, starting with Columbus. Naturally, with the Sea and the Ocean on three sides, seafood dishes have always been a principal part of the cuisine.

Spanish food is not highly spiced and there is only isolated use of hot (piquant) peppers. Majorca is one of the few areas where dried, hot red peppers are cooked whole in some dishes just like in two or three provinces of China.

So, with that, we shall try some of the recipes collected during our thirteen years living on that beautiful, tranquil Isle. Let's start with the Spanish salad, *Gazpacho*. Yes! Although it consists of liquified ingredients, Spaniards classify it as a salad. We have tried this unique dish all over Spain and finally settled on Lil's recipe.

LIL'S *GAZPACHO*

    5 large tomatoes, peeled
    2 green pepper, cleaned of stems and seeds
    1 medium onion
    3 to 5 garlic cloves
    2 cucumbers, peeled
    ⅓ cup olive oil, or vegetable oil
    ⅓ cup vinegar
    2 tbsp sugar
    2 tsp salt
    ½ tsp paprika
    5 cups water
    2 slices stale Italian or French bread (optional)

Chop the vegetables and put all ingredients through the blender or food processor. Chill overnight. Stir before serving in bowls. Often, there is an accompaniment of chopped onion, green pepper, tomato, cucumber and small croutons for topping.

MERLUZA SALSA VERDE (Fish with Green Sauce)

This is a regional dish found in the Basque country around Bilbao and San Sebastian.

Merluza is a large species of Whiting; Cod or other similar fish can be used. This fish is cut into steaks about one to 1 ½ inches thick, one per serving. Dredge in seasoned flour and saute quickly in hot oil, only long enough to brown lightly on each side; the inside will not be done. Place in a warm oven while preparing the following sauce.

1 minced onion
1 minced garlic clove; use more according to taste
2 tbsp flour, or cornstarch
2 tbsp butter
1 cup chicken or fish stock
1 cup white wine
1 cup parsley, finely chopped
½ tsp white pepper
pinch of ground nutmeg
salt to taste

Saute the onion and garlic in the butter until soft. Sprinkle with the flour or cornstarch and stir in the stock, over medium heat until sauce is smooth. Stir in the wine, parsley and seasoning. Add the fish in one layer and spoon over the sauce, at the same time, letting it simmer for five to ten minutes, until the fish flakes when tested with a fork. Serve with a crisp, green salad with a simple vinegar and olive oil dressing. Don't forget the chilled white wine and crusty bread.

ZARZUELA

This dish is named after the famous and very popular light musical opera, known as the *Zarzuela*. It is quite similar to the previous dish except the final cooking is done in a ceramic dish in the oven. In the restaurant, it is often brought to the table on a portable burner and served while it is bubbly hot. Fish steaks are usually used, but you can cut up fillets and avoid the bones. Calculate about four ounces of fillet per person. Dredge the fish pieces in flour and saute until lightly browned but not completely cooked. Keep warm in a ceramic dish in the oven; one that will be used for serving.

Make the same sauce as for the previous dish, except use only one tbsp parsley. Add one tbsp Pernod; if not availabe, use ¼ tsp anise seed and 1 tbsp sherry. In various parts of Spain, the sauce is varied by adding one or two tbsp of tomato sauce. Pour over the fish, lifting the pieces to allow some of the sauce to go underneath; sprinkle with olive oil. Bake at 375 degrees until bubbling and the fish just flakes with a fork. As usual, Spaniards have only a light green salad with a simple olive oil and vinegar dressing with fish dishes. A chilled white wine is essential.

PESCADO AL HORNO (Fish baked in the Oven)

This dish was a favorite in Palma.

Use a whole fish, slashed on both sides almost to the bone. Sprinkle with white wine. Prepare a mixture of:

1 or 2 chopped tomatoes
1 onion, sliced very thinly
1 clove garlic, minced
1 cup chopped spinach
1 cup chopped kale, or green lettuce
1 tsp oregano
½ tsp white pepper
salt to taste
olive oil

Place one-third of the mixture in the bottom of a baking pan, then the fish and, on top, the remainder of the mixture. Sprinkle with olive oil and bake at 350 degrees until the fish flakes with a fork; time depends on the size of the fish, but do not overcook. The toast is "Salud!" when raising your glass of wine.

One part of the Port of Palma was devoted to the Yacht Club where we whiled away many a pleasant hour in the sunshine having coffee and cognac and watching the yachts of all nations coming and going. Or, on the upper deck, enjoying an evening feast and taking in the lights of the Bay in front and the City in the background.

On the other side of the street that led down to the Club was the fishermen's area. At five o'clock on any morning, except Monday, the fishing boats docked after their all-night vigil at sea, bringing the fruits of their efforts into the large trading building alongside. Seafood of every size and shape was laid out for sale. In less than two hours, it would all be gone. The building was hosed down for the next day's onslaught. In the meantime, in about five minutes, one could drive to the huge city market where, along with meats and produce, the seafood was sold to the public.

On the waterfront, above the fish market building, were two cantinas specializing in the fresh seafood that was continually available. Many of the recipes given in this Part are for dishes that we enjoyed often in those restaurants. One of the delights was a simple Fish Soup.

SOPA DE PESCADO (Fish Soup)

Authentic Mediterranean fish soup requires fish stock as a base. You can use chicken stock, for convenience, but it's worth trying to make your own base for the real thing. Buy a whole fish and fillet it. Place the bones, head and skin in a pot and cover with water. Add: 1 chopped onion, 1 cut up carrot, a few stems of parsley, 1 chopped clove of garlic, ½ tsp pepper corns and salt to taste. Bring to a boil and simmer for thirty minutes. Let cool and pour through a sieve. This stock can be also used in making sauces for fish dishes.

The Fish Soup, itself, is very uncomplicated to prepare. Bring to a boil the desired amount of stock, add a cup of white wine and add the pieces of fish that were previously filleted. As soon as the flesh turns opaque, it is done. Add one or two tablespoons of Pernod (or ¼ tsp anise seeds), salt to taste and 2 tbsp chopped parsley. Place 1 tbsp Sherry in each soup plate before adding the serving portion. Often, a few raw, unpeeled shrimp are added to the soup at the same time as the fish. For *Sopa de Pescado con Arroz* (Fish Soup with Rice), add a couple of tbsp of cooked rice to each bowl. Crusty country bread and chilled white wine accompany this dish.

GAMBAS PIL-PIL

This is the Spanish version of *Scampi*. It is made in a flameproof ceramic serving dish, most frequently in a Tapa Bar. Since Spaniards have dinner at a very late hour, often not until ten or eleven o'clock at night, they will take something to hold them over at what we would call the cocktail hour. The Tapa is a small portion of food for one or more persons. If there is a group, a larger variety can be ordered. The score (or bill) is often kept in chalk on the bar which is rubbed off when payment is made. The best place for these delicious morsels is located in an area made up exclusively of *Tapa* Bars, within walking distance of the Palace Hotel of Madrid.

Enough olive oil is used to cover the bottom of the ceramic dish. The peeled shrimp, with the tails left on, are added in one layer with two or three small, dried, hot red peppers and three or four cloves of garlic, smashed with the skins left on; salt and white pepper to taste. When the oil boils, making the sound "*Pil-Pil*" for a minute, the dish is done; a dash of white wine is added, salt to taste. It is served in the cooking dish along with crusty country bread and a "*chato*" (glass) of wine. Since most

Tapas are served with red wine, you might find yourself having this seafood dish with that rather that white wine. If you eat the red peppers, you will find them very hot; but, the dish itself is not too hot because it is cooked so quickly that not much of the piquancy goes into the shrimp.

GAMBAS A LA PLANCHA

Plancha, in Spanish, is an iron plate, or what we would call a griddle. You can use large American shrimp, or prawns, as they are called in some areas; but, they will never have the taste or the texture of Mediterranean "*Gambas*." First of all, the shells of the latter, when cooked on a grill, are much more edible than the thicker and harder shells of our prawns. Also, after they are cooked, the flesh remains very tender and the taste is unique.

Use four or five prawns per person. Rinse under cold water and drain well. Marinate with olive oil, lots of chopped parsley and plenty of salt, about one teaspoon per serving. Place each serving on a hot griddle (or frying pan). A Spanish chef will always position the shrimp side-by-side so that he can turn them over with one sweep of the spatula. Timing is important, because the shells should be slightly charred while the inside of the flesh is just barely done. They may seem messy to eat and many of the deluxe restuarants will remove the shell for their clients. However, just grab a bunch of paper napkins and go at it. Do try some of the charred shell. And the "nectar of the gods" is in the heads, especially at a certain time of the year when a pink roe is present.

NOTE: An Oriental touch can be had by adding a dash of soy sauce and a little finely chopped ginger, during the marination.

MORE *TAPAS*

Bars that specialized in *Tapas* would serve dozens of different types, including all kinds of fish, prepared in many ways. The following are three of our favorite Tapas.

CALAMARES ROMANA

Don't tell your guests that this is squid! They will usually guess that they are onion rings. Use large squid, at least six to eight inches long. Clean the inside well, being sure that the plastic-like piece is removed. Scrape off the thin, purple outside skin. Cut crosswise so that the slices are circles. Dip in a batter of self-rising flour, an egg beaten with a little milk; add sufficient beer to make the consistency like pancake batter. Deep fry in oil at 375 degrees until golden brown. Serve with wedges of lemon. NOTE: Some cooks recommend blanching the rings, for a few seconds, in boiling water before applying the batter.

CHAMPIÑONES (MUSHROOMS)

Cut several large mushrooms into quarters. Have ready chopped garlic and chopped parsley. Saute the mushrooms quickly in very hot olive oil until starting to brown. Stir in the garlic and parsley, salt to taste. Give the pan a dash of white wine; stir and serve immediately.

HIGADO (LIVER)

Cut liver into bite-size pieces. Dredge in seasoned flour. Have ready chopped garlic and chopped parsley. Saute the liver pieces quickly in olive oil until lightly browned on each side; do not overcook! Toss with the garlic, parsley, salt and a dash of red wine.

NOTE: We found that a pinch of marjoram adds a special flavor to both the mushrooms and the liver during the final stage of cooking.

Toothpicks or small forks are the utensils used for eating *Tapas*.

LENGUADO (SOLE) COLMAR

There was a small restaurant, on Paseo Maritimo which ran along the west side of the Bay below the Hotel Mediterraneo, called Colmar. They specialized in *Lenguado* (Sole) and *Higado* (liver) and did them better than anyone else in the region. The cook worked on a little two-burner stove behind a counter where everyone could watch. He cooked each order as it was brought to him.

For the *Lenguado*, he took a large sole which had been skinned and had the side bones removed. He shook seasoned flour on each side and patted it on before placing it in a large saute pan with half butter and half olive oil. By the time it was golden brown, the fish was done. He put the fish on a large plate, added a little white wine and lemon juice to the pan and poured it over the delicious dish. Those who wanted only the fish usually had *Papas Fritas* (French Fried Potatoes) as an accompaniment. For trenchermen, just some green salad would do for the time being, because the *Higado* was coming up.

HIGADO COLMAR

The cook took a large slice of liver that covered more than the bottom of the frying pan. It had been dredged in seasoned flour and was frying in the butter-olive oil mixture. Browned on one side, it was deftly flipped to the other. The secret to a great liver dish is, of course, to start with a tender piece of meat; the flour coating, which makes it a little crisp and brown; and, at the end, smothering it with a mountain of seasoned, sliced onions which had been previously sauteed until brown, soft and tender, and to which a little flour had been added along with a generous shake of sherry. With a bottle of *Marques de Riscal*, you had to exclaim, *"Es Verdad?"* when they got the bill because it was less than a dollar for each dish!

TORTILLA ESPANOLA (SPANISH OMELETTE)

The so-called Spanish Omelette, with its tomato sauce filling, served outside of Spain is not what the Spaniards call a Spanish Omelette, which is made with fried potatoes. Sometimes, sauteed onions are added. The potatoes are fried until tender and brown on the outside. The onions, if used, are sauteed until soft but not brown. Beat the eggs as for any omelette and stir in the potatoes and onions with seasoning to taste. Fry in hot oil until brown on one side; shake the pan to be sure it is loose. Invert a plate over the pan and turn over onto the plate. Slide the omelette back into the pan with the brown side up; brown on the other side. Usually, a large omelette is made so that, when it is cut, the pieces are thick. The omelette is eaten hot or cold and is often taken on picnics. Also, served in *Tapa* Bars.

CREMA DE ESPINACAS (Creamed Spinach)

This is a side dish enjoyed all over Spain; Spaniards make one of the best. The secret is a Bechamel (white) Sauce to which white pepper and a dash of freshly ground nutmeg have been added. Use a package of frozen, chopped spinach; unless you want to got through the washing, cooking and chopping of fresh spinach like the Spaniards do.

BECHAMEL SAUCE

Melt 2 tbsp butter and add 2 tbsp flour; let bubble for a minute and add 1 cup milk. Stir constantly with a wire whisk over medium heat. When it has bubbled, add ¼ tsp white pepper, salt to taste and a dash of ground nutmeg. A variation is to add minced onion when first melting the butter. Drain the cooked spinach well and stir in the sauce; delicious with both meat and fish. Served on top of the latter, it is known as *Pescado Florentina*.

COCA

This is the Majorcan version of pizza, except no cheese is used. It was sold by the piece in bars, especially at the public food markets. The dough was the same one used for the crusty bread sold in all bakeries. The topping was very simple, sliced onions with some mashed tomato. Before putting in the oven it was drizzled with olive oil. The other variation was with fish.

The Majorcans have a poor man's version of *Coca*, called *Pa amb oli* A piece of country bread was browned by the open fireplace. Rubbed with garlic and smashed tomato, it was sprinkled with olive oil and salt to taste and eaten for breakfast! Sounds odd, but try it, you'll like it.

Potaje and Fabada

No recipes here, only explanations. Every restaurant and every home had its own version. *Potaje* is a thick soup. In some small restaurants, a large bowl and a whole loaf of country bread could be had for about twenty-five cents! A glass of hearty red wine would be only a few cents more. That could keep one going most of the day. The large pot of soup was cooked for hours and served the next day. The main ingredients were: beans (Spaniards love legumes), carrots, potatoes, parsley, bits of ham with bones, pig's ear and tail, tomatoes, onions and garlic, seasoned with pepper, oregano and thyme. On the Island of Ibiza, they made a liqueur of thyme, called *Frigola*, which was great in *Potaje* or in any stew.

Fabada is basically a bean stew, and the one from the Province of Asturias is most famous because of the large white beans and the pork products from that region. It is made like *Potaje*, cooked all day. The pig's ear and tail are essential and, often, the snout and the feet are thrown in, plus the Spanish sausage, *Chorizo*. The finished product should be thick and the beans must be very soft. With country bread and a heavy red wine, nothing else was needed to make a complete meal.

Rabbit

This was a favorite on Majorca. Rabbit was prepared in two basic ways. One was a stew with the liquid, red wine. Onions, carrots, garlic, thyme and tomatoes were essential. The rabbit was browned in a hot frying pan before putting in the stew pot. The cooking took about three hours until the meat was falling off the bones. A little sherry was often added at the end. Also, some cooks combined the red wine with brandy for the overall cooking. Be adventurous; combine the rabbit with a leg of lamb (or 2 or 3 shanks) and *Chorizo*. Brown the lamb, first, as with the rabbit.

The other way was sauteed. The pieces of rabbit were sprinkled with seasoned flour and browned quickly in hot olive oil with lots of whole unpeeled garlic cloves. Then the pan was flamed with brandy. When the flame died, a quantity of wine was added up to about ¼ inch in the bottom of the pan. Covered, it was sauteed until the meat was tender.

PAELLA (pronounced: pah-ELL-yah)

If you ask any American who has been to Spain what his favorite dish is, the answer will probably be, "*Paella*." It makes a complete meal. However, for Spaniards, it is usually the start of a Sunday meal where the entire family goes out for the day, all dressed up in their best. After *Paella*, they will have a main course.

The dish is made in a *paella* pan the size of which is designated by the number of persons it serves. Large parties are often held outdoors, especially at the beach, where the *Paella* is cooked over an open fire.

There is a *Paella de Mariscos* made with only seafood; but here we will deal with the usual type *Paella*. This is more of a procedure, rather than a recipe. Assemble the following for about six to eight persons:

1 Chicken, cut in pieces
2 or 3 Pork chops, cut in pieces
1 Squid, cleaned and cut in pieces
½ lb medium shrimp, with shells
8 Mussels, scrubbed
1 Onion, sliced
1 Tomato, chopped
½ cup peas
1 can Artichoke hearts
1 small jar Pimientos
2 cups Rice
5 cups Chicken stock
Olive oil and salt

Mussels are essential for an authentic *Paella*; if not available, use steamer clams. In the old days, when it was cheaper, saffron was used to give the rice a yellow color. Today, the Spaniards use a synthetic. A similar product can be purchased in Cuban stores under the name; Bijol. A small amount is stirred into the cooking stock to give the desired yellow color.

Brown the chicken and the pork in a *Paella* pan in olive oil. If such a pan is not available, use a large frying pan . If the pan is not large enough to hold all the ingredients, the fried foods can be transferred to a rectangular baking pan. Add to the chicken and the pork the onions, tomatoes and squid. Stir while frying until the onion becomes translucent, then add the rice. There should be sufficient oil to coat the rice, so it may be necessary to add a little more. After stirring and frying a few minutes, this is the point at which everything is transferred to the larger pan. Then, pour in the stock and cook over two burners, if the pan is too large for one. When the rice is almost done, it will be finished in the oven. Stir in the peas. Decorate with the mussels, shrimp, artichokes and pimientos. Sprinkle with olive oil. It will take only five to ten minutes in a 350-degree oven for the mussels to open and the shrimp to be pink. Serve with wedges of lemon for each person to squeeze on his *Paella*. A chilled white wine is essential; and, of course, the word is *"Salud!"*

NOTE: Spaniards like their rice under-done; so, if you are traveling in Spain and like your rice well-done, be sure to instruct the waiter.

PICKLED *JALAPEÑA* PEPPERS

Hot! Hot! If you like hot peppers this is it. They were used in our Mexican restaurant in Terreno (Palma).

There are many types of hot peppers but my favorite for piquancy, taste and texture is the Jalapeña. There may be some that are hotter, like the minuscule grain-size pepper from Thailand, but not better. Use the following recipe to preserve the peppers, not only to use on food as they are, but to be employed in other dishes.

1 lb *Jalapeña* peppers
1 onion
1 green pepper
Cut these three items into ¼" pieces and place in a saucepan.

Note: After cutting up the *Jalapeñas* wash hands thoroughly because an accidental touch on the eye, not to mention an abrupt trip to the bathroom, will sting for hours!

Add:
1 tsp sugar
½ cup vinegar

1 tbsp salt
Several cloves of garlic
½ tsp ground cumin (optional)

This last item is mainly for Mexican flavor; for general use, omit it. Add sufficient water to just barely cover. Bring to a boil, turn off the heat and cover. Leave out overnight then place in a jar and store in the refrigerator; will keep for two or three months.

Use as is as a condiment on food or, sparingly, when making Pizza. It makes the simplest Taco Sauce as follows:

Saute one chopped onion. Add one can of tomatoes, chopped. Simmer with the juice until the onions are tender. Add one or two tbsp of the pickled *Jalapeñas*, according to your taste for the piquant, and the sauce is ready for your tacos and other Mexican food.

GRAVAD LOX

On one of our several trips to visit friends in Denmark and my sister and her husband in Stockholm, I had occasion to try *Gravad Lox*, literally translated means, "buried salmon." It is basically raw salmon that is pickled with salt and dill. The classic method is with fresh dill; but, if that is not available, dried dill weed (not the seed) will work.

Any salmon will do, but the red variety produces a finished product that is bright orange in color. Use fillets that have the skin left on. Place in a glass or enamel pan that will hold the fillets in one layer. Rub both sides with brandy and sprinkle them with salt and pepper. Go heavy on the salt because it is the preservative and not too much of it will penetrate the fish. Cover both sides with chopped dill, then vegetable oil. If you like a smoky taste, shake on some liquid smoke. Cover the fillets with a layer of plastic wrap next to the fish to keep out the air. Then cover the container with another layer. Place in the refrigerator and after one week, turn the fillets over. Another week will see them ready to eat. Slice thinly, almost parallel to the cutting board, producing a nice, large slice. Serve with lemon wedges, pepper grinder and rye bread, toasted or not. Ice cold aquavit and beer should cause you to exclaim, "*Skol!*"

If you want to try something very special, cut the Lox into pieces about half an inch thick; dust with flour. In a frying pan, bring to a slow boil about ¼ inch of Bechamel Sauce. Place the pieces of Lox in the sauce in one layer. In one minute, turn the pieces and immediately remove from the heat, no further cooking is necessary. Place the Lox on a heated serving platter. Stir into the sauce some sour cream and you have *Lox a la Russe!*

VARIATION: Add sauteed mushrooms to the sauce . You can "gild the lily" by including some small shrimp.

SARMALE ROMANESTI LULU

These thumb-size, stuffed cabbage rolls, Romanian style are so delicious they can be eaten like peanuts. The recipe is from Lulu the sister of Jackie. Our dear friends the Lawrences (mentioned on Page 272) lived twenty miles on the west end of Majorca in a beautiful house on a hill overlooking the Mediterranean Sea. Many a good time we had with them and often partook of this delicacy.

You will need cabbage leaves, parboiled for five minutes, and vat-type (rather than canned) sauerkraut. Spinach leaves, softened in boiling water can be used in place of cabbage leaves.

Filling:

1 ½ lbs; ½ ground pork, ½ ground beef
1 slice bread, soaked in milk and then squeezed
½ cup cooked rice
1 onion, minced and sauteed soft
2 tbsp salt
1 tbsp each; Pepper, dill weed, parsley

If the cabbage leaves are large, cut them in pieces about 4 or 5 inches across. Place one tsp meat mixture in the center and roll halfway; fold over the sides and roll the rest of the way. They can be put in the cooking pan as they are made; it should be one that can be used on top of the stove and in the oven. Cover the bottom of the pan with a little tomato sauce, then some of the sauerkraut. Add a few pieces of chopped bacon. Position the cabbage rolls tightly together in one layer on top of the bed. Then make another bed, on top of the rolls, of tomato sauce, sauerkraut, bacon pieces, then another layer of rolls. The top layer also needs tomato sauce, sauerkraut and bacon pieces. Pour over all one cup of chicken stock to which one tbsp of sugar has been added. Cover and cook slowly on top of the stove for 1½ hours. Check during the cooking to be sure all of the liquid had not cooked away; it may be necessary to add more stock. Then add one cup of white wine, cover and place in a 350-degree oven for one hour. Let cool in the covered pan. Reheat when ready to serve; be sure to add more liquid, if needed, during the heating.

These rolls go very well with Italian *Polenta* (corn meal mush) or sour cream, or both. Try some ground lamb as part of the meat mixture and you will have a different taste.

PART VI: Stateside Terminus

Chapter 13: Great Smoky Mountains

Chapter 13

GREAT SMOKY MOUNTAINS

Stella Maris in the Bahamas is a long distance from Majorca. Situated two hundred miles from Nassau on the upper end of Long Island (appropriately named because it is seventy-five miles long and very narrow), it is a development done by German entrepreneurs. Somehow we got on their mailing list in Son Vida and, strictly from the brochures and maps, we purchased four lots, sight unseen! It has been said that an adventurer lives by his wits. But to some this was more like being half-witted. However, the price was very low and there were no interest charges for the installment plan offered. So, we took the plunge. After all, it was a romantic idea.

However, the trip over on the old tub which was employed as a mail boat was definitely not all that romantic. We and a few returning Bahamians were accompanied by, among other things, a flock of chickens, a small herd of goats and a few squealing pigs.

"I don't believe this." I announced to Lil as we anchored in the shallow water offshore and the crew slowly lowered a skiff over the side. It began to rain as an outboard motor was let down to complete our dubious mode of transport to the rickety wooden pier on shore.

"Do you think you can make it?" I asked with great doubt.

"I have to," Lil replied. "I'm not staying on this wreck," she added, as several hands were already assisting her in descending the wood and rope ladder hanging over the side.

Somehow, we made it to shore. There was not a vehicle in sight, although we had requested transportation from Stella Maris. A padre in black cossack helpfully advised us that on the day the mailboat arrives, a taxi usually comes by!

Doubtful as we were, one did come along. It was probaly the oldest taxi still running in all of the Bahamas. We did make it to the development but only after a flat tire on the way. We held our breath the entire journey for fear of a complete breakdown.

In spite of all that, Stella Maris did not prove to be a disappointment. On such a tropical island the plants and flowers were luxuriantly beautiful. In addition to many exquisite houses already built, the central, Spanish-style building was impressive.

Everyone was very hospitable and we were shown a short distance away to our accommodations right on the beautiful, turquoise Caribbean Sea.

In our dubious and rather weak financial situation, I said to Lil, "We might as well live it up while we're here because when we get to the States things are going to be rough."

And that we did, by changing our clothes and heading for the cocktail lounge. And that night there was a great outdoor barbecue party with exotic drinks and delicious food.

As we sailed out of Nassau harbor headed for the States, we had some fond remembrances of Stella Maris, even including the return trip on that old, scruffy mailboat. Yes, we decided to keep the property after inspecting it, even though the agreement was that our money would be returned if we were not satisfied. So, to this day, we still have that sort of Bahamian anchor on Long Island. Incidentally, it is said that Columbus actually visited there because it is only a few miles from San Salvador Island, his purported first landfall in the New World, October 12, 1492.

Although we did not realize it at the time, our landing at Ft. Lauderdale in June of 1972 started us on the road to North Carolina. But first we had to travel a rough road. Oh, yes! there were many fond memories. Like the time Marie came over from Spain with our first granddaughter, Kailani, and spent a year with us. Elder son, Joe, although situated in North Carolina after doing his service in the Navy, would occasionally visit. We certainly had many a glorious time during that period.

The rough part was working, at first, like janitors (we were called "Managers") at an apartment house in the Hialeah area. You have heard the expression, "We don't do windows." We did everything from cleaning toilets, scouring stove ovens, painting, repairing; all this in addition to renting the apartments and collecting the rents. You name it, we did it!

A slight improvement occurred just before Thanksgiving. We were moved to a new apartment complex that we were originally hired for. The place was so new that the gas service for the cooking stove had not yet been turned on. So, we cooked the turkey on our gas (bottled) chargrill which was the first purchase we made together with Joe when we hit Miami. He came, not then, but for our first Christmas together in the States. We still have the grill; and, of course, the set of China that he put under the tree.

The next year while we were in a new management job not far away, friends came to visit on their way to have a look at the Florida Keys. That opened up a whole new avenue. We visited our friends several times and it was not too long before we were on the road to the Lower Keys, not far from Key West. A Real Estate Broker's License was won after some nightschool work.

With that we located land on a canal to build a house. We put it on stilts to avoid the ravages of water damage from a hurricane and, therefore, from the porch we could look down the canal about a hundred yards and see the sea. We thought that was not too bad for a couple of waifs who arrived in the States only two years before with three suitcases as our only possessions!

Naturally, we were in debt for the house. But that burden seemed to have been overridden by the marriage of Joe to his sweetheart, Effie, from Navy days. They came to live with us. Bob was already there working for Sears during the day and going to school at night. So, for a time at least, we were one big happy family, again.

Also, this was another period in which to learn and practice some new culinary experiences. Seafood, as one can imagine, abounds in the Keys. In fact, it is one of the best fishing grounds in all the world. Then, there are the Cubans who have a cuisine somewhat akin to the Spanish but flavored with the influence of the Caribbean area. A few recipes of this period will be found at the end of this, Part VI, to help you to retrace our experiences in the region. Conch (pronounced "konk") is used in many specialties in the Keys as it is in the Bahamas.

You may wonder what a conch is; well, one meaning is: a longtime resident of the Keys of many generations. They got the name from communicating, many years ago, by blowing on conch shells which are very prevalent in the area. The conch is actually a species of snail that lives in the sea; the beautiful shells that are sold as ornaments are often bigger than the size of a football. Since the meat is very difficult to remove from the shell, it is usually purchased in stores already ground up. It is used to make fritters, chowders and salads, among other things. It may not be of great interest to know but the official name of the conch is *Strombus Gigas*. It is related to the whelk, another edible sea snail.

It is a moving experience to see the Great Smoky Mountains for the first time and they leave a lasting impression. Covering both sides of the border between North Carolina and Tennessee they are part of the Appalachian Range that angles from Vermont and New Hampshire to Alabama. My first crossing was in the Spring of 1940 driving from Philadelphia to the West Coast after receiving my Naval Aviator's wings in Pensacola.

That was an opportunity to compare these mountains with the Rockies in the West. First of all, the latter are rugged, comparatively new mountains, geologically speaking. The Appalachian Range is the oldest in the Western Hemisphere. They have been worn down with time, the highest peaks are just under seven thousand feet. That has something to do with an outstanding characteristic, they are completely covered with forest from the top down. From spring through summer, there is a luxuriant covering of green. In the Fall, they are aflame in a blaze of color.

Summer of 1963, after a complete circuit of the States; camping in our Volkswagen bus, across the North, down the West Coast, back across the South to Florida, I decided to show the family Western North Carolina. On the way from my sister's in Miami we stopped off for a couple of days to see "Moose" and Janie Moss in Doerun in the south of Georgia. Being a southern gentleman and an old Flying Tiger buddy, he and his wife showed us more hospitality than we could ever expect. The kids were especially impressed with the animals and equipment on their scientific farm. They were really wide-eyed to experience a ride in the truck with their ten-year old daughter!

On the way to Cherokee, in the heart of the Great Smoky Mountains, just after crossing from Georgia to North Carolina, we passed a small town, sitting on the top of a hill, called Franklin. We remarked, as we passed along Main Street, about the interesting low brick buildings, none more than two stories high. Little did we realize then that that would be our "home town" years later.

"The countryside is so green here in the mountains," Lil remarked as we journeyed through the Smokies.

"Sure is beautiful," I added. "Might be a good area to live in one day."

Lil smiled and that was a sign to me that this was surely to be one of our stopping places in the adventure of life.

In New York, as we embarked on the ship that was to take us back to Majorca, after our three months' vacation, we were still thinking of the Great Smokies and a possible future there. It seemed as though we had left a part of our hearts in that beautiful part of the Country.

Summer, 1976: Not only Bicentennial, the two-hundredth birthday of the United States, but also time for The Olympics. One night in the previous year, at our home on Cudjoe Key, we stayed up until very late excitedly going over the schedule of events, carefully selecting our seats. It was spring when we received the tickets.

Lil, Bob and I set out in our motor home early one summer morning; destination, Montreal, Canada. Just the sound of the name of that city gave us the feeling of adventure, once again. After visiting family along the way, we arrived at Portsmouth New Hampshire. One day's rest at a nearby campground saw us, the next night, boarding the ferry bound for Nova Scotia.

Once settled in the cabin, what's the next thing to do? Go to the dining room, of course; not only to have a look, but also to make reservations for dinner. The room was very elegant and when we arrived, after a session in the cocktail lounge, we were greeted by a very cheerful waiter; his name, Alfonso. After seating us, he indicated a long, food-laden table in the middle of the room.

"You might like to try our buffet dinner," he offered, his eyes lighting up as if he were going to indulge. "I think you will find that it has everything you might want for a splendid dinner."

After ordering a dry Portuguese wine, we approached the festive table. Alfonso had not exaggerated. There was everything imaginable: Smoked Nova Scotia salmon, numerous hors d'oeuvres, different kinds of stews and ragouts, roast beef, several kinds of fish and ...

"Here's my favorite," exclaimed Lil. "Red caviar."

That meant the large, plump salmon eggs that she enjoys so much. Not the small, pink, bullet-like things that one often encounters. Bob's eyes were getting larger as we moved along the table.

"I think we might come close to killing ourselves with this layout," he declared.

We had a lot of fun besides enjoying a sumptuous meal. The wine was especially good and the food left nothing to be desired, it was outstanding. We had a good feeling in our hearts as we said "Adios!" to Alfonso.

Unfortunately, we could not say the same for the remainder of the evening. We made the mistake of visiting the gambling room. Bob and I lost; he would not say how much. Lil won all of twenty dollars.

An uneventful and dismal, drizzly trip through Nova Scotia and the Province of New Brunswick saw us at the approaches to Quebec. Our luck returned as we located a nice campground almost under the bridge going over the St. Lawrence River to the City.

If one has the opportunity to visit only one Canadian city it should be Quebec. Situated on a promontory on the north bank of the River, it is an imposing sight with its provincial buildings surrounded by a massive wall which served in past history as fortifications. We strolled the narrow streets and enjoyed the ancient houses, having a cold beer in a small pub hanging on the side of a building whose steps connected the lower part of town with the upper.

Our stay was all too short as we had to make the two hundred miles along the River to Montreal. There is no speed limit on Canadian highways so cars went whizzing by our 55-mile pace as if the motor home were standing still. However, that afternoon, having passed surprisingly quickly through the City, we arrived at the expansive campground, twenty miles west of Montreal, where our home for two weeks had been reserved. The next day, Joe and Effie arrived in their new car which was to serve as our rather elegant transportation to and from the Games. So, there we were, a family of five all together in the motor home, "as snug as bugs in a rug."

If you have never been to The Olympic Games: Go! If you can possible work it out. The Canadians built an Olympic village like a futuristic fairy-tale land. It was as if another world. And Montreal was an ideal site especially with its Old Town section which was connected to the Games site by an almost noiseless 10-minute ride on the Metro. One should not miss partaking of the excellent French Canadian food served in any one of numerous small restaurants within walking distance of the main street of the section.

Well, chapters could be written about the Games. But, suffice is to say here, they are a great experience. However, we must move on to further adventure because there is more to come.

On the return trip to the Keys we just had to pass through the Great Smoky Mountains once again. The motor home was left at a campground outside Cherokee and Joe drove us on a tour of the area. This cursory inspection took us to Waynesville, Cashiers, Highlands, Franklin and Bryson City; all, except the first being small towns of about three thousand people and each approximately twenty miles from the other. That seemed to be the distance a horse and carriage could travel in the old days. Although casual, the tour gave us more of a feel for the area and built up the initial attachment for that beautiful mountain area which we had acquired on previous visits.

That fall, to our great joy, Marie and Kailani arrived for a three-month visit. Lil, with her great love for the holidays, spent most of the time preparing for Christmas. And what a glorious one it was! The festive board was covered with a golden brown turkey and all the trimmings. The entire family, including Mom, was there to partake and enjoy.

Unfortunately, that holiday season was the last big occasion that we were all together. But, celebrate the end of the year we did in a big way. The ladies made all kinds of unique and funny hats. Friends from nearby joined in. We danced and laughed and sang. Then, after ringing in the New Year we enjoyed a sumptuous dinner which, among other things, included a dish which has become traditional with us. Florida lobster, Keys shrimp and sea scallops, all laced with cheese and a wine cream sauce, were presented as a centerpiece.

It was almost dawn before we fell in bed, pretty much satiated. Before we did, Joe, Bob and I sat on the porch admiring the moon and the stars and discussed our next trip. Capt. Frank "Delo" De Lorenzo, a contemporary of mine in flight school (he started one month after me in Class 130-C) had sent out a flyer explaining an idea he had for a reunion in Pensacola of all pre-war Aviation Cadets.

"Sounds like a great idea." Bob and Joe each echoed the other.

"Sure does," I affirmed. "And Pensacola is beautiful in November. Besides we can continue from there to Western North Carolina to see if we can find anything interesting."

We had already decided that we might get into the campground business: so, the Reunion presented an excellent opportunity to further that idea. And, too, it is only about four hundred miles from Pensacola to the area.

November, 1977: The nostalgia of returning to Pensacola was almost overwhelming. After all, it had been thirty years since cadet days! We had stayed overnight on the beach at a State campground just west of Panama City. That enabled us to have a leisurely drive along the Gulf Coast, the next day. Before departing we had to sample the Apalachicola oysters in Pee Wee's, a hole-in-the-wall bar at portside in the City. At a dollar a dozen, we had to have two! Later in this story, we will have more of a dissertation on this delectable bivalve.

The entrance to the Pensacola Naval Air Station was not the old wooden guard house that I remembered. Crossing the bridge over the Bayou Grande, which comes off Pensacola Bay, we approached an impressive, red brick structure. The Navy guard directed us to a building off to the right where passes were arranged for our stay. It was unbelievable that no one seemed to know where the RV campground was located!

Although wider, the road south seemed familiar. After about a mile, we reached the Bay. The area on the left held the same old stately colonial-style buildings where we cadets had lived in 1939.

Turning right, the road (already a four-lane highway) ran along the beach area. The old charming wooden building with its tropical flavor that was the Mustin Beach Officers Club was gone. How sad that it had been replaced with a new brick building. Then, there was a modern structure on the beach which turned out to be the Non-Commissioned Officers Club. After a mile, another familiar landmark loomed up, the San Carlos Lighthouse: and, on the right the new Naval Aviation Museum. Straight ahead lay a huge jet airfield, called Sherman Forrest Field.

We almost missed the little wooden sign that directed us along a dirt road by the beach which led to our RV site. Well, it did exist even though we had to stop several times to ask where it was. The Oak Park Recreation Area was set up for retired personnel. As a former cadet, although not retired military, we got in only because Delo had worked it out with the powers that be. And that worked, even though illegal, on several future visits because the Manager got to know us.

The Reunion was a huge success. It was an extraordinary experience to renew ties with old friends after so many years. Bob and Joe joined me in enjoying the camaraderie.

There were eight of us Flying Tigers there including: Tex Hill, Link

Laughlin, Dick Rossi, Bus Keeton, Pete Wright, Jim Howard, Bob Layher and Bill Bartling.

Time to move north was approaching. But, not before the big banquet on Saturday night at the Officers Club. Dinner with wine and entertainment, beautifully emceed by Delo who surprised everyone with his stage presence, was the culmination of the Reunion. Delo had to get all of us Flying Tigers up on the stage to take a bow.

But, that was not the real culmination. We all had to go to Rosie O'Grady's in the newly restored area known as The Seville Quarter. It replaced the old rundown warehouse area a few blocks from the center of the City. A Dixieland band provided loud brassy music for listening and dancing. Pitchers of beer flowed like water. I realized this only the next morning when we woke up before dawn to get on our way.

"How do you feel, Dad?" Joe asked as I was trying to get organized.

"I feel fine," I lied. I didn't have a hangover but there was a woozy feeling. "Why?"

"When we were trying to change clothes to go to bed," Bob chimed in. "You got impatient and changed outside the camper. Did you think we were in the campground?"

We all laughed hysterically because, to get an early and quick start, we had stayed in the parking lot of the Sheraton Hotel right in the center of the City!

By nightfall we were in Knoxville, Tennessee. An all-day ride had fatigued us and we hurriedly bought some chicken and other goodies in a supermarket and headed for the Safari Campground in the hills north of town. A glass of wine and the aroma of the food cooking perked us up long enough to eat and get into bed.

In the morning the Safari people showed us their franchise setup with picture slides and a long spiel. After lunch they showed us one of their campgrounds near Seviersville a few miles north of the well-known ski resort of Gatlinburg.

The rain, interspersed with fog, made for an unpleasant ride over the mountains and through the Great Smoky National Park. Going down Highway 441 past Franklin, we hardly noticed the town because of the nasty weather.

The winding mountainous road eventually brought us to Highlands just as darkness overtook us. After buying a few provisions, our question about a campground brought negative replies. However, remembering the tourist sight, Dry Falls, about three miles back, we retraced our path and found the parking lot above the Falls. With a few glasses of wine, Joe and I had one of our long, argumentative discussions about absolutely nothing important.

Finally, with Bob shouting, "Shut up and go to sleep!" for about the tenth time, we heeded his command and went to bed.

The next morning, a real estate agent showed us several properties, one of which looked like a possible sight for a campground. As we headed out: destination...the Keys, no one was overly enthusiastic about what we had seen.

The long grind home left us exhausted. The next day was Sunday and we were hardly recuperated. Picking through the classified section of the Miami Herald I came upon an item which really caught my eye.

"Have a look at this," I exclaimed. "It may be something we are looking for and it's in Franklin!"

The ad was for the sale of a property: Restaurant seating seventy people, nine-unit motel, gift shop, Manager's house, duplex and fourteen acres of wooded land.

"It's a shame we missed that," Joe remarked. "It was right on our way, we must have passed right by it."

"Maybe we should go back," Bob interjected.

The thought of that long trip all over again made me sort of groggy. But after a family discussion and a call to the owner in Miami, we decided to takeoff the following Friday to see the place.

The trip north was the hard part. Our departure on Friday was at night after Joe and Bob returned from a full day's work. They took their turns driving during the hours of darkness. Each tried to catnap in between but not too successfully. When the sun came up I spelled them for awhile.

Upon arrival in the Franklin area we were greeted by a blast of cold air; winter had arrived there. A friend of Joe Del Buono, the owner, met us at the door of the restaurant which was perched on the side of a hill, as were the other buildings. With its decorative border running around the roof and the dark ornamental shutters contrasting with the light yellow exterior walls, it reminded me of an Austrian chalet.

The entrance led directly into the gift shop area.

"Mom will sure like this," I commented. Joe and Bob both assented without saying a word.

The open kitchen area was to the left and, off that, the door to the dining room which was semi-separated into two areas by a low divider. It was fully equipped as was the kitchen. There was even a deli display case in front of the latter, strategically located for clients to see as they were on their way into the dining room. In the basement was a huge walk-in refrigerator-freezer the size of two small rooms. Besides, gifts for the shop were stored away on shelves for the winter off-season.

We were silently pleased with what we had seen and headed outside to visit the other parts of the property. First, the manager's house. It really was not much of house being, rather, an old farm bungalow with crooked floors and somewhat rundown. But it seemed to serve its purpose because the manager and his family did live there.

The motel was a long, rectangular brick building which looked sturdy enough. Of the nine units, five had kitchens. The other four units were alright except one which had a cement shower; not too inviting. We could see that certain repairs would have to be made. But, its outstanding feature was the fantastic mountain view which was almost enough to sell the place.

The same view persisted and was even more spectacular when we stepped onto the porch of the duplex located behind and above the motel. Each unit had a substantial stone fireplace, living-dining-kitchen area, and four steps up, bedroom and bath. The building seemed to be the newest of all we had seen, probably four or five years old.

Outside, the caretaker told us that the backdrop of forest above and behind us made up the fourteen acres and completed the extent of the property. Before taking off, Joe took a series of pictures to show Lil and Effie when we returned home. At that point we were chilled to the bone and anxious to get in the camper and be on our way.

To reach home by Sunday night we had to drive all Saturday night and most of the next day. To imply that we were weary upon arrival would be an understatement, to say the least. Naturally, there were numerous questions.

"How was it?" The most important question was asked by Lil.

We all started to comment at once but Bob had the last word, for that day.

"You will like it, Mom," he stated quietly, but firmly and with conviction. That seemed to speak for all of us. After all, Lil always did want a gift shop, anyway.

Oh, yes; there was much discussion during the next few days but we all seemed to be saying that the place was what we wanted. One last meeting with all the family and that was it. I called Del Buono and told him we would take the property according to the terms Joe, Bob and I had discussed when we passed by to see him on our way back from inspecting it.

"A check will be in the mail tomorrow for the earnest money you requested." With that the deal was done and we were on our way to the Great Smoky Mountains!"

Yes, on the way...but not immediately. There were enumerable details to be put in order, especially those necessary to arrive at the point where we could go to the closing of the purchase of the property. We thought the day would never arrive; there was always something causing a delay. Then one day, toward the end of March, there was a call.

"This is Amoon," I recognized the voice of Del Buono's lawyer. "Can you be in my office on April tenth for the closing?"

The question needed no answer. It was an anti-climax because we had been biting our nails for the previous few weeks. However, there were still some important things to be done, like getting together the bulk of the down payment. Joe and Effie redeemed a Saving Bond that they had been saving for a rainy day and I arranged the balance that was required.

Outside of packing the motor home, Lil and I were ready. Since Joe and Effie both had jobs, they would come later. Bob was furthering his education at Community College and would continue that; besides minding the house. Marie, with Kailani, had returned to her nursing career in Majorca.

On the way, we picked up Mom at my sister Mary's.

I could see that Lil was getting more and more anxious as we passed Franklin and began the last few miles north.

"Are we getting close to the place?" she asked nervously.

"Just up the next mountain and around the curve." I replied, laughingly.

And, then, there it was. Being spring, the delicate new green leaves created an impressive backdrop for the contrasting colors and architecture of the restaurant and, above it and nestled a little farther back on the hill, the motel.

Lil was affected at the sight; but was really overawed when we entered the gift shop and she feasted her eyes on the hundreds of gift items displayed in the glass stands and on the shelves of the unique wooden cabinets with their little shingle roofs.

"It's wonderful," was all she could utter.

"There's plenty more stored in the basement," I disclosed, "Enough to keep you busy for months."

"It's what I've always wanted," Lil remarked as she eagerly went on inspecting the collection, item by item, holding up each and examining it as if it were a jewel.

After a tour of the buildings, we sat down in the living room of the duplex to have a glass of wine to celebrate our new adventure and to discuss plans for the operation.

"Besides handling the shop," Lil announced, "I'll be the dining room hostess and the cashier." (She liked to handle cash!).

"And I'll be the chef, besides doing the accounts." (I liked cooking and figures!). "Del Buono told me the motel manager is leaving but will stay on until we find another one. Also, there are two others available to help: Mike, an assistant chef; and Rosemary, an experienced waitress.

So, we have almost everything we need except a dishwasher and, if business builds as we expect, a second waitress."

"When shall we open?" Lil asked.

"How about Memorial Day weekend, the end of May?" I suggested. "We can start the operation off with a bang by inviting to dinner all those former and prospective clients on the list that the Del Buonos gave us."

As Lil agreed, I went on. "Macon County is dry, even in this day and age; and, though surrounding areas have voted out prohibition, it persists in forcing its people to go elsewhere, even to neighboring Georgia, for alcoholic beverages."

"What do we do?"

"Del Buono had a club license where members had lockers in which to keep their booze. The dinner party will be a good time to promote memberships. In fact, we can put in the invitations that we send out a notation that we are accepting renewals and new members."

Enthusiasm began to flow to the stage where all kinds of details were discussed including the menu. Mom said she would pitch in and make the cole slaw (her special pride and joy) and the marinated carrots.

In addition to talk, there was work to be done and plenty of it. But, by the time Saturday, May 24th arrived everything looked great. The grass had been cut. The little yellow chrysanthemums in the long stone planters on each side of the entrance, with two blooming rose bushes, set off the whole building. Inside, Lil, in her artistic fashion, had rearranged all the gifts to give a most imposing impression to all who entered. Looking over the counter into the kitchen, the pots and pans were gleaming on their racks and there was the hum of the equipment signifying that all was ready. That included the chef in white uniform and imposing *toque blanc* on his head.

The dining room, with checked tablecloths and flowers on each table (Lil's touch, again), looked imposing. But the *piece de resistance* of the entire arrangement was the long table at the end of the room near the entrance.

In the center were:

Golden Brown Roast Turkey

Clove-studded Roast Ham

Arranged on each side:

Liver Pate provided by Kay Del Buono

Grandmom's Marinated Carrots

Homemade Pickled Beets

Cole Slaw

Red Bean Salad with Onions and Sour Cream

Sliced Smoked Hot Dogs in Sour Cream

Lil's Marinated Tomatoes and Onions in Olive Oil
Stuffed Peppers
Eggplant Caviar
Vinegrette (Russian Potato Salad)
Cucumbers in Sour Cream with Dill
Sauteed Mushrooms with Marjoram in Sour Cream

The room was packed to the rafters with people from all over the area. Besides people and good food, one of the secrets of a successful dinner party is a sufficient quantity of liquid cheer. So, we made a punch in the largest container in the kitchen, a huge aluminum pot big enough for an army. We put everything in it but the kitchen sink. By the time the guests sat down for dinner, almost all of it had been consumed, thus insuring the outcome of the affair.

I contributed two main things: A huge sheet cheesecake with cream and toasted sliced almonds on top; and a short after-dinner speech to welcome all to the newest and most unique gourmet restaurant in the area.

We signed up a great number of Tiger Joe's Social Club members that evening. Tiger Joe's Gourmet Restaurant, Gift Shoppe and Motel was on its way.

Survival was the key word that summer. And survive we did. Joe and Effie came up and pitched in until October. The decision had been made to close after the change of the color of the leaves which is always a great time in the mountains. Lil and I had to leave early to head for the CAT Reunion in Santa Cruz, California. Joe and Effie would close the place and join us for the winter in the Keys after our return from the West Coast.

The Reunion was a huge success. But, first, on the way there were visits with old friends and associates: the Shrefflers in Nashville where we saw the Grand Ole Opry in full swing; the Rousselots on their Gray Oaks Ranch in Wagoner, Oklahoma (that's near Muscogee; if you don't know where that is, it's south of Tulsa); The Lewises in Pueblo, Colorado; John Fogg (CAT meteorologist) in Colorado Springs; the Fields (old Taipei friends) in Sonoma in the wine country of California and Nadia McCann (husband, John, one of the CAT Operations men) in San Francisco.

After the Reunion, our motor home took us south to Los Angeles where there were more visitations with friends. On the journey east, trouble struck as we approached Baton Rouge in Louisiana. The engine of "old faithful" heated up and then quit before I could get it off the Interstate. When the tow truck arrived at the garage, I called "Red" Probst, a Flying Tiger buddy from the same squadron I was in. In a short time we were in his apartment having a drink with him and his wife, Millie. Little did we know then that it would not be too long before he would be gone, a victim of a heart attack. After that, in her sorrow, Millie seemed to disappear and we were never able to make contact with her.

In spite of the delay, we made it home in plenty of time to prepare for the holidays starting with Thanksgiving. In the tranquility of the Keys, we had the opportunity to review the first year's operation of the North Carolina business. It had not been too bad, but not good enough.

"We will have to operate a longer season," I announced at a family gathering. "We lost some money this past year and I would like to see us in the black this coming season."

Everyone agreed. So, after a joyful and festive holiday season, we started making plans for the trip north, once again.

In the meantime, Joe laid out, for printing, a definitive menu developed during the previous year. The finished product was, I think, a masterful job. Dark brown lettering on an orange-colored paper made a pretty contrast. At the bottom, in the middle, was our logo of the Restaurant with mountains in the background. And at the top a cute little tiger cat with a chef's hat, marked "Joe," designed by Lil. To touch it off, Joe made a border of pine cones. But, of course, the most important element was the voluminous list of menu items. They will all be covered in the Recipe Part of this book.

This time, on the return journey to our second home in the mountains, we went back to Oak Grove Park on the Naval Air Station at Pensacola. We arrived with our safari; we in our motor home, Effie with her Volkswagen bus and Joe with his Granada. You may wonder why we went out of the way to visit Pensacola again. Well, first of all, Joe and Effie spent some time there as photographers in the Navy. They wanted to see the place again. But, the principal reason was that there is a seafood dealer there, Joe Patti, who has some of the best fish and shellfish on the entire Gulf Coast.

It was March, 1979, and there was still the chill of winter in the air as we went through northern Georgia and approached North Carolina. Among other things, there were two large coolers full of fresh Gulf shrimp in the bus.

Immediately upon arrival at the Restaurant, the first thing we had to do was prepare the shrimp for kitchen use. To start with, that meant grading them. The small ones were left in their shells to be packaged for serving as boiled shrimp. The jumbo size, also with shells, were for *"Gambas a la Plancha"*, Spanish for "Grilled Prawns." All the rest had to have the shells taken off, except for the tails. Placed six to the package, they would be used for: Scampi a la Tiger Joe, Fried Shrimp (done in a light batter) and Sweet n' Sour Shrimp (Chinese style). The latter was one of our specialties on the Chinese menu served on Mondays (Chinese Night) or, at other times, by special arrangement.

By the second day, our fingers were worn out and we were sick of the sight of shrimp. Effie, who had never eaten shrimp, let alone clean them, could not believe that she withstood the ordeal and actually became proficient at it. With the entire family working, we did manage to get everything done and put away by that night. Our efforts were more than rewarded during the season as we served all the shrimp to well-satisfied customers. I think that, for the next few nights, all we could dream of was shrimp.

Easter Sunday saw us putting the final touches on another opening extravaganza for Club members. It was Lil's idea to give them a Russian Easter feast. And, a feast it was! We spent several days preparing the food.

The long buffet table was, once again, pressed into service. It was burdened down with all kinds of delicacies:

Two varieties of Herring
Gefilte fish
Marinated Fish, two styles
Liver Pate' a la Tiger Joe
Eggplant Caviar
Stuffed Peppers a la Russe
Cucumbers in Sour Cream with Dill
Sliced Smoked Sausage in Sour Cream
White Bean Salad
Two kinds of Stuffed Eggs
Vinegrette (Russian Potato Salad with Beets)
Cole Slaw
Mushrooms in Sour Cream
Marinated Tomatoes and Onions
Rare Roast Beef and other various sliced meats

After all the guests in the jam-packed room had partaken of the expansive banquet, the table was cleared and the Russian *piece de resistance* was brought out and placed in the center of it.

Pasha, the creamy Russian delicacy in pyramid form
Kulich, tall cylindrical, semi-sweet, cake-like bread

The latter had been beautifully decorated by Lil in traditional Russian designs. It goes without saying that the *Pasha*, served with a slice of *Kulich*, disappeared in a matter of minutes.

Once again the gala affair had been a tremendous success which propelled us into the season with great momentum. We were then open seven days a week for breakfast, lunch and dinner. It was a hectic regimen and, towards the end of July, Joe suggested that we ought to arrange a day off. I thought that was strange for a tall, strapping young man who was always full of energy; I gave it little importance at the time.

In the meantime, a great event occurred. Effie had been heavy with child and on June 19th gave birth to a beautiful baby girl. Joe had passed around forms for a "name-the-baby contest." There was a flurry of entries but no one guessed that the name would be...what else, Effie! From then on the mother would be Eff and the little one, Effie. Her middle name was Marie after our daughter.

Needless to say, our new grandchild was the center of attraction wherever she was taken and the parents were justifiably proud.

"OK, we'll close each Tuesday for the rest of the year." I acceded to Joe's plea about a little respite. We had just passed Labor Day and things were slowing down a little.

"That's great!" Joe exclaimed. "I'm really bushed these days."

"Again that strange feeling." I thought to myself. "I wonder if he's really worn out or is he just beginning to get a little lazy?"

Soon, we went through the annual spectacular, the blazing color change of the leaves. That was during the third week of October. The last day of the month was Halloween and we had an amusing costume party in the restaurant. That led us into the holiday season; turkey dinner on Thanksgiving with all the trimmings and, of course, a festive Christmas dinner.

As if that were not enough, we planned a big blow-out to top off the year, a Happy New Year's party. My sister, Marie, and her husband, Ben (Bengt in Danish), came over from Stockholm. Sister, Eleanor and husband, Ted, arrived from Pennsylvania. Mom was with us; so, we had almost all of the family except Bob and Marie and our first grandchild, Kailani. The ladies made funny hats and the men all pitched in to decorate the restaurant.

We really rang in the New Year with plenty of good food, noisemakers, and a couple of cases of champagne which flowed freely all night. Then, early in the morning, I whipped up scrambled eggs with succulent Gulf shrimp to steady the minds of those who had to go on the road home. Upon departure, they were of one voice.

"Franklin has never seen such a fabulous gay affair as this on New Year's Eve."

"Happy New Year!" echoed through the mountains as each one departed for home.

Two days later, we all loaded into the motor home and headed south with our human cargo of eight souls. The bulging walls of the little old farm bungalow, which had served such a large gang of people during those few days, heaved a sigh of relief as it felt itself completely empty.

First stop; Satellite Beach and the Earharts, Eff's parents. They had prepared a christening for little Effie.

Effie's father, Bud, who was a deacon in the Church, got up and introduced us all to the congregation, including, "...Marie and Ben Jensen from Stockholm and Great Grandmother, Mae, originally from Delaware City, Delaware." Mom really felt good about that.

When Joe took little·Effie up to the altar to be christened, out from under her pretty little dress, especially made for the occasion, came two little feet clad in a pair of old dull-gray woolen socks. Those looking on could hardly suppress a giggle. To this day, Effie has those socks and we all laugh everytime the incident comes up.

The minister gave a very nice sermon, most fitting for the christening.

"We have to be very grateful," he ended, "that little Effie is surrounded by so many great family members who can watch over and look after her during her growing years."

Little did he know how prophetic that would be!

Joe, Eff and the little one headed back to Franklin to "watch the store." The rest of our family group continued on south to Cudjoe Key.

That was our last trip to the Keys. Our house had been sold. We had decided that the trip each winter was getting too much for us; so, we started packing. The amount of stuff that we amassed was just unbelievable considering that we had arrived in the States eight years before with only three suitcases!

Lil and I managed to get the motel and restaurant in shape to open for the season. Joe felt very bad that he could not pitch in and help because of the weak state of his health which had manifested itself at that time. He stayed home and took care of the little one while Eff went to work. He seemed to have some concern about going to the doctor because of the lack of medical insurance coverage.

He finally agreed to go for an examination and some tests after Eff had completed ninety days of employment, the time required to put the medical coverage into effect. He was given, literally, dozens upon dozens of tests. Not being able to find anything of significance, the doctor sent him to Emory University Hospital in Atlanta. Then the tests were expanded to include X-rays, CAT-Scans and God knows what else. The upshot of all that was the diagnosis that he had a cirrhotic liver. The treatment prescribed was of no help.

It was the middle of June and we were visiting Joe in the duplex. He was as white as a sheet and feeling considerable pain.

"We had better get you to the hospital." I advised.

"Alright." He murmured, agreeing reluctantly.

Two nights later, on the 21st, having arrived home from a visit to the hospital, Lil began to cry.

"What's the matter?" I tried to console her.

"Joe is going to die!" She exclaimed.

"Now, come on. He's going to be alright." I held her in my arms and tried to comfort her.

"No, it's true, the doctor told me." She sobbed.

"What do you mean?" I demanded; I was shocked.

"When I was out in the hall, I stopped him and asked what was going on. He told me then that whatever condition he has could cause him to bleed to death internally."

"I can hardly believe that." I went immediately to the phone.

"Hello. Dr. Johns?"

"Yes."

"This is Mr. Rosbert." I said rather brusquely. "My wife tells me that you told her tonight that our son could die, bleed to death, from his condition. Is that right?"

"Yes." I could hardly believe my ears. "We don't know for sure, of course, but those are the chances."

"This is unbelievable." I shouted, hanging up the phone, angrily. "Why couldn't he have gotten us together and given us the straight dope? All along they haven't known what's wrong with Joe but now they can say that he might die!"

I called our dear friend Sue Hacker (formerly Buol) in Honolulu and explained the situation asking her if the Clinic in Mexico where she was cured of "incurable" breast cancer might be able to help.

"Yes." She said confidently. "Besides cancer, the treatment is especially effective for liver ailments."

"Well, they have just about thrown their hands up here; so, short of any objection from Effie, I think we'll take him there."

"Alright. I'll call Charlotte and ask her to make the necessary arrangements. She is the daughter of Max Gerson, the medical doctor who set up the Clinic."

It was Dr. Gerson, a German, who successfully treated cancer, liver diseases and arthritis with diet, and little medicine, in Europe. Although he obtained a license to practice medicine in the States, he was precluded from using his method because the medical profession recognized only the traditional one for treating cancer; basically, chemotherapy and radiology. At least, that is, up until the early 1980's when the medical profession and the National Cancer Institute began acceding to the fact that diet does play a big part in the cancer picture. Even Vitamin C was being recognized as playing a part. Remember Linus Pauling? He was pooh-poohed as some kind of nut for his studies on the effectiveness of that vitamin. Now, the medical profession acts as if it has made some kind of a great discovery; Vitamin C does have a role!

Eff was all for the idea of the Clinic. A plane was chartered for the first leg of the journey, Franklin to Atlanta. The restaurant was closed. Lil said she would get the help of a maid and run the motel.

We got Joe out of the hospital the next day at one PM. It was Monday, June 23rd. About half an hour later we were in the air and after another 45 minutes landed in Atlanta. After a five-hour flight, we were met at San Diego by a young man driving a motor home. Joe stretched out on one of the beds and at eight PM that night we drove through the Spanish style entrance to the Clinic. Our double room with bath was near the end of a long, wide, covered porch. The medical staff gave Joe a physical examination; I noted that he weighed 203 pounds.

A very healthful dinner was served in the room: freshly squeezed carrot juice, vegetable soup, vegetable plate with tomato, green beans and baked potato; then, fresh fruit.

After calling home and Sue in Honolulu, off to sleep we went for a much needed rest. In the morning, no water, but herb tea was the drink and would be all day long. A lady-doctor appeared and she explained the treatment. Except for a daily Vitamin B-12 shot, Potassium and Vitamin C, there were only vegetables with lots of carrot juice (Note that today there is a big hullabaloo about Beta Carotene in the cancer picture!)

All went well for five days. Charlotte had been there with the American medical doctor in charge and they were both pleased with Joe's progress. But then disaster struck. During the early morning hours I was awakened by Joe moaning with pain. He was feeling very bad. I called the doctor on duty and, after a quick check, he said that Joe was bleeding again. It was the type of difficulty that the Clinic was not setup to handle; especially, they could not do major operations. There was nothing to do but get an ambulance to take him to a hospital, not too distant, between the border and San Diego.

At the Paradise Valley Hospital the doctors diagnosed the bleeding as an enlarged liver pressing on blood vessels in the area. They recommended Dr. Orloff, a surgeon at the University Hospital in San Diego. Joe was flown there in a helicopter. I took a taxi and arrived in time to see it land!

Since Joe had had eleven pints of blood in Paradise Valley Hospital and already two in the emergency room, the doctors wanted to arrange an immediate operation.

"If it won't jeopardize his situation," I offered, "can we wait until morning to confer with Dr. Orloff?"

After much consultation they agreed to delay until morning, all the while watching him carefully in intensive care.

It was after midnight when I arrived at the motel. My attempt at sleeping was less than successful. Upon arising, I immediately went to the hospital. There was a long wait before Dr. Orloff appeared. He explained a bypass operation which would eliminate the bleeding problem. That sounded good to Joe and me. The doctor would observe him for a day or two to be sure that the operation was necessary.

"In the meantime," he remarked, "the scans and other tests indicate some kind of an infection on the liver. When and if we operate, we should learn more about this.'

Joe seemed to be doing well all that day. So, I did get some sleep that night. I was ready to go to the hospital before eight AM; but, for some reason decided to call first. Joe had started bleeding again and they were giving him blood. Rushing to the Hospital, I found Dr. Orloff was just finishing an operation and had cancelled all others that day to operate on Joe.

At 10:30 I was called to the second floor where the operating rooms were located but it was not until 3:30 in the afternoon that the doctor called me. The operation itself had gone well and Joe had already been in the recuperating room for over an hour. I got to see him briefly, after which I was informed that the doctor would see me in intensive care later that afternoon.

At 5:30 he appeared leading his entourage of about six other doctors. Outside the room the terrible blow struck.

"A hepatome was found on Joe's liver." He announced very quietly. "Now, the test on the frozen section, although it shows a malignancy, is not thoroughly accurate."

I was completely crushed. "That's small consolation, I guess." I could scarcely get the words out.

"No, we'll hold final judgment for 48 hours until the definitive tests are completed."

I called Lil and Eff and tried to soften the blow by telling them the doctor's expectations. But I told Eff I would immediately arrange an airline ticket for her to come out; Joe was asking for her. When I called Mom, she was visiting her sister, my Aunt Anna. She gave me the phone number of my cousin, Arlene, who lived a short way out of town in La

RECIPES

"Worth their weight in gold." That's what the French say about truffles, the fragrant underground fungus prized worldwide for its delicate flavor, especially famous in Strasbourg goose liver pate. These days, truffles sell for many times the price of gold. Therefore, my *Poulet a la Truffe* has been replaced by this recipe using ginger instead of truffles.

Inspiration for this dish came one day when we received a package containing several fresh ginger roots and a jar of pickled ginger. It was from our dear friend, Etta Cummings (nee Bowen), who was in the CAT executive offices, first in Shanghai, then in Hong Kong. Now married to her girlhood friend, Gene, who was a doctor-teacher at the University of Florida. A friend in the Department of Agriculture sent them the original ginger root and they have been growing it and sending their surplus to appreciative friends. Now, let's try this succulent chicken.

TIGER JOE'S ORIENTAL ROAST CHICKEN

Start heating oven to 400 degrees.

Use quartered chicken, one piece per person plus an extra bonus piece, the usual Chinese custom. Ginger is commonly pickled in thin slices (see Page 227).Lift the skin of the chicken and slide in two slices per quarter piece; pat the skin back in place. Use a roasting pan large enough to hold the pieces, skin side up, in one layer. Grease it with oil.

Slice two onions, spread evenly in the pan. Sprinkle one tsp each of tarragon and salt on the underside of the chicken and place on top of the onions.

Prepare marinade:

1 tbsp each of honey, soy sauce, lemon juice, oriental sesame oil

1 tsp each of liquid smoke and Chinese mustard (can use 1 tsp dried dissolved in 1 tsp water)

Brush on the skin side of the chicken; then sprinkle with 1 tsp each of tarragon and salt. Pour one cup white wine into the pan. Place in the preheated oven and immediately turn it down to 325 degrees. After ½ hour, brush with marinade and add more wine to prevent burning of the onions. Repeat after one hour. After 1¼ to 1½ hours, turn off oven and leave another 15 minutes. The Chinese like their chicken moist; we would call it underdone. If you like your chicken dry (well done), use the longer time.

Remove the chicken to a hot platter. Add one cup of chicken stock to the pan. Heat while scraping and mixing. Stir in one tbsp sherry and strain through a sieve. For a thicker sauce add slowly, while stirring and

315

heating, one tbsp cornstarch dissolved in 3 tbsp water. Add only enough to obtain the desired consistency; serve on the side. Serve with rice and Chinese-style vegetables (see recipe, Page 210).

TIGER JOE'S SWEET & SOUR MEATBALLS

The Chinese make all kinds of mixtures of ground meat for meatballs, fillings for steamed dumplings and for *chiao tze*. The following recipe was developed for use in Tiger Joe's Gourmet Restaurant.

Use ½ pound ground beef with ½ pound ground pork.

Mix with:

1 egg
2 tbsp soy sauce
1 tbsp sesame oil
2 tbsp chopped bamboo shoot
1 tsp *cilantro* (Chinese parsley)
2 tbsp chopped green onion
1 tbsp chopped ginger
1 clove garlic, chopped
1 tbsp sugar
About 3 to 4 tbsp water to make a soft mixture

Form into balls about 1½ to 2 inches in diameter and flatten slightly. Roll in flour and fry on both sides in about ¼ inch oil. Keep warm in the oven while making the sauce.

In 1 tbsp oil, stir fry:

1 cut up green pepper
1 green onion, cut in one-inch pieces
¼ cup sliced bamboo shoot
1 tbsp ginger, slivered (julienne)

Add one cup chicken stock, cover and steam for a few minutes until the vegetables are barely tender. Stir in cornstarch in water until slightly thickened. Add 2 tbsp each sugar, vinegar and catsup. Pour over meatballs.

Making good bread consistently is an art which takes constant practice. If you lay off, even for a few months, you will have to get back into the swing of it. Try practicing the following recipe. It is for a rye bread but you can use all white flour for a French-type bread.

TIGER JOE'S RYE BREAD

For good old-fashioned bread, a sourdough starter, although not essential, should be used for texture and unusual taste. Instead of throwing it away, save 2 cups of the water from cooking potatoes. Stir in 2 cups of flour, 1 tsp sugar and 1 tbsp dried yeast which has been dissolved in ⅓ cup warm water. Leave this covered for at least 24 hours; the longer, the more sour. Then store in the refrigerator. Always use half when baking and restore by adding one cup water, one cup flour and ½ tsp sugar.

Using an extra large stainless steel bowl for mixing and kneading eliminates the use of a board. Put in the bowl:

2 cups rye flour
2 cups unbleached white flour
4tbsp oil
1 tbsp salt
2 tbsp sugar
3 tbsp dried yeast dissolved in ⅔ cup warm water and 1 tsp sugar
2 cups warm water
½ of the starter
2 tbsp caraway seeds
1tsp anise seed

Mix at medium speed for at least 5 minutes. Gradually add more unbleached white flour until too thick for the mixer. Continue to add flour while kneading until the dough is pliable and no longer sticky. This will require 2 to 3 cups more of flour. Knead for 10 to 15 minutes more until the dough is springy. Remove from the bowl.

Put one tbsp oil in the bowl. Roll the dough in the oil until covered on all sides. Cover and let rise in a warm place until double in bulk, about 1½ hours. Punch down squeezing out the air. This recipe is sufficient for two regular size loaves plus about six rolls or bread sticks; so, cut off a piece large enough for the rolls (can be kept in the refrigerator in a plastic bag for about a week). Form the main piece of dough into two loaves. Grease two bread pans and sprinkle with corn meal (can use corn bread mix). Let rise, covered, until double in bulk, about one hour. Bake at 450 degrees for 20 to 25 minutes, then at 350 degrees for the same time. The time is approximate and depends upon your individual oven. Turn off the oven and leave the door ajar for 30 minutes. Remove the loaves from the pans and let cool; uncovered if you want a crisp crust, covered if you desire it soft. For a darker crust, brush with egg wash before baking.

While still warm, cut a couple of slices with a serrated knife and smother them with butter. This is the test to see if your procedure was correct and the timing in the oven was just right. If you were lucky and all was perfect, remember what you did and follow it exactly the next time. Or, make whatever corrections are necessary. You've got it made when each time you say, "That was the best one I ever made!"

To make the rolls, cut the piece of dough that was saved into 6 equal portions. Roll into balls and flatten. Let rise, covered, on a baking sheet on which corn meal was sprinkled, about ¾ hour. Bake at 450 degrees for about 20 minutes. At the end, I always brown the tops under the broiler. The procedure is the same for bread sticks except that after forming the sticks, roll them in salt and caraway seeds before letting them rise.

ENGLISH MUFFINS

To make your own use the above dough recipe or one made of all white flour. Form into balls as for rolls. Flatten and, with your fingers, make the sides vertical. Cook, one at a time, in a small frying pan sprinkled with corn meal, on low heat. Place a small pie pan on top with a weight. This keeps the muffin flat and from rising beyond the thickness desired. Especially the first time, check the cooking of each side to avoid burning. Split wih a fork and, if you like, brown under the grill.

THE REUBEN

Tiger Joe's Restaurant served all kinds of sandwiches for lunch including two sizes and five varieties of Hoagies (see Part I, page 23 for background and recipes) but the most famous was the Reuben. Here's how we did it.

Take 2 slices of Jewish sour rye bread (recipe on page 316).If not available, use any kind of rye.

Slice cooked cornbeef (or, better still, pastrami) very thin and place on one slice.

Place 2 slices of Swiss cheese on the other slice.

On the cornbeef, spread enough sauerkraut to cover

On the sauerkraut, sprinkle 1 tsp Russian Dressing

Turn the cheese-covered slice over on top of the other

If a sandwich grill is being used, butter both sides and grill until golden brown.

If you do not have a grill, use a frying pan. Butter one side and brown in the pan, covered. Butter the top, turn over and brown, covered.

Cut the sandwich in half and garnish with a wedge or two of pickle. In the Restaurant, we standardized on Clausen Kosher Dills; sometimes we made our own when fresh dill was available. Don't forget the mustard and the horseradish.

The secret ingredient is the sauerkraut. Most restaurants just use it out of the can. Horrors! We spent some time and prepared it this way. Empty the can or package of sauerkraut into a colander and rinse under cold water. In a frying pan, saute one sliced onion until translucent. Add the sauerkraut and cook for 30 minutes on LOW HEAT, stirring occasionally to prevent burning. During the cooking add: half cup white wine, 1 tbsp sugar, couple of shakes of celery salt, quarter tsp white pepper, 1 tbsp caraway seeds and, if desired, a shake of garlic powder. Use this recipe wherever sauerkraut is called for, especially to garnish German sausages, pork chops and other such goodies.

Now, we have an old cooking-and-eating buddy from CAT who sent us the ultimate recipe for a genuine HOMEMADE Reuben; that means everything from scratch except, of course, the Swiss cheese. For his explanation and recipes, see Part 4, Page 256.

During the periods that we were serving breakfast, the most sought after, and most requested, item was Tiger Joe's Eggs Benedict. Our menu portion was two poached eggs, each on its own toasted half of English muffin; but you may want to do just one per person. Use a slice of ham and one of Swiss cheese per muffin. Have all prepared and at hand to put the dish together quickly. Make a Bechamel (white) Sauce by melting 1 tbsp butter or margarine, stir in 1 tbsp flour until the mixture is uniform and bubbles. Add half cup of milk and stir rapidly until well mixed and thickened. Add a dash of ground nutmeg, white pepper and salt, to taste. A tsp of sherry adds a desirable touch. Warm the ham in a pan and on top of each slice melt a slice of cheese. At the same time, have the toasted muffins hot. Place in the bottom of a serving dish, cover with the ham and cheese, carefully place a poached egg on top and cover with the sauce. Serve immediately with a sprinkle of grated Swiss cheese on top. Enjoy! For Sunday brunch, champagne goes very well with this dish.

For lunch, our salads; Tuna, Salmon and Egg were pretty much standardized but always made from fresh ingredients; chopped onions, celery and parsley bound together with mayonaise, a little lemon juice, white pepper and celery salt. But the Chicken Salad had an added ingredient, a little chopped pineapple. The diner usually did not know what it was but found the salad a little different than that dispensed in other places.

Tiger Joe's Pizza was a worthy effort to duplicate the pizzas I knew in South Philadelphia in the thirties. Use any recipe for yeast bread dough; or, even use the recipe for Tiger Joe's Rye Bread (Page 316 of this Part). After the dough has risen and been punched down, spread a sufficient portion in the bottom of the pizza pan. If you do not have a round one, use a shallow, rectangular cookie pan. The canned pizza sauce of today is alright, but I prefer one made from fresh tomatoes, or canned ones, cooked with chopped onions and green peppers. Then do your own concoction. Remember, this is supposed to be one of your adventures in cooking; no exact recipe is given, only ideas. When all is ready be sure you add two things; crushed oregano leaves and a sprinkle all over of olive oil. The oven must be very hot, about 450 to 500. For that reason, the pizza will be bubbling and the dough rim will be a nice brown, in about ten to twelve minutes.

The recipes and instructions, so far in this Part, have only been to whet your imagination. Now, we get into the Dinner Menu. All of the main items, except the spaghetti sauce, were prepared only at the time the order was given to the kitchen by the waitress. And we never put the food, once it had been prepared, under a warming light. In fact, we put away the one left by the previous owner. The food was always taken to the dining room and served immediately. Many of the recipes used in the restaurant, mainly Russian and Chinese, are in Part IV.

Now, for the recipes.

TROUT

Two kinds of trout abound in the streams and lakes of the mountains of western North Carolina. The most prevalent is the common brook trout, also known as the speckled trout. It is the closest species to the brown trout of Europe. The other is the rainbow trout which really is a native of the mountainous areas of the west. It has been introduced, not only in the east, but also in other parts of the world. There are hatcheries all over The Great Smokies region that stock every conceivable fishing area and small trout farms. The latter supply the restaurants, netting the fish when they are about twelve ounces to one pound. These trouts are not to be confused with ocean trout which come from the sea and are much larger in size.

TIGER JOE'S TROUT AMANDINE

Both kinds of trout mentioned above have very small scales. These cook as part of the skin and, therefore, do not have to be removed. Leave the head and tail on but gut the fish with an incision in the forward half of the belly. Rinse under cold water. Cut three or four diagonal slits almost to the center bone, both sides of the fish. Salt and pepper inside and out.

Prepare a Bechamel Sauce with 1 tbsp each of flour and butter. When these are mixed and bubbling in a sauce pan, add one half cup of milk and stir briskly until mixed and thickened. Add: a dash of nutmeg and white pepper, salt to taste, 1 tbsp sherry and 1 tbsp toasted chopped almonds (make 2 tbsp and keep one to sprinkle on top of the finished dish).

Have a frying pan hot on high heat with a tbsp each of oil and butter. Roll the fish in flour and shake off the excess. Never do this ahead of time, but just before cooking. Place in the pan and partially cover, using an aluminum pie pan or foil. As soon as the fish begins to fry, turn the heat down to medium. When nicely browned (Only takes about three or four minutes), carefully turn on the other side. With the slits in the fish, it should be done when the outside has browned. However, it is best to check by opening one of the deepest slits with a fork. The flesh should have just reached the opaque stage; DO NOT OVERCOOK. If not, turn to low heat and cook, covered, another minute or two. Place on a warm plate, cover with the sauce and a sprinkling of the reserved almonds. Peas and boiled potatoes with chopped parsley complete the dish.
NOTE: If a long oval-shaped frying pan is not available to hold the fish, cut it in two halves to fry. When finished, place the two pieces together on the serving plate; the sauce will cover up the incision!

LASAGNA

Before putting together Lasagna, you will need Spaghetti Sauce. You can make your own, buy it in a jar or use the following recipe.

TIGER JOE'S SPAGHETTI SAUCE

Saute 1 chopped onion and 1 green pepper in oil until limp. Add ground meat and brown.

Add: 1 minced garlic clove, half can (small) tomato paste, 1 can tomato sauce, 1 can tomatoes (chopped), 1 tbsp each of Basil, Oregano, black Pepper and sugar. Simmer on the lowest heat for one hour. We kept our sauce all season! You have to boil it every few days being very careful not to burn it. We added to it whenever necessary to fill the pot.

Now, the Lasagna.

Four kinds of cheese are needed for a good Lasagna: Ricotta, Mozzarella, Provolone and Parmesan (for the top). We used the Provolone to make the dish distinctive, but you can do without it.

Cut the Mozzarella and Provolone into small dice, mix with the Ricotta, about equal quantities of all three. If the Ricotta container has half pound, then, that determines the amount of the other two. Add: 1 egg, 3 tbsp chopped parsley, 1 clove garlic (minced), dash of white pepper and nutmeg. Mix and set aside while the noodles are cooking. Lasagna noodles are wide and long with krinkles down each side. Put a tbsp of oil in the water to keep them from sticking. Boil until almost done, about ten to twelve minutes. When draining, leave sufficient water to cover. This will facilitate handling.

If possible, choose a baking dish that has one dimension equal to the length of the noodles. That will avoid the necessity of cutting them. Spray the dish or coat with oil. Cover the bottom with Spaghetti Sauce. Arrange the noodles side-by-side to cover the sauce. Distribute half of the cheese mixture on the noodles, cover with Spaghetti Sauce, another layer of cheese mix, Spaghetti Sauce, final layer of noodles, Spaghetti Sauce and a generous sprinkling of Parmesan cheese. All of this can be done ahead of time, even a day or two.

About an hour before serving time, heat the oven to 350. Sprinkle the top of the dish with Oregano leaves and olive oil. Cover with foil and bake 45 minutes. Just before serving, you can remove the foil and brown the top, lightly, under the broiler. Serve with garlic bread and a tossed green salad. A glass of red wine goes beautifully with this dish. After freezing, it is just as good, if not better.

TIGER JOE'S SAUSAGE AND PEPPERS

With the Lasagna, we garnished the dish with two pieces of our home-made Italian sausage. For those who were limiting their caloric intake, there was Sausage and Peppers, baked in the oven and presented in the same dish. We tell you how to make the sausage itself in the section on sausage-making in this Part on Page 330 . The dish itself is very simple and quick to make.

While the sausage is browning in the pan, boil a green pepper cut up into bite-size pieces with a pinch of sugar and salt. Drain. Cut the sausage lengthwise and then into one-inch pieces. Coat the bottom of the baking dish with Spaghetti Sauce and one layer of sausage and peppers, cover with Sauce. Sprinkle with Parmesan cheese, Oregano leaves and olive oil. Bake until bubbling, about 15 minutes. Serve in the same individual baking dish with spaghetti and sauce on the side, garlic bread and salad

TIGER JOE'S *SCAMPI*

Since *Scampi* is the Italian word for shrimp (or prawns, if you like) it is superfluous to include the word "Shrimp." However, we did, as do most restaurants, because it helps those patrons who are not quite certain what "Scampi" means.

Use six large shrimp per person. Remove the shells except for the tails. Cut a slit down the back, half way into the shrimp. Rinse under cold water and drain.

Mix together: 1 tbsp chopped parsley, 1 clove minced garlic, grated rind from half a lemon, pinch of sugar and a pinch of Italian Seasoning. Reserve the juice from the half lemon.

In a frying pan over high heat, melt 1 tbsp butter with 1 tbsp oil until the bubbles disappear. Saute the shrimp, stirring constantly until they just change color, a matter of only 2 or 3 minutes. Add the seasoning mixture, the lemon juice, a tbsp of Vermouth or Sherry and toss only enough to coat the shrimp. Serve immediately, pouring the pan juices over the top. In addition to a salad, you can serve a side portion of spaghetti or noodles with a butter sauce a la Alfredo; that is, melted butter with minced garlic and parsley. Toss the mixture with the pasta and, towards the end, Parmesan cheese. With garlic bread and a glass of chilled white wine (or rose, if you prefer): *Mama Mia!*

TIGER JOE'S SHRIMP TEMPURA

Use six large shrimp per person. Remove the shells except for the tails. Cut a slit down the back about halfway through, rinse under cold water and drain.

Make the coating by mixing: 1 cup self-rising flour, 2 tbsp cornstarch, 1 egg, enough milk (2 tbsp or more) to wet the mixture and sufficient beer to get the consistency desired. Some like a thin batter, others a thick one. If you are aiming for a Tempura-like result, use a thin one.

Make a sweet and sour sauce (this part Page 329) or an apricot sauce as follows: mash the apricots from a small can, mix with 1 tsp chopped ginger, 1 tsp sugar, 1 tbsp sherry. Mix apricot juice with 1 tsp cornstarch and stir over medium heat until thickened. Mix all together.

Have a deep fryer (or other suitable vessel) with the oil hot, 375 degrees. Holding the shrimp by the tails, run them through the batter, letting the excess drain off, and drop them in the oil. Move them around to prevent sticking together. As soon as they change color, about 30 seconds to one minute, remove and drain on a paper towel. Serve with either sauce over or on the side. Prepared this way, they also make up the Chinese dish, Sweet and Sour Shrimp.

SEA SCALLOPS

Rinse the scallops under cold water; sometimes they have sand. One pound should be sufficient for about four persons. Shake them in a bag, about six at a time, with some cornstarch and a tsp of salt. Then dip in an egg which has been beaten with 2 tbsp of milk. Shake in a bag, this time with bread crumbs. At this point, they can be placed in one layer on a shallow pan and frozen; and, later stored in bags. Or, whenever all is ready for dinner, drop them in the deep fryer, oil at 375 degrees, for about two minutes, or for three minutes if frozen. Test one for doneness; they should be opaque, not translucent, and tender. Serve with tartar sauce; or, for that Oriental touch, with sweet and sour sauce.

The classic, French way of doing scallops is in the style, *Coquilles Saint Jacques. Coquille* means shell and refers to the scallop and also to the scallop shell, itself, in which the dish is presented. If you do not have such shells, use individual baking dishes. In the first step, prepare Bechamel Sauce (Page 319 this Part); and, when it is bubbling add about 4 tbsp grated Swiss cheese and 1 tbsp sherry. Shake the scallops with flour and 1 tsp of salt. Saute them in 1 tbsp each of oil and butter over high heat until lightly browned but not cooked through; takes about one or two minutes. Cover the bottom of the individual serving shells, or dishes, with some of the sauce, 4 or 5 scallops and apportion the remainder of the sauce on top. Sprinkle with Parmesan cheese, a little oil or a few dots of butter and place under the broiler, but in the middle of the oven. All is ready when the tops are a golden brown. With a chilled white wine: *Que Magnifique!*

NOTE: Sauteed sliced mushrooms and a few peeled shrimp go well in the sauce.

TIGER JOE'S VEAL *SCALOPPINE*

The scallops of veal employed in the Restaurant for all veal dishes were individually wrapped 4-ounce slices from a meat-packing company in Philadelphia. This was not only convenient but also insured a standard portion everytime. The slices should be about one quarter inch thick and flattened with a cleaver. Dust with flour seasoned with salt and pepper. Brown on each side in the frying pan (once again, half oil and half butter). At the point of turning over to brown the second side, add 3 or 4 mushrooms, sliced or cut up in pieces. When the meat is done (takes not more than about three minutes), sprinkle with a pinch of Italian seasoning and 1 tbsp white vermouth. On the serving dish, pour the pan juices over the meat, add chopped parsley. Fresh green broccoli makes a good accompaniment as does a side dish of spaghetti with a white cream sauce or a la Alfredo (butter, garlic, parsley and Parmesan cheese). With a chilled glass of Rose: *Che Exquisito!*

TIGER JOE'S VEAL *PARMIGIANA*

This time the veal slices are pounded with a kitchen mallet until almost twice their size, dipped in beaten egg to which 2 tbsp of milk have been added, then in Italian-seasoned bread crumbs. Pat each side to make the crumbs adhere better. Saute in the usual butter and oil over high heat until golden brown on each side; takes not more than two minutes. When doing breaded meat like this, lift it up with the spatula every now and then to allow the hot oil to run underneath. Place on an oven-proof plate, top with Spaghetti Sauce, 3 strips of Provolone or Mozzarella cheese, a sprinkle of Parmesan and brown under the broiler. Serve with a vegetable and a portion of pasta with Spaghetti Sauce.

TIGER JOE'S *WIENER SCHNITZEL*

Prepare the veal slices exactly as for Veal Parmigiana up to the point of completion of the frying of the breaded meat. Serve, topped with a Bechamel Sauce (recipe page 319 to which has been added sauteed mushroom slices and a tbsp of sour cream. Goes well with Tiger Joe's Sauerkraut (Page 318 this Part), apple sauce and Parsleyed boiled potatoes, mashed potatoes, or hot German Potato Salad. The latter is prepared from the Potato Salad recipe on Page 327 of this Part, adding crumbled bacon and some of the bacon drippings; serve hot. Of course, you need some of Tiger Joe's rye bread (Page 316 this Part) and a chilled mug of beer. Sehr Gut!

NOTE: In place of the very expensive veal in all of the foregoing meat dishes, try thinly sliced beefsteak; or, better still, sliced pork loin, taken off the bone. You will find the latter very tender, especially after it has been pounded.

DESSERTS

Besides the usual sweets; such as, pies, cakes, ice creams, etc., there were three specialties. Here are the recipes.

TIGER JOE'S CHEESECAKE

Cheesecake-making is an old European custom. The Italian version is made with Ricotta chese; Russian, with cottage cheese; and others with various mixtures of cheeses. The highly touted "Lindy Cheesecake" uses only cream cheese. Ours has a mixture of cream and cottage cheeses.

First, prepare the pan. A cheesecake pan which is about 3 inches high, or a tube cake pan can be used. Mix with a fork: one and a quarter cups Graham Cracker crumbs, quarter cup sugar, half tsp ground cinnamon, half stick melted butter. Press three quarters of the mixture in the bottom of the pan and refrigerate.

Set out one and a half pounds of cream cheese to soften and two cups of cottage cheese to drain in a sieve.

Place in a blender or food processor: one and one quarter cups sugar, a lemon wedge and an orange wedge both roughly chopped. Add 2 tbsp milk and blend again for a few seconds.

Place the sugar mixture in a large bowl with the cheeses. Add 2 tbsp flour, 1 tsp vanilla, quarter tsp ground nutmeg, 4 eggs and 3 egg yolks. Blend in processor or blender until all the cottage cheese curds have broken down and the mixture is smooth.

Pour mixture in prepared pan. Sprinkle the remaining crumb mix over the top, placing the majority of it near the outer edge. Place on a shallow pan in a pre-heatad oven, 425 degrees for 12 minutes, without opening the oven, reset temperature to 275 degrees; bake for 45 minutes more. Turn off oven and leave door closed for at least an hour. Partially open the door and leave overnight, then refrigerate. When completely chilled, can be topped with cherry or strawberry pie filling. Another good topping is pineapple with a little of its own juice thickened with cornstarch. In any case, many purists want the cheesecake with no topping.

NOTE: For variations; try Ricotta cheese in place of the cottage cheese and add a tbsp or two of Amaretto to the entire cheese mixture. Put one tsp anise seeds in the crumb mixture. With toasted, sliced almonds on top of the finished product, you have a cheesecake with a genuine Italian flavor.

TIGER JOE'S WALNUT RUM CAKE

For presentation, the Bundt-type cake pan is the best for this recipe. It must be well greased so that the cake will come out easily when it is done. For a nice decorative effect, place candied cherry halves and pieces of pineapple in the bottom of the pan. Use the crumb mix as for Cheesecake, add half cup of chopped walnuts. Press in the bottom and up the sides of the pan; refrigerate.

Use your own yellow cake recipe or a box of cake mix. Add half cup of chopped walnuts and follow the instructions for the mix. Sprinkle rum on the crumbs in the refrigerated cake pan, pour in the batter and bake at 375 degrees for 30 to 35 minutes. When cool, turn over onto a serving dish. At the time of cutting the cake, sprinkle each slice with rum and cover with the rum sauce.

RUM SAUCE

Mix together: 2 cups water, 2 tbsp cornstarch, 1 cup sugar and 1 tbsp honey. Bring to a boil while stirring until thickened and the sugar has completely dissolved. Remove from the heat and add: 1 tbsp rum, 1 tsp vanilla, quarter tsp each ground nutmeg and powdered ginger.

SHANGHAI LIL'S PARFAIT

Lil always had great fun putting together parfaits with their various multi-colored layers. A parfait glass gives the best effect because of its height. But any tall glass is satisfactory. Use vanilla custard, strawberry or blueberry jam and ice cream in layers topped off with whipped cream, chopped nuts and a cherry.

MISCELLANEOUS RECIPES FROM TIGER JOE'S

COLE SLAW

Shred one head of cabbage, one carrot and one green pepper. Mix equal amounts of sugar and vinegar sufficient to moisten the vegetables. Add one half to one tsp of mustard (quantity depends upon taste and the amount of vegetables). Season with celery salt and white pepper to taste. This mixture will keep well in the refrigerator. When ready to serve, take out the amount needed; add a few drops of oil and enough mayonnaise to coat the slaw. Serve with a dash of paprika on top. A variation is to mix in celery seed.

POTATO SALAD

Boil potatoes with the skins on. Drain, let cool, peel and cut into cubes. If you use five large potatoes, add the following: 1 tbsp chopped parsley, 2 tbsp each of onion and celery, 1 tsp sugar, 1 tsp mustard, juice from a quarter wedge of lemon, celery salt and white pepper to taste.

Mix sufficient mayonnaise to coat the potatoes, about 2 tbsp. Sprinkle paprika on each serving.

It is noted that, in another Part of the Book, this recipe is employed for hot German potato salad by adding crumbled bacon and a little of the bacon drippings. The salad is warmed before serving.

TIGER JOE'S BLUE CHEESE SALAD DRESSING

Mix the following: 1 cup mayonnaise, 1 cup sour cream, a little mustard to taste, 2 tsp sugar, 2 tsp vinegar or lemon juice, 1 tbsp of oil, celery salt and white pepper to taste and a dash of garlic powder. Then fold in half cup Blue Cheese crumbles. Refrigerate.

JUMBO GOURMET HOT DOG

This grilled, quarter-pound, fat, smoked hot dog was a very popular item, served in two ways. In each case it was slashed on both sides at about one inch intervals, before placing on the grill. One of the ways was on a hoagie roll with a choice of one or all of the following: mustard, chili, sauerkraut, onions or relish. The other way was with honey baked beans in a boater, the hot dog in the center.

HONEY BAKED BEANS

For each serving: heat an 8-ounce portion of Pork n' Beans in a frying pan. Add 1 tsp bacon crumbles, 1 tsp minced onion, dash of Worcestershire sauce, 1 tsp brown sugar, 1 tsp honey and a few drops of vinegar. When the mixture is bubbling, pour in the boater and place the grilled hot dog down the center. As an added touch, sprinkle grated cheese on top.

TIGER JOE'S GIANT HAMBURGER

The pattie used in the Restaurant was one-third pound or 5.3 ounces. Two pounds of ground chuck will produce more than six hamburgers because of the added ingredients. Mix the meat with: 3 tbsp oil, 1 tbsp water, 1 tbsp sauteed minced onion, 1 tsp sugar, 1 tsp soy sauce, 1 tsp salt, 1 tsp celery salt and half tsp black pepper. Form into patties and freeze. That way they are much easier to handle on the grill. From the frozen state, paint each side of the pattie with Bar-B-Q Sauce. When one side is done, turn and place another coat of the Sauce. Add whatever accompaniments are desired; thinly sliced onion and tomato, lettuce, etc.

TIGER JOE'S BAR-B-Q SAUCE

The quantities are determined by the cook. Heat the following in a large sauce pan: Catsup, chopped green pepper, onion and celery, brown sugar and an equal amount of vinegar, Worcestershire sauce, a dash of liquid hickory smoke and tabasco sauce. Simmer for about half an hour.

TIGER JOE'S SPAGHETTI AND MEAT BALLS

The recipe for the sauce is in this Part on Page 321.
For the meat balls mix: 4 parts of ground beef to one of stale bread which has been moistened with water and squeezed out. For 2 pounds of beef, add: 1 onion chopped and sauteed, 1 tbsp chopped parsley, 1 tsp sugar, 1 tbsp soy sauce, 1 egg, salt and pepper to taste. Mix in water, a little at a time, until the meat has lost its stiffness and feels very pliable. This will make the meat balls tender and juicy. A dash of garlic powder enhances the flavor. Roll into balls and bake in a 350-degree oven until brown.
Or, roll the balls in Italian-seasoned bread crumbs and fry in oil on top of the stove.

SWEET AND SOUR SAUCE (for pork, shrimp or scallops)

Mix, in equal amounts: Catsup, sugar, vinegar and water. Bring to a boil and simmer until sugar is dissolved. Add: a dash of ginger powder and Worcestershire sauce. Can be thickened slightly by stirring in a little water in which a tsp of cornstarch has been mixed. Will keep in the refrigerator.

TIGER JOE'S HOAGIE SAUCE.

"This formula is confidential. It is the property of Tiger Joe. It is not to be released, loaned, sold or stolen, under any circumstances.
Mix Italian Salad Dressing (oil and vinegar type) with Italian Seasoning."
NOTE: This was from son, Joe's cookbook notes and was one of his last humorous contributions.

SAUSAGE MAKING

In Majorca, we made a Mexican *Chorizo* that was all-beef, stuffed in sheep casings which we located in a small factory in Palma. One almost needed a gas mask to go there to pick them up. There were girls cleaning the fecal matter from the intestines and one visit would be enough for most people never to eat sausage again. However, we struggled through that and the second cleaning operation in the restaurant, and the sausages were a huge success.

Here in the United States, casings can be purchased by mail. They are very clean and packed in salt so that they can be kept in the refrigerator for a couple of months. To use them, it is only necessary to wash off the salt and run water through them and they are ready for stuffing. The usual quantity is enough for making over one hundred pounds of sausage. Of course, you can make a small amount at a time; or a large one that can be frozen. There are several places from which to order casings. We always use: The Sausage Maker, 177 Military Road, Buffalo, New York 14207. They have many varieties of casings and all kinds of equipment.

Believe it or not, sausage can be made without any special equipment at all! That is, if it is made into patties. The first recipes here are for that kind of sausage. If you want the sausage in casings, a meat grinder is needed with a funnel-like fitting that goes on the front of it for filling the casing. That's all we had in the restaurant and we made one or two hundred pounds at a time. So, start out modestly with the first recipes. Read a book or two on sausage making and experiment with different mixtures and combinations.

QUICK "HOMEMADE" SAUSAGE

Buy the cheapest pork sausage when it is on sale. It will cost one-half to one-third the regular price. Recipes are for one pound. Add multiples of one pound for freezing larger quantities. If the seasonings are not to your liking, use plain ground pork.

TIGER JOE'S ITALIAN SAUSAGE (See Page 332 for our regular

recipe)

In a bowl place 1 Pound of pork sausage. Add:
½ tsp sugar
¼ tsp white pepper
1 tbsp fennel seed, crushed

1 tsp rosemary leaves, crushed
Dash of nutmeg
2 tbsp water
Mix well. Note that meat absorbs water. Add enough to make a soft, workable mixture; it makes the sausage juicy. To make hot sausage, add ¼ tsp (or more depending upon hotness desired) crushed red pepper. Form into 12 patties or balls. Freeze in one layer on a cookie sheet and wrap individually. When ready to use, fry from the frozen state, at a medium heat, until cooked through

TIGER JOE'S BREAKFAST SAUSAGE (regular recipe on

Page 332)

In a bowl place one pound of pork sausage. Add:
½ tsp sugar
¼ tsp white pepper
1 tsp rubbed sage
1 tsp rosemary leaves, crushed
2 tbsp water
Dash of nutmeg
Mix well. For hot sausage, add ¼ tsp (or more depending on hotness desired) crushed red pepper. Form into 6 patties. Can be frozen and wrapped individually. Fry from the frozen state, at medium heat to cook through and brown nicely on the outside.

RECIPES USING CASINGS

The quantities are large because it is not worth getting set up for smaller amounts. The first part of the operation is to prepare the casings. We used medium sized hog casings. After all the salt is washed off and water has been run through the casings, hang them in separate strands in a bucket of water with one end hanging over the side. It may be necessary to put a lid on the container to keep the ends from falling in.

Set up the grinder with the grinding disk that has coarse holes, about ¼ inch. There are two grindings to be performed: the first with just the meat; and, the second with the ground meat and the other ingredients. For the second grinding, the disk is sometimes changed for one with smaller holes, about 1/8 inch. The tube fitting that takes the casing is installed in front of the disk. The entire length of the wet casing is fed onto the tube. When the grinder is "ON" the sausage will feed into the casing which has to be held onto the tube and assisted in the feeding by letting it go off the tube at the same rate that the ground mixture is moving. This may sound complicated but will simplify itself when you try it. So, let's go make some sausage.

TIGER JOE'S ITALIAN SAUSAGE

The cut known as "Pork Butt" is best for this sausage. Cut the meat off the bones of 25 lbs and cut it into pieces that will go into the mouth of the grinder, about 2 inches. Do not remove the fat but do take off whatever little gristle there may be. Run it through the grinder with the coarse holes. Add to the ground meat:

6 oz salt
6 oz fennel seed, crushed
3 oz white pepper
1 tbsp MSG (optional)
4/5 gallon water
If you want hot sausage, add 4 tbsp crushed red pepper.

Make the second grind with the same coarse grinding disk with the tube fitting and the casing on the front. The finished product should be cut into one-pound pieces and rolled flat in a spiral to make a package like you see in the supermarket. Wrap well in plastic and then in freezer paper and freeze; will keep several months. Now, aren't you proud of this first effort? You can really impress your friends serving them this sausage in spaghetti, sausage and pepper with Lasagna or in a hoagie with spaghetti sauce. It's much better than any you buy in the store. Remember, professional sausage makers add 30 to 40 percent fat to their formulas; it is much cheaper and acts as a filler. Of course, a little fat will make the product juicier.

TIGER JOE'S BREAKFAST SAUSAGE

As you did for Italian Sausage, run 10 pounds of pork butt meat through the coarse disk of the grinder. Mix with:

3 oz salt
3 tbsp each rubbed sage and crushed rosemary leaves
1 oz white pepper
1 ½ tsp thyme
½ tsp each nutmeg and mace
1 cup water
MSG can be added but we did not use it in the restaurant. If you want hot sausage, add crushed red pepper to taste. Run the mixture through

the same coarse disk with the casing on the tube. If desired, sheep's casing can be used and that will produce little links, if you tie them off with string. In the restaurant we made only patties, thus eliminating the casing. One of the specialties was Tiger Joe's Sausage on Toasted English Muffin. Now you can duplicate that at home.

TIGER JOE'S POLISH SAUSAGE

This sausage is better smoked giving it a nicer flavor and color. Instead, to approximate the flavor, we used liquid smoke. For color, potassium nitrate can be used, but the paprika in the recipe gives it sufficient redness.

Put 10 lbs pork butt meat through the coarse disk and mix the ground meat with:

½ cup salt
2 tsp each black and white pepper
10 cloves garlic, minced
1 ½ cups chicken, beef or pork stock
1 oz sugar

MSG is optional. Run the mixture through the coarse grind with the casing in place. The sausage can be frozen as is or boiled. In the restaurant we immediately immersed the sausage in a large container of boiling water for 10 minutes. Before serving, it was put on the grill to brown lightly. With horseradish, sauerkraut and mashed potatoes: Oh Boy!

TIGER JOE'S BOCKWURST

This was always the hit of any German Dinner Party, especially Oktoberfest. Run 25 lbs of pork butt meat through the coarse disk. With the ground meat, mix:

1 gallon water or stock
12 cups dry powdered milk
1 dozen eggs, lightly beaten
7 oz salt
4 onions, minced
2 cups chopped parsley
4 tbsp chopped chives, or tops of green onions
3 oz white pepper
3 oz sugar
½ tsp ground cloves
2 tbsp celery salt or 1 tbsp of ground celery seed

MSG is optional. Change the grinding disk to the small hole (1/8 inch) and put the casing in place. Run the mixture through; it will go more slowly than with the coarse grind. Twist the finished sausage into links or tie them off with string. Immerse in a large container of boiling water for 10 minutes. Brown on the grill, or in the frying pan, before serving being careful not to burn. Serve with hot mustard, sauerkraut, mashed potatoes and a good sour rye bread (recipe page 316). A stein of cold beer is essential. Prosit!

TIGER JOE'S BRATWURST

Run 3 pounds of pork butt meat through the coarse grind. Mix with the ground meat:

1 tsp nutmeg (can use ½ mace)
1 tbsp salt
1 tsp white pepper
1 tsp liquid smoke
2 tbsp chives or the tops of green onions
½ cup bread crumbs moistened with a little milk
½ cup dry powdered milk
1½ cups stock; chicken, pork or beef

Change the grinding disk to the smaller hole (1/8 inch), put the casing in place and run the mixture through. Twist into links or tie them off. Immerse sausage in a large container of boiling water for 10 minutes. Use the same as Bockwurst.

Warren Jamieson is a retired Eastern Airlines pilot. He and his wife, Edie, spend their summers in the beautiful home which they built in the mountains near Franklin. He dabbles in furniture-making and his wife in the culinary arts. She has parted with four of her most interesting recipes; three of them are from the Middle East.

HOMOS CHICK PEA DIP

1 can garbanzos (chick peas)
juice of 2 lemons
1 onion, minced
2 tbsp sesame paste
1 tbsp olive oil
1 clove garlic, pressed
salt and pepper, to taste
1 tbsp pine nuts, browned

Blend onion and lemon juice; add chick peas, olive oil, sesame paste, garlic, salt and pepper. Mix until smooth; thin with chick pea juice as necessary. Garnish with pine nuts and some chopped parsley.

NOTE: Vary the taste with lime juice instead of lemon. We like to add a little sugar to take away the acid bite.

TABULEE - CRACKED WHEAT SALAD

¾ cup cracked wheat
2 tomatoes, diced small
1 medium onion, minced
2 bunches parsley, minced
2 tbsp mint leaves, minced
½ cup lemon juice
2 or 3 tbsp olive oil

Soak wheat in water 45 minutes, until fully expanded; drain. Mix with vegetables. Add oil, lemon juice and spices. Garnish with mint. Serve on lettuce leaves.

NOTE: A tbsp or so of sugar does wonders for the taste.

KIBBEE - LAMB WITH CRACKED WHEAT

1 cup cracked wheat, soaked for 45 minutes
1 ½ lbs ground lamb
4 tbsp pine nuts, browned
3 tbsp butter
1 onion, minced
1 tsp each salt and pepper
¼ tsp allspice
2 tbsp mint leaves, minced

Knead grains of wheat like dough. Brown pine nuts in oil, remove and then brown the onions. Combine meat with wheat and spices; mix and knead for 10 minutes. Divide in half. Put half in greased baking dish, spread mixture of onion and pine nuts over it. Place the other half of meat mixture on top, sealing the edges. Make two cuts all the way through to form quarters. Distribute butter on top and bake 20 to 30 minutes at 375 degrees, until brown.

ALMOND MACAROONS EDIE JAMIESON

You might like these better than the more common ones made with coconut.

1 8-oz can almond paste
1 cup sugar
2 egg whites
pinch salt

Cut almond paste in small pieces. Add sugar and egg whites. Mix until smooth, no lumps. Drop by tsp onto paper-lined cookie sheet. Press in the center of each an almond half or a sliver. Bake at 325 degrees 25 minutes, or until lightly browned.

INDEX — PEOPLE